A LIBERAL STATE AT WAR

*English Politics
and Economics during
the Crimean War*

A LIBERAL
STATE AT WAR

ENGLISH POLITICS
AND ECONOMICS DURING
THE CRIMEAN WAR

OLIVE ANDERSON

M.A., B.LITT. (OXON.)

Lecturer in History,
Westfield College, University of London

MACMILLAN
LONDON · MELBOURNE · TORONTO

ST MARTIN'S PRESS
NEW YORK
1967

MACMILLAN AND COMPANY LIMITED
also Bombay Calcutta Madras Melbourne

THE MACMILLAN COMPANY OF CANADA LIMITED
70 *Bond Street Toronto* 2

ST MARTIN'S PRESS INC
175 *Fifth Avenue New York NY* 10010

Library of Congress catalog card no. 67–11670

PRINTED IN GREAT BRITAIN

TO MY HUSBAND

Contents

Contents

List of Illustrations

Acknowledgements

I HAVE to acknowledge the gracious permission of Her Majesty the Queen to make use of material from the Royal Archives, Windsor Castle.

I am also indebted to a number of private owners for permission to examine and quote from material in their possession: to the Earl of Clarendon for the Clarendon Papers deposited at the Bodleian Library, Oxford; to the Trustees of the Broadlands Archives for the Palmerston Papers; to Sir Feargus Graham, Bart., for the microfilm of the Netherby Manuscripts deposited in the University Library, Cambridge; to Russell Ellice, Esq., for the Ellice Papers deposited at the National Library of Scotland; to the Trustees of the Newcastle Estates and the Department of Manuscripts of the University of Nottingham for the Newcastle Manuscripts; to the Master and Fellows of Balliol College, Oxford, for the Urquhart Manuscripts; and to the National Trust for the Disraeli Papers at Hughenden Manor.

My thanks are also due to the Department of Palæography and Diplomatic of the University of Durham for permission to examine the papers of the third Earl Grey deposited in the Prior's Kitchen; and to the Librarians of University College, London for the Chadwick Papers, the British Library of Political and Economic Science for the Harrison Papers, the Bishopsgate Institute for the Holyoake Collection, and the National Library of Wales for the Harpton Court Collection. I must also express my gratitude to the custodians of the manuscript collections in the British Museum and the Scottish Record Office, and to the Controller of H.M. Stationery Office, by whose permission quotations are made from Crown-copyright records in the Public Record Office; and, finally, to the Editors of the *Economic History Review* for permission to use material which originally appeared in that journal.

Great Expectations

IT is impossible to understand its vast impact upon contemporary Englishmen if the Crimean War is dismissed as the abortive and futile episode it has seemed to be ever since the peace preliminaries were signed at Paris in March 1856. Almost to the end contemporaries expected something very different from what actually came to pass. They expected a long and global war, terrible in its scope and decisive in its outcome — decisive not only with regard to power relationships but with regard to the great contemporary issues of liberalism and nationalism as well. It is essential to understand these heroic anticipations at the outset in order to comprehend how a mere two years' war of limited and ineffective operations almost entirely confined to the Baltic and Black Seas could loom so large in the domestic history of one of the world's great powers at the very peak of its strength.

Around the middle of the nineteenth century opinion-making in England was remarkably evenly divided between those who judged the present by looking back to the past, and those who judged it by looking forward to the future. The country was poised between Coleridge's 'Principles of Permanence and Progression', between 'the wisdom of ancestors' and 'the march of intellect'. As it happened traditionalists and progressives alike had their own equally good though entirely different reasons for regarding the approach of the Crimean War with awe and foreboding. Those who looked to the past — and they were the more numerous and more powerful politically — almost instinctively thought of war in terms of the great struggle between 1793 and 1815 against Revolutionary and Napoleonic France. They did not do so simply because this was the last European war in which Britain had been

involved, and because each war is customarily fought with the
ideas of the last. Throughout the forty years' peace the continuing influence of the French wars in shaping men's political
and even economic outlooks was a phenomenon to be reckoned
with. Part at least of the explanation lies in the prestige of
modern history as a moral science and its commercial success
as a form of literature. Political debate was then almost habitually conducted in terms of historical parallels, and for many
reasons the years between 1803 and 1815 were a particularly
favoured quarry for such parallels. The apotheosis during his
lifetime of the Duke of Wellington had concentrated attention upon the Peninsular campaigns, while prolonged partisan exploitation of the legends of Pitt and Fox nurtured
an abiding memory of the bitter political background of the
struggle. In the years immediately before the outbreak of the
Crimean War Sir William Napier's *History of the War in the
Peninsula* and Wellington's *Despatches* were among the leading
best-sellers.[1] Thus the period of the Napoleonic Wars had
become the most familiar chapter in English history to a very
historically minded generation, and the new European war
which was clearly threatening throughout most of 1853 was
inevitably expected to be cast in the same impressive mould.

But if this was a historically minded generation it was also,
though in different quarters, a technologically minded one.
The 'men of the Age' marked themselves off from the traditionalists by their certainty that the coming war would be
totally different from the last. To them it was the pace of
change in the forty years' peace which was important, and
above all, the achievement of speedy and certain transport
and communications. In technological progress it was taken
for granted that England led the world, and that of all the
great powers Russia lagged furthest behind. The modernists

---

[1] The former was first published between 1828 and 1840, but was
abridged and reprinted in 1852 and 1853; the latter was first published
between 1834 and 1849, reissued between 1844 and 1847 and again
in an abridged form in 1851.

expected, therefore, a war which might indeed be bloody, but which would certainly be rapid and decisive. The electric telegraph, railways, shell-firing guns, rifled and breech-loading gun barrels, innumerable inventions ranging from daguerreotype pictures and gutta-percha bivouacs to that most significant development of all in English eyes, the screw-propeller steamship, convinced them that a new and impressive chapter in the history of warfare was about to be written. 'Short and sharp' was their prophecy and their hope, a prophecy and a hope shared by almost the entire business world.

Political radicals and their moderate liberal sympathizers were convinced by yet other reasons that Europe was on the brink of a tremendous and epoch-making struggle. To them the war was destined to be a sequel to the events of 1848–9, a final struggle which would end the 'war of opinion' begun two generations ago, the war between despotism and liberty, or (to some) between universal empire and national independence. Such convictions were strongest furthest to the left. Karl Marx predicted on 2 February 1854 that the coming war would inevitably raise again a 'sixth Power of Europe', the Revolution.[1] The Polish refugees and their numerous English sympathizers were confident that this was to be no mere war for the balance of power, and full of renewed activity accordingly. The very pacifism and caution of Lord Aberdeen's Coalition Government of Whigs and Peelites convinced the extremists that the Government too believed that the war would bring revolution and that nothing could prevent it from becoming 'a war of nationalities'. 'The war may be short, but cannot be trifling.' This editorial opinion of the leading radical dissenting newspaper, *The Nonconformist*, was the common belief of the political Left. Few, perhaps, were as logical as the positivist journalist who declared that the alliance with Bonapartist France must be ended forthwith so that England could work wholeheartedly for the dissolution of the Austrian Empire and the liberation of Hungary, Italy

---

[1] *The Eastern Question*, ed. A. M. and E. Aveling (1897), p. 220.

and Poland.[1] But very many repeated the attractively simple argument that since Russian military power had been responsible for the course of events in 1848–9, the absorption of the Russian Army in a war of its own would allow 'the Revolution' to continue where it had been obliged to stop half a dozen years before. Middle-class liberals warmed to the theme of England's renewed leadership in an age-old struggle for constitutional liberty, in which the Tsar Nicholas I embodied the ancient enemy of despotism, as Napoleon I had done earlier. Indeed of all the many conceptions of what the war was to be about, this notion that it was to be one of a constitutional system of government against the despotic principle was perhaps the most widely accepted by the general public. True, this view was difficult to reconcile with alliance with Napoleonic France and the Ottoman Empire. Moderates, however, were satisfied by allusions to the Bonapartist doctrine of the referendum, and the Turkish system of government could be regarded as a special case. Moreover this view accorded particularly well with the type of Russophobia which had developed in England a generation earlier. That most orthodox of Whig organs, with a solidly upper-middle-class readership, the *Morning Post*, declared more than once that the war would really be one between opposite principles of government. Thus even in the most moderate circles, provided the question of 'the nationalities' was excluded, and provided liberalism was understood to imply the rule of middle-class opinion, the war was welcomed as the culmination of an ideological struggle which had been going on for many years.

Russia is the leader and archetype of the system of policy under which restricted bodies — mere administrative sections — act in the name of vast nations, and use the brute weight and force of masses of humanity as the blind instrument of their will. England and her allies are the exponents and the defence of that means and result of the highest civilization, which consist in the self-government and independent action

[1] *The Leader*, 7 January 1854.

of intelligent communities through the constitutional medium of ascertained public opinion. It is to this same antagonism of the constitutional system by which national intelligence grows and acts, to the bureaucratic management under which brute force is the all-powerful agent, that we must trace all the menaced dangers and actual convulsions of Europe for the many years during which the sagacity and firmness of certain leading statesmen have succeeded in maintaining peace. . . . The supremacy of political intelligence or of brute force in the great community of civilised nations is what is really at stake.[1]

This magisterial concept of the principles at stake was not always subscribed to, but there was wide agreement that what was coming was a war of opinion, a continuation of a war of principles which had in some sense been endemic for a couple of generations. Only to the inner ring of working politicians was any such ideological notion of war anathema — and to that arch-Russophobe, David Urquhart, to whom the coming war was a mere sham engineered by Palmerston, the traitor bought by Russian gold, and bound therefore to be a feeble, inconclusive affair. Immediately before the outbreak of war, however, Urquhart's peculiar views of Palmerston were at their least influential and he could find few to agree with him in denouncing the Government's public moves as a mockery.

One last factor which induced a not inconsiderable section of the public to believe the coming war would be a profoundly important event in the history of the world, was the popularity of certain eschatological interpretations among so many devout evangelicals and nonconformists of the day. Many Christians were then much concerned with the interpretation of Biblical prophecy about the end of the world, and regarded the Eastern Question from the special point of view of the return of the Jews to their national home in the last days. One of the most popular preachers in London, Dr. John Cumming of the National Scottish Church in Crown Court,

---

[1] *Morning Post*, 7 January 1854.

Covent Garden, repeatedly declared (as did many others) that the 'last vial' of the Apocalypse was to be poured out between 1848 and 1865, that the fall of Turkey was symbolized in the prophesied 'drying up of the Euphrates' and would prepare the way for the return of the Jews to Palestine, and that only after this would Russia, Ezekiel's great power 'out of the Northern parts', be destroyed. She might be checked in the coming war, he conceded, but not permanently destroyed. Another, less popular, interpreter thought differently — for him, not only was the mission of the Russians to bring about the fall of the Turkish Empire, but in the course of the coming struggle Britain would be invaded and defeated, in order to usher in 'the reign of liberty in the New World'. Armageddon was to be fought in Britain.[1] But however much they diverged in their application of prophecy, the prophetic school united upon the common theme that 'the last times are now opening out', and those who heard and read their arguments were too numerous and varied a section of the public to be dismissed as a lunatic fringe.

Contemporaries then undoubtedly expected the war to prove a great, almost a portentous event in the history of the world. What did they believe Britain's special role would be as a belligerent in that war? What did they expect to prove her peculiar strengths and weaknesses? What policies and preparations were thought to be appropriate? Public expectations about how Britain would fare as a belligerent are as important for an understanding of the actual impact of the Crimean War as are public expectations about the nature and significance of the war itself. They constitute moreover the first attempts to foresee the military significance of liberalism and industrialization in the only country which could as yet provide any evidence upon a question which was to be fundamental for the next hundred years. In particular those who were most conscious of the pace of change in Britain since

[1] Anon., *The Downfall of Despotism* (1853) (catalogued in the British Museum Library, s.n. E. B. Elliott).

1815 and of her dissimilarity from other great powers, when they speculated at length upon British fitness for a major war gave quite as much attention to political and economic conditions and to the moral state of her people, as to the state of her armed forces. Here were the first early perceptions that the organization of a modern nation for war is not basically a military matter, and as such they deserve careful analysis.

From the beginning it was the fitness for war of the British system of government which attracted the most attention. Since the collapse of the European revolutions of 1848, British self-consciousness about her unique political institutions had become yet more intense than before. In October 1852, for example, an *Edinburgh* reviewer developed the theme that Britain was 'now the only great Power in Europe in which a Parliamentary system is in active operation'. Mr. Punch made the same point less weightily in January 1852:

> Ordnance the subject multitude for ordinance obey;
> The bullet and the bayonet debate at once allay:
> The mouth is gagg'd, the Press is stopp'd, and we remain
> alone
> With power our thoughts to utter, or to call our souls our
> own.[1]

Yet one of the oldest political equations in history was that of despotism with military success, representative government with military weakness. Was it possible for a country governed by representative institutions to fight a major war with a great despotic power and win? This was a fundamental problem which was to be raised more than once in the next century. In the months before the Crimean War began, however — months on the whole of optimism and hope — there were few who doubted that it could and should be Britain's role to demonstrate the unique blessings of her constitution in war as well as peace. The classic objection to parliamentary government and untrammelled public discussion in time of war was that it impeded vigour and unanimity; the executive was

[1] *Punch*, xxii. 13.

fettered by its relationship with the legislature, and the legislature fell an easy victim to faction and demagogy, while
demos itself was notoriously unstable. But before the war
began these failings seemed to be avoidable, and the picture
had another side. 'Our free constitution is a source to us both
of strength and weakness,' explained *The Times* on 11 February 1854. 'The strength is perpetual, the weakness periodical.' The strength was the tremendous popular backing which
representative institutions and liberty of speech gave a
government, valuable above all in solving problems of manpower and finance, and supremely valuable in a long-drawn-
out struggle. The weakness was the familiar one of disunity.
Patriotism therefore demanded that as war approached, controversial issues should be shelved. The historically minded
educated public was all too familiar with the bitter party
struggles which distinguished the politicians of the Napoleonic
War — they had indeed become part of the Whig myth. In
1854 such recollections helped to make the theme of national
unity a source not only of earnest adjurations but of complacent comparisons as well. How fortunate that the political and
social tensions which had been so acute a few years earlier had
now relaxed! Only one fertile source of political dissension
threatened — from Lord John Russell's new Parliamentary
Reform Bill, long expected, and announced in the Queen's
Speech at the opening of the session on 31 January 1854.
'The duties of a War Ministry and a Reform Ministry are
totally incompatible,' urged *The Times*.[1] 'It is the clear duty
of every patriotic Government in time of war to do nothing
which may diminish confidence in its stability . . . , which may
present it to foreigners as the head of a party rather than of
the nation.' The parliamentary opposition was given an even
more difficult part to play. 'Mere retrospective criticism',
again explained *The Times*,[2] could not be condoned, for 'all
endeavours to weaken the Government without seeking its
dismissal are really co-operation with the enemy'. So astute a

[1] 11 March 1854.   [2] 3 April 1854.

A STRUGGLE BETWEEN DUTY AND INCLINATION.

GALLANT LITTLE JOHN TAKING LEAVE OF HIS PET TO SERVE HIS COUNTRY.

(*Punch*, April 22, 1854)

politician as the leader in the Commons of the parliamentary opposition of the day, Benjamin Disraeli, could not fail to conform to these patriotic adjurations in the most flamboyant way open to him. Nicholas I, he promised the House, unlike the first Napoleon, would have no party in the British Parliament;[1] the Conservatives would loyally forswear factious opposition for the duration of the war. When Lord John reluctantly and tardily dropped his Reform Bill on 11 April 1854, the way seemed to be clear for a demonstration of that real national unity which it was fashionable to believe could be shown only by free men.

The British system of government then, it might well be hoped, could be turned into a military asset and one of the great arguments of the opponents of liberty thus refuted. But could this optimism be extended to the British system of administration, above all of military administration? Greater efficiency of personnel in the Civil Service might perhaps be looked for from the new system of recruitment by competitive examination announced in the Queen's Speech on 31 January 1854 (though this was highly controversial), but the failings of British military administration were notoriously not failings of personnel but of departmental organization. In this branch of government the principle of checks and balances through division had run glaringly to excess. In the years since Howick's famous Report on the administration of the Army in 1837 this had become one of the most well-worn topics of English public life. Now the imminence of war inevitably revived the cry for a single powerful Minister of War, if only to allow the country to match the administrative advantages which were associated with the autocratic Russian form of government. Once again *The Times* took up the cry. 'We want a real Minister of War,' it thundered, 'military administration is more decisive in war than diplomacy in the Cabinet or courage in the field'; and again, 'we need the superior intelligence in administration as much as

[1] 3 *Hansard*, cxxx, col. 1029 (20 February 1854).

the master mind in science'.[1] A glance at the Russian system of government seemed to dispose of the argument that unity of administration should halt where the capacity of a single chief to give direct superintendence ended.[2] In the House of Commons a few weeks before the declaration of war, a major debate on military administration was brought on by the leading financial reformer, Joseph Hume, who had been concerned for many years with attempts to get the jungle of military administration cleared on grounds of economy. Now more urgent reasons could be exploited. It was clear at once, however, that this was one of the subjects upon which Aberdeen's Coalition Government was divided. Upon so stale a subject the veteran politicians who sat in the Cabinet had long ago taken up rigid and conflicting attitudes. The Leader of the House, Lord John Russell, an old military reformer, now readily admitted that 'a more efficient and more direct authority is required,' whereas the Peelite Sidney Herbert, who as Secretary at War was the Government's official spokesman on military matters in the House of Commons, urged that it was human capacity that mattered, not systems, and that settled routines should not be tampered with in time of war. No one mentioned what was well known to be a chief obstacle to change: the fear of the professional soldiers and of the Court of increased parliamentary control over that historic royal preserve, the command of the Army. The last word clearly lay with that veteran reformer, Edward Ellice, who roundly told the House that there was no concealing the fact that opinion out of doors was convinced that 'it was impossible in a rational country long to continue a confused and perplexed administration' like that under discussion. In the Lords the still-determined Howick, then third Earl Grey, had stressed the urgency of reform on the very first day of the session.[3] Lord John

[1] 8 and 27 February, 8 and 10 April 1854.
[2] 8 February 1854.
[3] 3 *Hansard*, cxxx, cols. 223–59 (2 March 1854), and col. 62 (31 January 1854).

Russell's bathetic announcement that another Under Secretary would be appointed to assist the Secretary of State for the Colonies (the minister constitutionally responsible for the conduct of war) by acting as Military Secretary was so obviously a mere stop-gap that it could only rouse impatient indignation. Thus at the very outset of the war it was obvious to many informed people that only remarkable good fortune, remarkable good will or bold reorganization could make one important branch of the British system of government a match for the authority, unity and precision which were assumed to flow from autocracy. If, then, Britain's unique political system was widely regarded as a potential asset to the nation in time of war, in certain circles at least this optimism was qualified by serious reservations in the all-important matter of military administration.

What was to be expected from Britain's other distinguishing feature — her uniquely industrialized, free trade economy, already closely geared to world trade? How would the workshop of the world fare in what promised to be a world war? Would the currency arrangements made in 1819 and 1844 with the return to cash payments and the passing of the Bank Charter Act stand the strain? Could the fiscal policy of reducing Customs duties and simplifying taxation be retained in view of the greatly increased revenue which would now be required? Were British imports of raw materials from Russia now so essential to her manufacturing economy as to dictate business as usual and not trade war with the enemy? From an economic point of view there could be no doubt whatever that vast changes had taken place since England was last on the verge of war. Yet in this field, too, a historical outlook was ubiquitous. Although there was a fundamental (and one would have thought disquieting) disagreement about whether the economic history of the last war offered a dreadful warning or a guide to be followed, much confidence was expressed that the financial and commercial lessons of that war (whatever they might be) had been mastered. Undoubtedly at the outset it was the 'men of the age' who had the better of it. Their economic policy for the war was clear. Maintain cash payments and the restriction of the note issue; raise revenue by taxes, especially the income tax, and not loans; avoid foreign subsidies and enforce strict accounting. As far as trade was concerned, the country should abandon its traditional practice of trading with the enemy under licence combined with the vigorous assertion of maritime rights, for this ancient custom brought the worst of both economic and diplomatic worlds. The traditionalists at this stage were somewhat in eclipse. But men's attitudes depended above all upon their assessment of Russia as an enemy. Even the most progressive wondered whether some of their number sufficiently realized that only an overwhelmingly sharp or improbably lucky war could be a really short one. Thus both Gladstone's first war budget, confined to financing the expeditionary force sent out to the East a month before war was declared, and the Government's announcements foreshadowing abandonment of the right to search neutral vessels, aroused disquiet even in these quarters. The many traditionalists who expected an immensely long and costly struggle were even more uncertain about the feasibility of avoiding borrowing and maintaining a convertible currency for long. It is not surprising that the advent of war sparked off a renewed debate on both fiscal and currency questions, with the protectionists and banking school alike hoping to exploit the crisis to convert the moderates to their side.

To that generation the prospect of war from a monetary point of view suggested not internal inflation, but external drains of bullion. News of the expeditionary force to the East at once gave fresh significance to memories of the legendary suspension of cash payments in 1797. Indeed within a few weeks of the destruction of the Turkish fleet at Sinope, all the old currency arguments had been revived, and the gold standard itself as well as the Bank Charter Act attacked. The evils of the war would be amply repaid, one anti-bullionist pamphleteer exclaimed three months before war materialized, 'if they served to free our legislators from the leading strings of the old school of London Bankers '.[1] A week before war was proclaimed the House of Commons was assured in debate that 'there would be found no enemy so deadly to us as the Bank Charter Act of 1844 ',[2] and some of that Act's firmest supporters feared the war would offer a challenge which would be hard to meet. This still controversial Act forbade the Bank of England to issue notes except against the gold reserves in its Issue Department (apart from a fiduciary issue of £14 million), and was intended to check automatically any drain of gold by restricting the currency. Its opponents denied that drains were always caused by monetary circumstances and therefore that contracting the currency was always the appropriate remedy. The Crimean generation felt confident that subsidies and loans abroad in the style of Pitt would be avoided, but the expeditionary force sent to the East in February was obviously only a first instalment and considerable drains of bullion must be expected. Under the Act financial stringency must inevitably follow. In any case, any Government in wartime might find itself obliged to draw largely on the Bank, and in the coming war if it did so the Bank might not be able to assist private individuals in time of need, because of the restrictive provisions of the Act of 1844. Even the wisdom of the gold standard itself was questioned again as memories of the years from 1797 to 1818 were revived. Doubt and despondency spread so fast that by 24 March 1854 George Arbuthnot of the Treasury felt he should write a memorandum emphasizing, as he put it, 'the contrast in present circumstances and those which led to the suspension of cash payments in 1797'.[3] One simple fact, however, proved far more

[1] *The Bank Screw; or, War and the Gold Discoveries in connexion with the Money Market. A Letter to W. E. Gladstone . . . by Malagrowther the Less* (January 1854). A copy of this pamphlet is in the Goldsmiths' Library, University of London.

[2] 3 *Hansard*, cxxxi, col. 1106 (21 March 1854). Cf. ibid., col. 391 (6 March 1854).

[3] British Museum, Gladstone Papers, Add. MS. 44096, fo. 37.

reassuring than any Treasury memorandum could have been: the steady influx of gold into the country ensured by the gold discoveries in California and Australia. This, many people felt, would carry the country's monetary system through.

What of the fiscal system? Would Peelite methods of raising revenue prove adequate for the sinews of war or would the country have to turn back towards indirect taxation? Memories of the Napoleonic experience were as green in this field as in that of currency, and quite as alarming. The enormous growth of the permanent Debt in Pitt's day had been denounced as an intolerable millstone round the nation's neck throughout the forty years' peace. Was there now to be another vast accumulation of Debt which would cripple posterity even more? In one of his most telling speeches Gladstone as Chancellor of the Exchequer took the first opportunity to associate himself in the House of Commons with this emotional attitude towards the National Debt, and preached a heroic gospel of financing the war by taxation alone. His budget for the expeditionary force relied upon doubling the income tax for six months.[1] Pride and confidence in the country's wealth, united with a determination to avoid Pitt's widely condemned financial errors, created a moralizing arrogance which matched Gladstone's own and induced a widespread belief that England could impress the world by paying for a major war out of income. But from the very beginning there were some who disagreed with either Gladstone's premises or his conclusions, or both. Conservative politicians naturally predicted that the war would vindicate their party's fiscal policies and reverse the trend towards free trade, and they were not alone in this. Those who believed in making families still exempt from income tax contribute to the nation's revenue, those who believed government borrowing under proper safeguards to be to the country's economic advantage, above all those who believed Gladstone was seriously underestimating the probable length and scope of the

[1] 3 *Hansard*, cxxxi, cols. 370–89 (6 March 1854).

war, all doubted whether it would prove possible to finance the war from income tax alone.

Indeed the only part of the Government's slowly emerging economic policy for the coming war which won universal support in the early spring of 1854 was its decision not to issue letters of marque. Privateering seemed obviously futile against an enemy with so little seaborne trade as Russia, which yet might commission American privateers to prey on Britain's abundant shipping. It was moreover genuinely repugnant to a generation so devoted to humanitarian progress and the rule of law. But the other great question of maritime warfare, whether to seize enemy property on neutral ships or whether to allow the flag to cover the goods, was controversial from the first. The traditionalists remembered the events of 1810–12 when the Continental Blockade impelled the great Russian landowners to force the Tsar into an anti-French policy, whereas Napoleon's military attack proved futile. For Britain to inflict similar injuries on Russian trade by means of a strict blockade and control of neutral carriers was widely assumed to be possible and even easy, and to be a sure way of undermining Russian morale and currency as well as trade. Those who were impressed by Russia's inaccessibility to military or naval attack — and they were many — attached particular importance to an economic blow against her. But others insisted on a comparative approach: would Britain suffer even more than Russia by a vigorous application of her traditional maritime policy? Would Britain's own economic well-being be jeopardized? Would her relations with the neutral powers be seriously strained?

It was expertly argued that the loss of Russian markets would not be significant, since only one seventy-eighth of British exports went to Russia in 1852.[1] British imports from Russia were more substantial, but good alternative sources of supply were believed to exist, except in the case of grain. In any case the innumerable amateur political economists of the

[1] *The Economist*, 4 March 1854.

day were convinced that if the usual outlets for Russian produce in demand in England were closed, economic forces
would open up others. Thus many believed that to try to intercept the whole maritime trade of Russia was not very worth-
while in itself and would moreover be defeated by the play of
economic forces. Strong arguments could be produced in
favour of allowing even British subjects to trade with the
enemy. If they were forbidden to do so, devious routes and
neutral middle men would produce a rise in prices to British
importers of Russian produce, and thus weaken Britain's
competitive position as an exporter. More generally, any prohibitions which jeopardized England's newly established position as 'the great Emporium of the Commerce of the World'
would jeopardize what many believed to have become the
real basis of British world power. From all this it followed that
Russian imports could be stopped without loss to England,
but not Russian exports. Translated into naval terms, this
implied a policy of blockade, but of non-interference with
neutral shipping otherwise.

As war drew nearer, able use was made inside the Cabinet
of precisely such arguments, particularly by the influential
Peelite First Lord of the Admiralty, Sir James Graham. With
ministers, however, diplomatic considerations inevitably
loomed far larger than with the general public, always less
sensitive to these arcana of public business. They naturally
dominated the outlook of the Foreign Secretary of the day,
that alert and enlightened Whig, Lord Clarendon, and even
Sir James Graham was unhappily aware that the adoption of
steam had made any Baltic fleet heavily dependent upon the
use of Danish and Swedish harbours for coaling purposes.[1]
More important even than the benevolent neutrality of
Scandinavian powers, however, was the attitude of the United
States. If Britain continued to seize enemy cargo on neutral
ships, she would probably find herself fighting the United

[1] Cambridge University Library, Graham Papers, Microfilm 44,
Memorandum for the Cabinet, 22 January 1854.

States as well as Russia. It was very obvious that Russia was
hoping yet again to exploit quarrels about the maritime rights
of neutrals precisely as she had so often done since the days of
Catherine II and the Armed Neutrality of 1780.[1] Thus to the
Cabinet the problem was clear: how could Britain's over-
whelming naval strength be used so as to cut off Russia's
imports totally, and her exports in so far as this would not
damage Britain's economy, while not allowing any Russian
ships out of their ports or offending the all-important neutral
powers? Outside the Cabinet the picture was more confused.
The diplomatic dangers seemed less, the efficacy of economic
weapons against Russia greater, and the danger of backlash
upon Britain's own free trade economy grew or shrank according to individual alignment in the bitter financial and commercial debates of the last few years. All that was certain was
that the Government's war trade policy would be carefully
calculated, but also inescapably controversial.[2]

With so much attention paid to the monetary, fiscal and
commercial consequences of Britain's unique economic position, it is the more striking (at least to the modern mind) that
its effect upon Britain's military manpower was ignored. On
all sides British prosperity was regarded as a source of un-
qualified strength in the coming struggle, and the probable
repercussions of full employment upon military recruiting
neglected. The ancient problem of manning the fleet had indeed
been kept in the public mind by the introduction of long service
in the Royal Navy in 1853 and by the Maritime Militia Act
of the same year. But recruiting the Army was still envisaged

---

[1] This was clear not only to Clarendon (Graham Papers, ibid., Clarendon to Graham, 16 February 1854) but also to Karl Marx: 'Russia in
the event of war with England bases her hopes upon eventual quarrels
about the maritime rights of neutrals involving dangerous situations
and pushing the United States towards Russia' (*The Eastern Question*,
p. 264).

[2] A more detailed discussion by the present author can be found
in the *Law Quarterly Review* for July 1960. Subsequent study of
additional manuscript sources has only served to confirm the argument
put forward there.

"RIGHT AGAINST WRONG."

(*Punch*, April 8, 1854)

simply as a question of inducing the Government of the day
to propose larger military establishments to Parliament. Such
blindness can only be explained by another, no less striking,
feature of the weeks before war began: implicit faith that as
soon as war was declared an outburst of patriotic devotion
would galvanize into heroism every level of society.

The effect of war upon the country's morale was indeed
expected to be as substantial as its effect upon the country's
prosperity was expected to be slight. It is almost too well
known that the Crimean War was widely welcomed as an
opportunity for the nation to purge itself of sordid utilitarian-
ism. It is less often appreciated that this did not mean that
there was any widespread cult of war for its own sake: the war
was held to offer tremendous moral opportunities only because it was believed to be a just war and an event of profound
significance in the divine scheme of things. This has perhaps
been obscured by the customary quotation of certain lines
from Tennyson's *Maud* (published in 1854) to illustrate and
indeed exhaust the topic of the public's attitude to the
Crimean War:

> For the peace, that I deem'd no peace, is over and done,
> And now by the side of the Black and the Baltic deep,
> And deathful-grinning mouths of the fortress, flames
> The blood-red blossom of war, with a heart of fire.[1]

In fact what occurred in 1854 was a very articulate revival of
the ancient belief that to fight a just and necessary war would
purify and elevate any nation thus entrusted by God with the
task of defending the moral order. Some much less familiar
lines at the end of the same poem illustrate this well enough:

> We are noble still —
> It is better to fight for the good than to rail at the ill;
> I have felt with my native land, I am one with my kind,
> I embrace the purpose of God, and the doom assign'd.

[1] Quoted, for example, in E. L. Woodward, *War and Peace in Europe,
1815–1870* (1931), p. 12, and *The Age of Reform, 1815–1870* (Oxford,
1938), p. 251; A. Briggs, *The Age of Improvement* (1959), p. 377; W. L.
Burn, *The Age of Equipoise* (1964), p. 55.

But in any case the speaker of these lines is a madman, and the poem itself was unfavourably received. A far better guide to the state of opinion than *Maud* is to be found in the editorial and correspondence columns of the Press, in the pamphlets and ballads and doggerel verse of the day, and above all in the sermons of popular preachers and in the religious press, since the direct and active interference of God in the day to day events of private and public life was still taken for granted by most people in this period. Indeed many Evangelicals and Dissenters explicitly believed the war to be God's scourge for the nation's sins, a divine punishment for personal, social or political shortcomings. From the pulpit the coming war was seen either as a divine trust or a divine chastisement. The strong religious cast of mind of the day contributed more than anything else to making the war appear as a providential moral stimulus.[1] Quite apart, however, from this widely diffused religious or quasi-religious interpretation of the war, there was one other though much less important source of these expectations that the war would prove a great moral challenge: the Carlylean cult of the hero and the nation. Thomas Carlyle himself thought only 'fools and loose-spoken inexperienced persons' were war-mad in the spring of 1854,[2] but many of those who had responded to his *Latter-Day Pamphlets* and were vaguely dissatisfied by constitutional liberalism and party politics, welcomed the war as likely to further strong government and national unity. Few went as far as William MacCall, the former Unitarian minister who preached his own version of the Carlylean religion of 'Individualism'. MacCall rhapsodically hailed the war in his public lectures not as for the establishment of freedom but 'to bring about the reign of realities. . . . Oh to be done with phrases and traditions and diplomacies and constitutionalism and all

---

[1] The attitude of the churches to the war is discussed in detail by the present author in the *Journal of Ecclesiastical History*, xvi (1965).

[2] D. A. Wilson, *Carlyle to Threescore and Ten* (1929), p. 93.

c

the other rubbish!'[1] To most people 'realities' were not what the war was *for*, but they trusted that these would come in its train. On the other hand the moral evils which war might also bring were never ignored. The secular as well as the religious press offered frequent warnings against arrogance and pride, brutalization and 'the hardening of the feelings'. A few radical organs predicted an increase of pauperism and crime[2] and even the most moderate people were prepared to admit that war tended to destroy the spirit of order and legality. Indeed this admission was merely the corollary of the idea that it tended to promote patriotism, chivalry, ingenuity and energy.

But quite as striking as any of these predictions about the consequences of war for the community's moral fibre was the widespread agreement about its probable effect upon the nation's attitude to its social and political problems. In the months immediately before the war the public had been forcibly reminded that these problems were still unsolved by the debate provoked by Lord John Russell's long-expected Parliamentary Reform Bill, and by the long-drawn-out strikes of the engineers at Sheffield and cotton-spinners at Preston, quite unprecedented at that time. Yet here too the potent though distorted stereotype of the experiences of the Napoleonic War gave a clear shape to most men's expectations. They were convinced that the nation was about to enter a period of inactivity in all things domestic; a period when it would be undesirable and indeed impossible to divert the country's attention and resources from the struggle abroad. Those with radical sympathies tried indeed to urge that the national unity and self-sacrifice which war demanded made it the very time when political rights should be extended and the well-being of the citizens attended to, but their arguments had little chance of success. The march of progress must clearly be post-

---

[1] *National Missions* (1855), p. 184, a lecture delivered on 11 December 1853. The positivist journal *The Leader* also believed like MacCall that war was good in itself, apart from its specific object (25 February 1854).

[2] e.g., *The Nonconformist*, 4 January 1854.

poned at home in order to ensure its advance abroad; or (as it seemed to another school of thought) the country's slide towards democracy and extravagant public expenditure upon improper social benefits must be halted in order to defend its security and the balance of power in Europe. England's political and social problems would and should be shelved for the duration of the war. This would be acceptable, the argument continued, because it would be so obviously part of the cost of the war, and the war was 'the People's War'. A great upsurge of national unity was confidently predicted. Class barriers would be lowered and class antagonisms overcome by the outpouring of unselfish patriotism released by common effort and common suffering. The very familiarity of this line of thought made it the more convincing. A political and social pause, made acceptable by patriotic emotion — this was what was most often believed to be in store for the nation.

Long before it began the Crimean War was thus expected to put the nation on trial. To the functioning of government, to the economic policy of the state and to national morale it was expected to present a searching challenge. Exactly how serious the challenge would be, above all how successfully it would be met — these were matters for dispute. On the whole the optimists had the better of it, but even at the beginning optimism was far from universal, and among the informed and reflective rarely blind. But however this may be, the intense contemporary preoccupation with what the war would mean for Britain surely does not deserve to be dismissed as proof of war hysteria or of a strange lack of proportion.[1] Men thought themselves about to live through one of the great events in the history of the world. Some expected an epic struggle along Napoleonic lines, others foresaw the first manifestation of scientific warfare. They shared a certainty that its effects

[1] These are the points of view expressed respectively by B. Kingsley Martin, *The Triumph of Lord Palmerston* (1st ed., 1924, reissued 1963), *passim*, and W. L. Burn, op. cit., p. 56.

might well be profound — for the whole population, not for
the armed forces and diplomats alone. They expected that
there would be a civil history of the war to be written, as well
as a military one. They looked to the country's wealth and
morale for victory; they realized that, as *The Times* put it,
'It is less in the actual magnitude of the force displayed than
in the inexhaustible resources for renewing and supporting it
that the power of this country will be shown.'[1] To a generation
innocent of any experience of what their descendants understand by total war, this highly articulate realization that war
could not be divorced from the life of the community — least
of all when that community was a liberal, industrial state such
as they knew theirs to be — could not fail to be a disturbing
experience. A modern student of war may indeed be impressed by their total unawareness of certain common consequences of modern war, especially in the economic field. But
to the historian it is on the contrary the breadth of their concept of the impact of war which is impressive. In England in
1854 there was already visible in many different social groups
a practical sense that a great war is not a purely military
matter. This is a phenomenon which deserves attention and
respect. That it has not received either is no doubt because in
the Crimean War reality was even less like anticipation than
is usual in human affairs.

In the event the war proved to be a mere two years' affair.
Neither on sea nor on land were there any really major operations. The casualties among combatants amounted to no more
than 95,000, of whom only 25,000 died in battle. When the
student of warfare seeks to study the first substantial military
exploitation of railways, ironclad ships, gunboats or rifled
small arms, it is to the American Civil War in the next decade
that he turns. It is true the Crimean War provides some inter-
esting and significant precedents, foreshadowing on a small
scale what was to come — for example, in the construction of
the first military railway from Balaklava to the heights above

[1] 14 February 1854.

LORD A——N.   LORD J. R——L.

A HOME AND FOREIGN QUESTION.

Johanna. "WHEN'S THE FIGHTING GOIN' TO BEGIN, GEORGE-ENA?"

(*Punch*, June 24, 1854)

Sebastopol and the use of ironclad gunboats at Kinburn and of steamships as transports. Nevertheless the fact remains that it was no Armageddon. It was a great war which failed to materialize.

It would however be a great mistake to conclude from this that it was an insignificant episode in English domestic history, still less that it made little impact on English public life at the time. In these brief two years the English public ran the gamut of many emotions, confidence, frustration, hysterical enthusiasm and even more hysterical rage and despair. As far as the public at home was concerned, the war had four quite distinct phases, each of which provoked its own response. Until the news of the landing in the Crimea in September 1854 it was a war which seemed to refuse really to begin. The Baltic fleet sailed in March 1854, but saw no action. Neither the Baltic nor the Black Sea was blockaded. By the time the military contingent which sailed to the Levant in February 1854 reached Varna, the Russians had left the Danubian Principalities and withdrawn to the Pruth. Odessa was bombarded in May, but on a very small scale — only military objectives were attacked. Thus six months after the outbreak of a war that was expected to be uniquely short and sharp, practically nothing had even been attempted: the fighting had virtually not begun. The public's sense of anticlimax was enormous.

Then at last came the news of the expedition to the Crimea and, one day after the landing, of the victory of the Alma. On 1 October a false report of the capture of Sebastopol spread throughout the country, and three weeks later news of the battle of Balaklava and the immediately renowned charge of the Light Brigade. For almost two months patriotic excitement, dismay at the casualty lists, and confidence in quick success were at their peak. It was only after the battle of Inkerman (5 November) that the public began to realize that the campaign would be a long and taxing one, and that the troops would have to spend the winter in the Crimea.

The shock was immense when just before Christmas 1854 *The Times* began its famous revelations about the state of the troops then settling down to besiege Sebastopol. The confidence and optimism so widespread (except in very well-informed circles) before the war began, the frustration of the first six months of the war and the excitement of the autumn all contributed to the spate of hysterical accusations and recriminations, the gloom and extremism, the impatience with all things established, which prevailed for the first difficult months of 1855. This third phase ended when in June 1855 the news of the war began to improve. The successful expedition to Kerch at the mouth of the Sea of Azov cut off the main source of Russian supplies. At Sebastopol, the Mamelon redoubt was captured although the Malakoff was not. In the Baltic the fortress of Sveaborg was taken and at last on 16 September 1855, Sebastopol itself. This last phase saw a mood of more sober confidence based on the belief that at last the nation's resources were being mobilized for a full-scale effort. It was a mood which was abruptly broken when the peace negotiations unexpectedly begun in January 1856 produced the Treaty of Paris two months later. To the end the public expected a spring campaign in 1856. The coming of this unimpressive peace was far more of a shock than the advent of war had ever been.

Thus in one of its phases the war enforced for several months a mood of national self-searching which can hardly be paralleled at any other time in the mid-Victorian 'age of equipoise'. For the first six months of 1855 at almost every articulate social level and to men of totally different outlooks, the war represented an inescapable challenge which stripped away the shams and compromises and time-honoured habits which gave English society its stability and cohesion. What Bagehot was to call 'the cake of custom' seemed to be breaking into fragments. Here then is one of the significant crises in national life, short perhaps, but revealing aspects of the state of things normally obscured. This does not mean that these months alone deserve attention. The significance of any crisis is made plain only by a study of its antecedents and its aftermath, and those antecedents are notoriously often unlike what contemporaries declare them to be. Wars in particular have sometimes been blamed for more, though often for less, than they deserve. What follows is an attempt to discover the impact (both psychological and practical) of the Crimean War upon the country's public life, with its unique political and economic institutions, not only during the crisis of 1855 but in each of its other phases as well.

PART ONE

Constitutional Government
on Trial

To the Crimean generation the essence of constitutional government was first and foremost the free expression of public opinion through the machinery of parliamentary representation, public meetings and the Press; and secondly, the restriction of the Crown's choice of ministers to members of either House and their continuous collective responsibility to Parliament for the conduct of affairs. It was only this second aspect of constitutional government whose compatibility with war was suspect from the beginning. For the distinction between parliamentary criticism and parliamentary control of the executive was obviously often hazy; and even when it was not, parliamentary criticism could easily become factious and improper rather than judicious and apt. It was this latter danger which most struck the mid-Victorians, whose memories of the Napoleonic War provided all too many examples of factious parliamentary opposition during a major war. Moreover they found it disturbing that in the war about to begin, Britain's enemy was the arch-autocracy of Europe and her ally a power that had recently returned to authoritarian rule. It was a platitude that speed, unity and decision came readily to authoritarian systems of government, while to a representative government they came not at all — or so at least the educated British public had recently found much reason to believe. Thomas Carlyle's diatribes against 'Downing Street men of straw' and 'parliamentary talking shops' were only the most colourful and widely discussed expressions of a discontent with British political institutions which had been growing since the end of the 1840s. The supreme value of the free expression of opinion, on the other hand, was increasingly a shibboleth with nearly every section of the public, bound up as it was with contemporary confidence in the wisdom of the average man, and

31

above all in this particular case with the far greater enthusiasm for the war shown by the public at large than by the governing group. Inevitably therefore it was chiefly the organization of the executive and its relationship to Parliament which aroused doubts as to the compatibility of the British constitution with military success, and not the free expression of opinion. Indeed the pressure of intensely patriotic opinion was widely expected to neutralize the weaknesses of representative government and collective responsibility; the willing support and enthusiasm of the country at large would provide a source of war-time strength which would counter-balance the hesitation and delay cabinet government might bring, especially as exemplified by Aberdeen's half-hearted Cabinet. Arguments and assumptions like these can be seen in a vague and disjointed form in nearly every circle of English society except the most eccentric and the most closely familiar with the daily exercise of political power: free institutions would be made to work by the moral qualities which they themselves fostered in the citizens who lived under them. Indeed if the war should prove long and arduous, the articulate and informed patriotism of a free country would, it was believed, contribute far more to military success than lack of executive authority took away. Were these anticipations correct? Did the Crimean War vindicate constitutional government along these lines and prove that whatever weaknesses English political institutions might have in war, they were cancelled out by the strength springing from the free expression of public opinion?

CHAPTER ONE

The Machinery of British Government under the Strain of War

THE principle enshrined in the machinery of British government was the ancient one of checks and balances, exemplified at the top by the formation of policy by the Cabinet, which then assumed collective responsibility to Parliament for the measures decided upon, and at the level of administration by a multitude of small but independent departments, often under the direction of a board. Yet 'the principle of war is authority',[1] and never was this more widely recognized than in 1854. Indeed (though this was not yet appreciated) the recent development of the electric telegraph, which made possible the continuous control of distant operations by the home authorities, made speed and decision in the government more vital than they had ever been before. Yet England entered the Crimean War with a Coalition Cabinet which contained more than one chronic trouble-maker, and with a notoriously complex system of military administration which had been considered ripe for reform for over twenty years. It was obvious from the beginning that changes of some sort were essential. But precisely what should they be, and could they be accomplished without sacrificing the essentials of the constitution?

The obvious solution was to hope for the emergence of an inspiring war leader within the Cabinet, and calls for a second Chatham soon began to be raised on all sides, reaching a climax in the winter of 1854–5 when the news from the front became grave. But which of the politicians was to fill this role? The men who held the two offices from which most might

---

[1] *Edinburgh Review*, ci (January 1855), 285.

be expected, those of Prime Minister and Secretary of State for War, were both at this time entirely unfitted to play any such part. Aberdeen was an exceptionally weak Prime Minister, incapable of bringing Cabinet discussions to a head, not attempting to co-ordinate the work of the departments, and moreover afflicted with 'want of manner and knowledge of how to deal with mankind, as well as lack of courage'.[1] Quite rightly, he always rejected as absurd any suggestion that he should direct war measures himself. The Secretary of State for War and Colonies (after June 1854 for War alone), the fifth Duke of Newcastle, was immensely industrious and not lacking in self-confidence, but he had a slow mind and was quite as deficient as Aberdeen in knowledge of how to deal with mankind.[2] There were however two politicians who might conceivably have taken their places, Lord John Russell and Palmerston. Lord John was fascinated by warfare, would have liked to be War Minister (or so at least he gave a close friend to believe),[3] and was restive about his position as second to Aberdeen. With these mixed motives he constantly nagged Aberdeen to achieve greater energy and efficiency. But in practice his energies proved more of a liability than anything else in the conduct of the war, for Lord John was impatient of details, very changeable, and had no sense of the practicable. His forays provoked constant Cabinet crises, and yet he was personally too far apart from the heads of the departments directly concerned with the war to exercise any influence upon them. In the end he had to learn from bitter experience that he lacked enough support to form a Cabinet of his own and try his powers as a great war leader. There remained Palmerston. The country at large was prepared in February 1855 when he first became Prime Minister to find in Palmerston

---

[1] Newcastle to Gladstone, 8 December 1851, J. Martineau, *Life of Henry Pelham, Fifth Duke of Newcastle* (1908), p. 106.

[2] Cf. *The Greville Memoirs*, ed. H. Reeve (1903 edn.), vii. 224.

[3] O. W. Hewett, '. . . *and Mr. Fortescue*' (The Diaries of Chichester Fortescue, Baron Carlingford) (1958), p. 67.

the second Chatham they had so long desired.[1] But the politicians were far more dubious; after all, his talent was clearly for diplomacy and not administration. As his speeches and ministerial appointments progressively revealed how little he had grasped the hysterically sensitive public mood of the moment, his stock fell steadily. Even inside the Cabinet, one of his ministers gave as his verdict: 'I cannot say we have improved in order and regularity under the new chief.'[2] Gladstone's (admittedly prejudiced) description of Palmerston's first Cabinet meeting was a gloomy one: 'It was more acephalous than ever; less order, less unity of purpose: Charles Wood had twice cried "*Will* the Cabinet decide *something* upon *some* point?" P., though he had appeared more éveillé than usual, had taken no lead. . . .'[3]

Admittedly the Cabinets of the early 1850s were exceptionally difficult to control, with their plethora of highly experienced and articulate politicians, ready to dogmatize about half a dozen departments. After the final resignation of the Peelites and the disgrace of Lord John Russell, Palmerston was able to treat his rather second-rate Cabinet very differently, and by October Sidney Herbert believed that 'Palmerston is master of his Cabinet now'.[4] In practice there was an inner Cabinet of Palmerston, Lansdowne and Clarendon, and the rest were little consulted.[5] Nevertheless Clarendon was probably right when he described Palmerston 'as not a good man for general business' (he disliked the details of the Home Office, for example, and was often careless), and doubted whether he had precisely the qualities necessary for leading

[1] G. Hamilton to Disraeli, [7?] February 1855, Hughenden MSS., B xx 98.
[2] Sir Charles Wood to Lord John Russell, undated, but about 26 February 1855, Public Record Office, Russell Papers, P.R.O. 30/22/12.
[3] Add. MS. 44745, fo. 63.
[4] Herbert to Gladstone, 7 October 1855, Add. MS. 44210, fo. 210.
[5] M. C. M. Simpson, *Many Memories of Many People* (1898), p. 214; Hewett, op. cit., p. 113. Panmure later came to take Lansdowne's place.

the House of Commons;[1] and these weaknesses in the field of administration and parliamentary debate were to be serious drawbacks when he became Prime Minister in the crisis of the war.

In short, no 'hero', no 'great man', was forthcoming among the public men of the day to demonstrate reassuringly that the right man could make the most cumbersome machinery of government to work. Nor was one forthcoming among the soldiers: the risk of military dictatorship, though often talked of, was in England quite non-existent, if only because of the total lack of even moderately competent generals. For England, though not for her French ally, the Crimean War was beyond dispute a civilians' war, and not one run by a group of professional soldiers. The Cabinet contained no military man and took no professional advice; Newcastle merely showed the despatches he thought important to the aged Commander-in-Chief, Lord Hardinge, who was by this time very irresolute and timid.[2] Hardinge's chief merit, as one Cabinet minister, Lord Granville, realistically confided to Lord John Russell at the beginning of the crisis of the war, was that 'Newcastle, Sidney Herbert and Prince Albert can bully him and make him adopt improvements which old military men of sterner stuff would resist'. Raglan, the commander in the East, was so extremely reticent about his circumstances and plans that, to quote Granville again, 'the War Office and the Cabinet derive no assistance from their general in the East'.[3] Yet after he died no better successor could be found than General Simpson (a complete nonentity), and when Hardinge too had to be replaced in 1856, Prince Albert could only comment about the appointment of the Queen's cousin the Duke of

[1] Sir H. Maxwell, *Life and Letters of George, fourth Earl of Clarendon* (1913), ii. 62. As Prime Minister, Palmerston 'left the Departments pretty much to themselves' (Lord Broughton's Diary, 19 April 1856, British Museum, Broughton MSS., Add. MSS. 43759, fo. 93).

[2] Simpson, op. cit., p. 152; Hewett, op. cit., p. 67; *Parliamentary Papers* (hereafter *P.P.*), 1854–5, ix. i, question 20749.

[3] P.R.O. 30/22/11, 23 December 1854.

Cambridge to succeed him, 'The sad thing is that there should not have been even a choice, so completely have we run out our stock of Generals competent to command.'[1] Thus even in the midst of the Crimean campaign the Cabinet had no military adviser of any weight to fall back upon; the civilians were obliged to go it alone, and the confident optimism of the larger public that mysteriously 'the hour would call forth the man' received a rude shock. Despite public hopes and indeed confident expectations, the Crimean War failed to throw up either a soldier or a politician of outstanding force. It ruined the reputation of many men, and made the reputation of none. Many people would have echoed Sir George Sinclair's lament to the aged Croker: 'There seems to prevail a fatal mediocrity in every department — in the Cabinet, no Chatham; in the Navy, no Nelson; in the Army, no Wellington; in the Church, no Luther.'[2] Inevitably, therefore, more than ever depended upon governmental machinery; and in this field no miracles could even be hoped for. Despite the impatience which many contemporaries felt with Cabinet government, despite the contempt which the English system of military administration had for long attracted, willy-nilly the conduct of the Crimean War hinged upon the efficiency of their functioning.

It was, however, not until the invasion of the Crimea at the very end of September 1854 that the compatibility of the English cabinet system with war was really put to the test. Unluckily the invasion coincided with the annual dead season in English political life, when Parliament was in recess and London deserted by Society. Throughout the vital first weeks of the Crimean expedition the Duke of Newcastle was the only Cabinet minister in London, and Cabinet meetings were suspended entirely in the normal way. (The Court, too, was absent,

[1] Prince Albert to Granville, 14 July 1856, Public Record Office, Granville Papers, P.R.O. 30/29/31.

[2] 20 November 1855, *The Croker Papers*, ed. L. J. Jennings (1885), iii. 354.

D

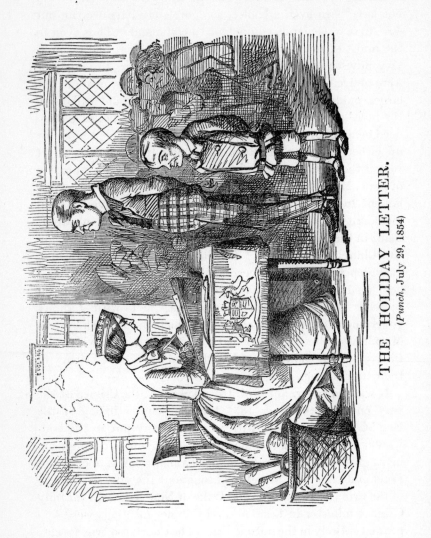

THE HOLIDAY LETTER.

(*Punch*, July 29, 1854)

at Balmoral.) When the Cabinet did meet again early in November, it was already clear that the expedition had run into difficulties, and recriminations were beginning. Lord John Russell was by that time established again at his grace-and-favour residence in Richmond Park, Pembroke Lodge, but as his father-in-law Lord Minto warned him, 'Even Pembroke Lodge is too distant to enable you to learn how very great is the clamour of indignation gathering against the government for its neglect of timely and sufficient exertion in the conduct of this war.'[1] As the situation deteriorated, so it became increasingly obvious that either the Cabinet or the war departments must be drastically revitalized. But which? Even the fabled Peelite administrators had proved to have feet of clay, and some Cabinet ministers felt it was essential for the Cabinet not to leave the departments to run the war themselves. As the Duke of Argyll confided to Lord John, recent experiences over transports for reinforcements had shown him that 'Departmental ideas of *the possible*' ought not to be relied upon; 'there are innate tendencies in all Departmental administration which require the vigilance of those who look upon the subject from other points of view'.[2] Sir George Grey felt the same.[3] But Lord John (no doubt partly for personal reasons) felt that it was from the departments and not from the Cabinet that something could be hoped. 'A cabinet', he told Aberdeen, 'is a cumbrous and unwieldy instrument for carrying on war. It can furnish suggestions, or make a decision upon a measure submitted to it, but it cannot administer.'[4] As the leader of the Whigs, Lord John was in no position to urge on the Peelites who were in control of the war departments and he soon produced a plan to reorganize military

[1] Minto to Lord John Russell, 16 November 1854, P.R.O. 30/22/11.

[2] Argyll to Lord John Russell, 17 November 1854, ibid.

[3] Memorandum of Sir George Grey, 8 January 1855, P.R.O. 30/22/12.

[4] Lord John Russell to Aberdeen, 28 November 1854, British Museum, Aberdeen Papers, Add. MS. 43068, fo. 205.

administration in order to strengthen a new War Minister, who should be Palmerston.[1]

The difficulties were not to be so easily resolved. The Coalition Government fell, and with it these proposals. Palmerston's method after he became Prime Minister in February 1855 seems to have been to by-pass the Cabinet upon important questions and to settle nearly everything himself in collaboration with the two key departmental ministers, Clarendon at the Foreign Office and Panmure at the War Office.[2] This 'inner Cabinet', however, was probably the result not of any views Palmerston entertained about the machinery of government in time of war, but of his own informal personality and habits and the fact that his Cabinet could be not unfairly described as a 'Ministry of all the mediocrities'. One significant development in Cabinet organization did, however, come about in 1855. The violent criticisms of the suspension of Cabinet meetings in the autumn of 1854 which had appeared in the Press and which were repeated by the notorious Select Committee on the state of the Army before Sebastopol, was one large factor in the setting up of a War Committee of the Cabinet — an anticipation of the small War Council set up in November 1915 in the midst of the Gallipoli expedition. It was to these War Committee meetings, which began as soon as Parliament rose in August 1855, that what *The Times* called 'the more immediate conduct of the war' was now entrusted. Yet this Committee was clearly far more than a mere face-saving formal substitute for meetings of the full Cabinet during the recess.[3] It continued to meet when the

[1] Sir Charles Wood to Lord John Russell, 11 December 1854, British Museum, Halifax Papers, Add. MS. 49531, fo. 92; Memorandum by Lord John Russell, 2 December 1854, P.R.O. 30/22/11.

[2] One member of the Cabinet reported that Palmerston 'never expressed any definite opinions or intentions to the Cabinet at all' (Herbert to Aberdeen, 30 November 1855, Add. MS. 43197, fo. 144), and another that since the resignation of the Peelites 'there is no longer anything deserving the name of discussion' (Add. MS. 44207, fo. 17).

[3] Unknown to the public, four ministers (Newcastle, Aberdeen, Clarendon and Graham) had privately met quite often in the critical

Cabinet was also meeting. Full Cabinet meetings were not wholly suspended in the autumn of 1855, despite the meetings of the Committee. It was thus a genuine administrative device for the more efficient conduct of the war, as well as a political manœuvre. Its membership was small (four: Palmerston himself, Wood of the Admiralty, Panmure of the War Office and Lord Granville, the President of the Council), but no doubt all the more efficient for that, and it summoned professional experts freely to its meetings according to the business to be discussed. There is no evidence that its decisions had necessarily to be endorsed by the Cabinet, though no doubt major ones were.[1] In these last months of the war it was dealing not only with strategy but with administrative points as well. Its very frequent and lengthy meetings in January 1856 to brief the British representatives at the Allied council of war in Paris show that this was the body which was to plan and provide for the campaign of 1856 which was never fought. Its continued existence even after the end of the war[2] suggests that it had proved of value in securing some at least of that departmental co-operation at Cabinet level whose absence in nineteenth-century England has often been lamented.[3]

Thus the shortcomings of the Cabinet system which the autumn of 1854 made all too obvious, were overcome not by the expedient of a war-time 'strong man', military or civilian, nor by some miracle of patriotic unity within the Cabinet, but by the device of a small *ad hoc* Cabinet Committee. Constitutional principles had certainly not been jettisoned,

---

autumn of 1854 (Nottingham University Library, Newcastle MSS. Ne C 12245, Newcastle to Mrs. Sidney Herbert, 1 May 1856).

[1] The evidence cited to the contrary in J. P. Mackintosh, *The British Cabinet* (1962), p. 138, seems inconclusive.

[2] It was in existence at the time of the Trent crisis in December 1861 (B. Connell, *Regina v. Palmerston* (1962), p. 299, quoting Palmerston to the Queen, 5 December 1861).

[3] Some further details and evidence upon this War Committee of the Cabinet are furnished by the present author in *English Historical Review*, lxxix (July 1964), 548–51.

although the cry for drastic changes had been loud in the hysterical spring of 1855. The efficiency of cabinet government depends, however, not only upon the internal organization of the Cabinet, but also upon the relations between Cabinet and legislature. This was the aspect of cabinet government on which contemporary doubts were gravest before the war began, and with good reason. The perennial problem of securing ministerial responsibility to Parliament without weakening ministerial authority can only be smoothly solved when the conventions of the constitution accurately reflect the political realities of the day, and with a fortunate conjuncture of political personalities. In the Crimean War both these conditions were lacking. Only one way out was seen: unfailing support of government on all matters connected with the war. Yet it should have been obvious that although abstention from opposition would furnish an impressive demonstration of national unity, it would also deprive the nation of a valuable safety-valve and the executive itself of a useful goad or deterrent. In any case no such self-denying ordinance was likely to survive the strain of set-back and defeats, and so indeed it soon proved.

In the opening months of 'phoney' war, before the parliamentary recess began in August 1854, the relationship between executive and legislature was put to no more searching test than Gladstone's financial proposals provided. But the atmosphere was already very different when Parliament reassembled on 12 December for a brief emergency session in order to pass a government Bill allowing the enlistment of foreign mercenaries — proof in itself to many members that military recruiting had been bungled. The Government took refuge, as had become its habit, in a threat to resign if the Bill were rejected. These tactics properly provoked the opposition to claim that 'It is a privilege of Parliament freely to canvass the conduct of Government without being forced to incur the responsibility of asking the House of Commons to sanction a change of Ministry.' Their leader Disraeli now insisted that his promise at the beginning of the war had been only to abstain from criticism of the country's naval and military commanders, not of the Cabinet.[1] Finally the Bill, much amended, scraped through, but this short session had made it clear that in this war no more than in any other would the legislature escape charges of lack of patriotism or the executive accusations of suppressing parliamentary freedom of speech. By the time Parliament reassembled five weeks later, *The Times*'s strongly phrased revelations about the deplorable condition of the expeditionary force in the Crimea were arousing such excitement that it was obvious that ministerial authority was likely to be entirely submerged beneath the enforcement of ministerial responsibility to Parliament. For the next two months the executive plumbed depths of weakness in its relations with the legislature rarely paralleled in modern British history. 'Tear 'em' Roebuck, a chronic malcontent whose reputation was far higher with the public than with his fellow members, immediately gave notice of a motion for the setting-up of a Select Committee to enquire into the state of the Army before Sebastopol, whereupon Lord John announced his resignation. On 29 January Roebuck's motion, although made a matter of confidence by the Government, was passed by 305 votes to 148 (a defeat frequently described as one of the most shameful ever inflicted upon a British Government), and the Aberdeen Cabinet resigned. For the next week the Queen sent for one political leader after another and shuttled back and forth between Windsor Castle and Buckingham Palace on 'our eternal Government hunting errand'.[2] Finally on 6 February Palmerston kissed hands as First Lord of the Treasury. At the end of this prolonged ministerial interregnum and in the midst of war, Parliament was adjourned for a week while ministers sought re-election. When on 16 February a Government at last confronted the House, excitement out-

[1] 3 *Hansard*, cxxxvi, col. 200 (12 December 1854).
[2] Elizabeth Longford, *Victoria R. I.* (1964), p. 246, quoting the Queen's Journal, 5 February 1855.

doors was still so intense that Roebuck's motion could not be dropped, although many of its original supporters inside Parliament had regarded it merely as a device for getting rid of the Aberdeen Ministry.[1] The Peelite members of Palmerston's Cabinet thereupon resigned a second time. Not until the beginning of April were all the posts at last filled, often by second-rate or little-known men and after many refusals. Nor were the Government's troubles even then over. In the spring a peace conference was held at Vienna at which Lord John Russell was the British plenipotentiary. Not long after his return, without peace with honour, it emerged that he had been prepared to accept peace terms very different from those which he had officially insisted upon and defended in the House. The uproar over his renewed duplicity — this time to his country as well as to his colleagues — obliged him to resign on 16 July. Once more Palmerston had to reshuffle and augment his scratch crew. When the House finally dispersed on 13 August 1855, the Government's majority had on one important measure for the prosecution of the war (the guarantee of the second Turkish loan) sunk as low as three. On this inglorious note the war-time confrontation of executive and legislature virtually came to an end. By the time Parliament reassembled on 31 January 1856 peace negotiations had already begun.

Thus in the event Parliament had quite failed consistently to support the Government's conduct of the war or to rise above political faction. The prolonged ministerial interregnum and subsequent parliamentary adjournment, after the House of Commons had forced the resignation of the Aberdeen Cabinet on 29 January, seemed to show all too clearly that a system of cabinet government might well leave the nation with no government at all, even in the midst of war. The activities of Roebuck's Select Committee and the resignation of the Peelites and later of Lord John Russell drove the lesson

[1] See, for example, Palmerston to the Queen, 20 February 1855, Royal Archives, Windsor Castle, A 24/1.

of the intrinsic instability of responsible government yet further home. On both sides of the Channel this lesson was taken very much to heart. On the Continent British prestige sank very low in the first half of 1855 as British military incompetence in the Crimea and political instability at home broke the spell of Wellington's victories and of the cult of *Parlamentarismus*.[1] In England, generations of constitutional smugness, accentuated since 1848, made the shock and disillusionment all the greater. Everywhere it was felt that a demonstration in applied political theory was being furnished by the war — a feeling which did much to heighten the emotional intensity, but not the clarity, of debate. Precisely why had the British system of government apparently failed to stand the test of war? Had British representative institutions in reality succumbed to extraneous pressures which had nothing to do with the war? or were they themselves incompletely representative or otherwise defective? If so, it could be argued that these disturbing events proved nothing about the intrinsic merit of representative institutions in time of war.

The discussion focused upon the two most dramatic political failures. Where should the blame be placed for the obviously deplorable delay in finding a government to replace the Aberdeen Coalition? Secondly, was the setting up of the Sebastopol Committee indeed either unconstitutional or unwise? On the first issue, it was clear that the delay was the result of the conventions the Crown felt obliged to observe and of the attitudes of the country's political leaders. It was pointed out that the conventional restriction of the Crown's choice of ministers to members of either House imposed a limitation particularly irksome in an emergency. But it was argued that this could be overcome without jeopardizing the essentials of representative government if the Crown were allowed to make

---

[1] *The Times* pointed out on 3 April 1855: 'Our institutions and proceedings attract more attention abroad now than in any former war.'

a certain number of ministers Members of Parliament *ex officio*, perhaps with the right to speak but not to vote. To those of logical mind, the decline of party feeling since 1846 clearly implied a return to the ancient ideal of government by a coalition of the wise and good chosen by the Sovereign on grounds of individual aptitude for the post concerned, and accordingly the substitution of individual for collective ministerial responsibility.[1] On the other hand it could be argued that the weakness lay in the personal qualities of the politicians, not in the conventions of the constitution. Had the Reform Act of 1832 created a shortage of potential ministerial material? Conservatives liked to argue that many of the representatives chosen by the new large urban constituencies were quite unsuitable for office, and in any case a business or professional man's time would often be too precious to allow him to accept office if it were offered. Those with more radical sympathies naturally preferred to find the fault in a tacit restriction of office to the old governing class. They raised again the well-worn cry against a selfish aristocratic monopoly of power, and this time their cry was made highly effective by the obvious truth in charges of cliquishness, rancour and egoism among the politicians of the day.[2] To those who argued in this way the favourite remedies were an extension of the franchise, the introduction of the ballot, or the improvement of the political judgment of the existing electorate either by fancy franchises or by general processes of education and moral improvement. In short, there was a strong feeling that much was amiss with 'the System' in England; yet although both legislature and executive had suffered a severe loss of prestige, representative institutions themselves were not usually considered to have been proved defective. Naturally those

[1] W. R. Greg argued thus in 'Government by Parties or by Statesmen?', *North British Review*, xxiv (November 1855), 183–96. See also ibid. xxv (May 1856), 103–7.

[2] For example, even Lord Clarendon felt these charges were justified (Clarendon to Stratford Canning, 23 February 1855, Public Record Office, Stratford Canning Papers, F.O. 352/42).

who were already convinced of the inefficiency of representative government — Carlyle the hero-worshipper, Richard Congreve the positivist, for example, and many professional soldiers — hailed the experiences of the Crimean War as proof of their rightness. But most people were able to deny that representative institutions themselves had been found wanting, on the grounds that English institutions were not truly representative, or were bedevilled by aristocratic social institutions, or, more moderately, because their operation was distorted by the peculiar political circumstance of the 1850s.

No such evasions were possible with regard to the setting up of the Sebastopol Committee. This was a decision which clearly called in question the functions and calibre of the House of Commons alone, taken as it was in the teeth of the advice of two successive governments. Was the appointment of the Committee in accordance with constitutional principles, or was it an improper encroachment on the sphere of the executive? Was it of service to the British war effort, or a foolish, unpatriotic blunder? On both counts the Peelites damned the Committee so whole-heartedly that they twice resigned office in protest against its appointment. Since the enquiry was to be into a situation still existing, and not into a past disaster, it seemed to them an unprecedented infringement of the constitutional convention that Parliament's control over the conduct of administration was indirect only, and must be exercised through the ministers of the Crown. Most people, however, found their ideas on this, as on many other issues, unduly pedantic[1] and realized, moreover, that some of

---

[1] Later constitutional historians have shared this view that the Peelites were mistaken (Alpheus Todd, *On Parliamentary Government in England* (1867), p. 334; Sir William Anson, *The Law and Custom of the Constitution*, 5th edn. (1922), i. 399; A. Berriedale Keith, *The Constitution of England from Queen Victoria to George VI* (1940), i. 361). The judgments of two more specialized studies (H. Clokie and J. Robinson, *Royal Commissions of Inquiry* (1937), pp. 71–2 and G. W. Keeton, *Trial by Tribunal* (1960), p. 39) are distorted by misapprehensions about the political situation at that moment.

the leading Peelites had a fairly obvious personal bias against a committee — Newcastle, Graham and Sidney Herbert were the heads of the service departments most likely to come under fire. Less obviously Gladstone, always prone to obsessions, happened to be deeply involved in a patronage dispute which had already convinced him that the House of Commons was steadily encroaching upon the executive through the device of select committees of enquiry.[1] Their practical objections, however, carried more weight, particularly their emphasis upon the strain which a public enquiry would impose both upon the maintenance of authority and discipline in the armed forces, and upon good relations with the French, who it was believed would be shown to deserve much of the blame. The decisive debate on 23 February 1855 was studded with arguments from precedents, comparisons with the French Convention of 1792 and vague threats of despatching representatives *en mission* to the seat of war, but the real issue was plainly whether a government conducting a war needed to be immune from official enquiry or not. To some, Sir George Grey seemed right in insisting that this was 'a period when greater confidence should be placed in the hands of government than under ordinary circumstances, and when it is essential that the hands of government should be left free and unfettered'. Consequently, as a Peelite pamphleteer argued, the Committee had 'dealt a blow on the cause of constitutional government, by affording reasonable grounds for the fear entertained abroad that a ruling power which holds office at the will of public opinion, is too weak for energetic action'.[2] But many others agreed with Spencer Walpole that 'publicity and enquiry are the life and soul of representative government' and

[1] Several weeks earlier, Gladstone as Chancellor of the Exchequer had dismissed a distant connexion of Lord John Russell, one J. T. Kennedy, from his post as Commissioner of Woods and Forests, and a movement was afoot among Kennedy's influential Whig connexions in the House for the appointment of a Select Committee of Enquiry. The Gladstone and Aberdeen papers for this time are full of this affair.

[2] Peter Benson Maxwell, *Whom shall we hang?* (1855), p. 18.

that the setting up of a committee would represent merely the active exercise of an admitted historic function of the legislature.[1] Only a few, however, went so far as to support Roebuck's claim that 'vigorous parliamentary action alone could overcome the *vis inertiae* of administration', and there was no real repetition of the parliamentary encroachments of the seventeenth century dreaded by Gladstone. In 1855 the key to the situation was not that the legislature was strong (it was not), but that the executive was weak. The effects of the Parliamentary Reform Act of 1832, the withering away of party issues and party discipline and the growing weight of public opinion had all combined to create in Members an attitude of independence with regard to the executive which was well appreciated in political circles. Moreover this particular Parliament contained exceptionally large numbers of 'loose fish' who (in the words of an *Edinburgh* reviewer), 'as a narrow view of their interest prompted, were ready to serve or overthrow the government of the day.'[2] and from its first session it had used both Select Committees and Questions very freely, often merely to satisfy curiosity or attract personal notice.[3] It was thus entirely predictable that under the strain of military failure a Parliament as undisciplined as that of 1852 confronting an executive as heterogeneous as Aberdeen's and then as unimpressive as Palmerston's, would prove fickle, pliable and uncertain.

But the subsequent history of the Sebastopol Committee made very plain how hollow the threat of legislative usurpation of executive functions really was. As early as 23 April even *The Times* denounced the Committee as merely another example of the jobbery which permeated the country's political life. Its members had been chosen in reality by agreement

[1] 3 *Hansard*, xxxxvi, cols. 1743–864 (23 February 1855).
[2] 'The Past Session and the New Parliament', *Edinburgh Review*, cv (April 1857), 553.
[3] [Erskine May], 'The Machinery of Parliamentary Legislation', ibid. xcix (January 1854), 252.

between the Government, Roebuck and Disraeli, and the lack of method, concert and preparation shown at its meetings completed its ineffectiveness. Little that was new emerged from its 'desultory and rambling' proceedings, it 'asked the wrong questions from the wrong witnesses' and 'furnished innumerable specimens of impotence', if not of malice.[1] Thus in the event the dreaded Committee failed to act either as judge or goad of the executive, or even to provide a safety valve for public discontent and indignation about the situation in the Crimea. In fact the true significance of this most notorious of the House of Commons' Crimean War activities lay in the sphere of relations between the House and the public without doors, and not in that of relations between the House and the executive. Many politicians openly acknowledged that the real reason why the House insisted upon setting up the Committee on 23 February 1855 was the clamour for it outside Parliament. The insignificant upshot of the Committee's sittings, however, merely furnished additional proof of a state of affairs whose existence was becoming all too obvious: the failure of Parliament effectively to reflect the moods and wishes of the public and the consequent resort of the political public of the mid-nineteenth century to extra-parliamentary pressure groups, leagues and associations and to political journalism of many kinds. Thus the Sebastopol Committee both expressed and encouraged one of the most deep-seated trends of the period: that away from parliamentary government and towards a kind of direct democracy.

Neither the legislative nor the executive branch of the machinery of government, then, had come triumphantly through the test of war. What of military administration itself? The fact that the newly created War Committee of the Cabinet performed some administrative duties of a kind that

[1] *The Times*, 16 May 1855; Peter Benson Maxwell, op. cit., pp. 21, 24.

would scarcely have come before the full Cabinet, suggests in itself some degree of failure satisfactorily to reorganize military administration. In reality it was in this highly complex field, and not in that of Cabinet organization or the relationship between legislature and executive, that the main effort to adapt the machinery of government to the strain of war was made. What was the nature and significance of this effort?

Probably the most familiar of all commonplaces about the Crimean War is that it 'disclosed' or 'revealed' the faults of the 'cumbrous' machinery of British military administration.[1] Only slightly less familiar is the view that the changes made as a result were 'swift and sweeping', 'the headlong expedients of a Cabinet of terrified men'.[2] All of this is quite misleading. Nothing could be a greater mistake than to suppose that it needed the sufferings of the troops in the Crimea to make it obvious that the British system of military administration was in need of reform. On the contrary, this had been widely recognized for at least twenty years. The recommendation in 1837 by Lord Howick's strong Commission in favour of consolidation of the numerous military departments — a report signed by Palmerston, Lord John Russell and Edward Ellice among others — was repeated in 1850 by the Select Committee on Naval, Military and Ordnance expenditure. In fact British military administration suffered in the Crimean War not from having been ignored, but from having been debated too often and too long. As soon as war seemed inevitable, it was widely agreed that unity and promptness of action were essential, and that the existing system did not promote these qualities. The old argument in favour of reform, that it would save public money, was replaced by considerations of military efficiency; everyone saw that war would force some decision upon this

[1] See, for example, Woodward, op. cit., p. 259, and Briggs, op. cit., p. 382.
[2] Hampden Gordon, *The War Office* (1935), p. 51; Sir John Fortescue, *History of the British Army*, xiii (1929), 171.

well-worn controversy. But here agreement ended. Exactly what changes of organization were desirable and which of them should be effected immediately? Both the discussion and the accomplishment of reform were continuous throughout the war, but since the leading politicians were already committed to one plan or another, it was almost impossible to debate these questions on the merits of the situation as it existed between 1854 and 1856, or to settle them expeditiously. Moreover the fact that the Press, the military departments themselves and the Court also had reforming ideas, made progress all the more difficult. Thus it was not apathy or even conservatism which bedevilled British military administration, but the very staleness of the question, combined with the variety of the changes recommended in so many different quarters. Unfortunately this combination of a widespread expectation yet slow accomplishment of change led to the adoption of temporary expedients, failure to replace officials on active service abroad, and a general feeling of improvisation and insecurity. Thus the much-publicized Crimean disasters did not begin a debate upon military administration; rather, they made it imperative to end a debate which had already been unduly prolonged. In so far as they thereby accomplished what the Cabinet should have achieved long before, they did indeed reveal — or rather offer further proof of — the weaknesses of the British system of government. But the Aberdeen Cabinet's inactivity was the result of indecision, not of ignorance or apathy. Ultimately, it was the lack of any single undisputed war leader who could overcome the evils of collective responsibility which was to blame for the excessive discussion and scanty action of the Coalition Government. In this sense alone — of too much talk and not too little — was the unhappy history of military administration in 1854–5 indeed an indictment of cabinet government, and even in this sense the aftermath of the crisis suggests that the indictment was not altogether just.

Long before the war began, then, there were already a variety

of well-formulated proposals for the reform of military administration. No one was surprised when early in February 1854
The Times launched a campaign for greater simplification,
consolidation and unity in the military departments.[1] In
Parliament, too, the need for consolidation of the military
departments was debated as soon as war appeared likely.
Nearly four weeks before war was declared, the division within
the Cabinet between the veteran consolidators (led by Lord
John Russell) and the more pragmatic Peelites, had been made
plain to the House. The spokesman of the latter, Sidney
Herbert, asserted in debate that circumstances had entirely
changed since the Report of 1837 was drawn up, that regular
inter-departmental meetings would increase efficiency far
more than consolidation, and that in any case good will
mattered more than machinery. He wanted some reorganization within the Ordnance and the Commissariat (these two
departments had long been the black sheep of military administration) and the creation of a supervising authority, but not
consolidation, not, that is, a single war department under a
Secretary of State.[2] Once more, however, the Peelites were in
a minority, although probably an enlightened one. Certainly
in Parliament and in the Press, consolidation under a real
Minister of War was the watchword. Despite their lip-service
to the virtues of practical experience, the men of that generation were in fact exceptionally addicted to belief in a few
simple dogmas, and in the 1850s 'sound administrative
theory' denounced boards and committees and the prolifera-
tion of independent departments. It therefore seemed in
this case to dictate consolidation under a Secretary of State.
Throughout May 1854 *The Times* thundered forth its impatience.[3] Finally the pressure of public opinion obliged

[1] See above, pp. 10–11.
[2] 3 *Hansard*, cxxxi, cols. 233–45 (2 March 1854). There was an
important debate in the Lords on the administration of the Army
on 7 April 1854 (ibid. cxxxii, cols. 606–69).
[3] *The Times*, 6, 20 and 24 May 1854.

E

the Government to announce a measure of reform of some kind.

It was Lord John Russell — not only a veteran army reformer but also as Leader of the House constantly suffering from the impatience of the House for consolidation — who forced the question before Aberdeen and then before the Cabinet. Lord John listed three possible courses: to upgrade the Secretary at War, to create a Military Board on the lines of the Admiralty, or to create a new Secretary of State for War alone (not for War and the Colonies) with control over the Commander-in-Chief, the Secretary at War, the Ordnance and the Commissariat. In the midst of war he considered the last plan the most practicable, as well as intrinsically the best.[1] But he was prepared to admit that ' this is not the moment for consolidating and re-arranging departments which have at least practice and experience in the conduct of military affairs ', and therefore that the new Secretary of State should merely survey and examine these four departments with a view to consolidation at a more fitting time.[2] To the creation of this fourth Secretary of State the rest of the Cabinet agreed, if only because otherwise, as the Foreign Secretary put it, 'The first untoward event that arises in either [the Department of War or of Colonies] will be attributed, and perhaps not un-justly, to our obstinately attempting, contrary to public opinion, to do what is impossible.' But the exact scope of the new Secretary of State's powers and the wider implications of the decision remained undecided. To Wood, Molesworth, Sir George Grey and Lord John Russell himself the change was to be the beginning of the consolidation of all branches of military administration under a Secretary of State. On the other hand, Sidney Herbert, that redoubtable enemy of consolidation, hoped the new Secretary of State would give

---

[1] Memorandum of 24 April 1854, Add. MS. 43068, fo. 28; Lord John Russell to Aberdeen, 5 May 1854, ibid., fo. 55.

[2] Memorandum of 20 May 1854 (circulated to the Cabinet), P.R.O. 30/22/11.

only 'the supervision of one recognized authority' over the military departments.[1] Herbert evidently won some substantial success, for in his third Memorandum of 31 May 1854 Lord John mentioned only the new minister's control over the Commander-in-Chief and the Ordnance; the Secretary at War was 'to retain his present functions'.[2] Again, to Aberdeen, and equally to Newcastle also, the step was reluctantly conceded only as a means of postponing consolidation, in short of 'allaying the anxiety of the publick Mind, and of preventing any desire of further change for some time to come'. It was in this light that Aberdeen always presented the measure to the Queen.[3] Nevertheless, she only consented to the step because she failed to focus her attention upon it until it was too late to resist. Since the beginning of April she and the Prince had been preoccupied with the much more far-reaching proposals which the third Earl Grey was propounding in the House of Lords. Ever since he had presided, as Lord Howick, over the Royal Commission of 1837, Grey had urged the remodelling of military administration on the lines of the Admiralty Board, with one of the three existing Secretaries of State controlling the use of the Army precisely as they controlled the use of the Navy. To him, there was 'no distinction between the military and any other branch of the executive authority of the Crown', so far as the prerogative was

[1] Sir George Grey to Lord John Russell, encl. in Lord John Russell to Aberdeen, 5 June 1855, Add. MS. 43068, fo. 76. Various memoranda of Cabinet ministers on Lord John Russell's Memorandum of 20 May, dated 22 and 23 May 1854, P.R.O. 30/22/11.

[2] Memorandum of Lord John Russell, 31 May 1854, Add. MS. 43068, fo. 70.

[3] Aberdeen to the Queen, 30 May 1854, Add. MS. 43049, fo. 123; See also Aberdeen to Lord John Russell, 30 May and 5 June 1854, Add. MSS. 43068, fos. 66 and 84. However a year later in giving evidence before the Sebastopol Committee Aberdeen claimed to have thought this step 'certainly only initiatory to other changes that were to follow' (P.P. 1854–5, ix, i, question 21367). Newcastle's attitude is described in Sir Charles Wood to Lord Grey, 7 June 1854, Prior's Kitchen, Durham, Grey MSS.

concerned,[1] and what was needed was 'not a new Minister for *War*, but a new organization of the office for the management of the *Army*' — a much more disturbing proposal.[2] The Queen as late as 29 May was still concentrating upon explaining to Aberdeen her strong objections to this plan and her alarm lest her government by condemning the existing system should seem to support Grey.[3] A few days later an ultimatum from Lord John in face of the perilous parliamentary situation carried the Cabinet and then the Queen 'by storm', as Prince Albert wrote indignantly. She had to be content with Lord John's undertaking that further changes should be an open question and Aberdeen's assurance that he and Newcastle (who as the new Secretary of State for War would be entrusted with working out the inevitable readjustments) were 'determined not to break down the present arrangements'. Thus the decision announced on 8 June 1854 to create a fourth Secretary of State was 'carried without a definite plan, leaving everything to the future!!', as the Prince rightly noted with horror.[4] Between them the anti-consolidationists for their various reasons had ensured that the creation of the fourth Secretaryship did little more than relieve Newcastle from the demands made upon his time by colonial business. It might well seem, as Karl Marx brutally put it, that 'the only merit of the change is the creation of a new ministerial place'.[5]

Indeed it could be argued — and soon was — that the confusion of military administration had actually been increased

[1] Prince Albert to Aberdeen, reporting a conversation with Grey, Add. MS. 43049, fo. 7, 2 April 1854; 3 *Hansard*, cxxxii, cols. 606–39 (7 April 1854); Aberdeen to Lord John Russell, 29 May 1854, Add. MS. 43068, fo. 61.

[2] Grey to Henry Drummond, 5 June 1854, Grey MSS.

[3] The Queen to Aberdeen, Add. MS. 43049, fos. 119–20, 29 May 1854.

[4] Minute by Prince Albert, 8 June 1854, *The Letters of Queen Victoria*, ed. A. C. Benson and Viscount Esher, iii (1907), 42.

[5] Leader in the *New York Times* of 9 June 1854, *The Eastern Question*, p. 373.

by the creation of a Minister of War without transferring to him full powers over at least every civil department of military administration; above all, that by leaving the War Office with a Cabinet minister at its head, a duality had been created between Secretary of State and Secretary at War.[1] It is not surprising that the general opinion was that the new arrangement had been dictated by personal considerations,[2] nor that before the estimates for the new department came before the House, Lord John Russell felt it necessary to call a meeting of the Government's supporters to justify what had been done.[3] Lord John himself had tried once more to get his colleagues to accept a more comprehensive plan, arguing in favour of a six-member Army Board to assist the new Secretary of State, but without success. When the debate came on a fortnight later he could only assure the House yet again that reorganization was under discussion.[4] One small change was announced however: the transfer of the Commissariat from the Treasury to the new department. The anomaly of allowing the supreme controller of expenditure to have under it one of the chief spending departments had been denounced for the last twenty years, and the creation of the new War Department made it impossible to resist parliamentary pressure for its transfer any longer.[5] On the other hand another obvious move was definitely rejected, namely, the transfer of the

---

[1] *The Times*, 9 and 16 June 1854; 3 *Hansard* cxxxv, col. 333 (17 July 1854). Benjamin Hawes, the civil servant who was the mainstay of military administration in the fifties, repeatedly complained of the folly of failing to combine the financial and general administration of the Army under one head (Hawes to Grey, 12 August and 13 November 1854, Grey MSS.).

[2] *Leaves from the Diary of Henry Greville*, ed. Viscountess Enfield, second series (1884), p. 105.

[3] Ibid. pp. 110–11; Aberdeen to the Queen, 17 July 1854, Add. MS. 43049, fo. 195.

[4] Lord John Russell to Newcastle, 2 July 1854, Newcastle MSS. Ne C 10291; 3 *Hansard*, cxxxv, col. 325 (17 July 1854).

[5] Newcastle to Aberdeen, 5 July 1854, Newcastle MSS. Ne C 12515; J. Martineau, op. cit., p. 133 (Aberdeen to Newcastle, same day).

disembodied militia from the Home Office to the new department.[1]

Thus the only structural alteration as a result of the creation of the new War Ministry was the removal of the Commissariat from Treasury control, and this was decided upon in the interests not of military efficiency but of financial economy and administrative regularity. Moreover even this step was not actually taken until 22 December, over five months after it was promised. The opinionated assistant secretary to the Treasury, Sir Charles Trevelyan, fought obstinately against its being taken at all.[2] Gladstone, then Chancellor of the Exchequer, and always anxious to bring all public accounts under Treasury control, agreed that the supply duties of the Commissariat should be removed, but insisted that its pay and banking functions should be retained under the Treasury's control. Furthermore Gladstone's theoretical cast of mind appreciated the constitutional purists' objection that such detailed duties were inappropriate for a Secretary of State, an officer whose role was 'direction and superintendence and not execution'. He would have preferred, therefore, to make the Commissariat a distinct subordinate department related to the War Department only in the way that the Revenue Departments were related to the Treasury.[3] Fortunately he was enough of a politician to realize that such evasion (as the long-suffering Newcastle rightly called it)[4] was politically im-

[1] Palmerston persuaded the Cabinet that the ancient argument that the militia must be kept as a civilian bulwark against the military was still valid (Palmerston to Aberdeen, 8 July 1854, Add. MS. 43069, fo. 257).

[2] Trevelyan to Aberdeen, 8 July 1854, and Memorandum, Newcastle MSS. Ne C 10541, a and b; Gladstone to Trevelyan, 23 August 1854, Add. MS. 44529, fo. 134. Trevelyan had also opposed the creation of a separate Secretary of State for War, Memorandum of 27 May 1854, Newcastle MSS. Ne C 10535, a.

[3] Gladstone to Trevelyan, 14 August and 30 October 1854, Add. MS. 44529, fos. 130 and 164; Memorandum by Gladstone, 17 November 1854, Add. MS. 44744, fo. 82.

[4] Newcastle to Gladstone, 3 and 6 November 1854, Add. MS. 44262, fos. 157 and 160.

practicable, and therefore finally consented to the Treasury Minute of 22 December whereby the 'entire responsibility' for the Commissariat was transferred to the Minister for War.[1] Gladstone was convinced, however (as he assured the indignant Trevelyan), that Newcastle had verbally agreed that where the financial duties of the Commissariat were concerned the War Department would be simply the Treasury's instrument.[2] Thus yet again what appeared to be a clear-cut decision concealed nothing but ambiguity. Conflict and friction were bound to follow. The new arrangement continued to fall under a double fire from the 'Treasury traditionalists' who wanted the Commissariat back and the constitutional purists who wanted to create some kind of independent department.[3] In reality this first instalment of consolidation had substantial disadvantages, and it was neither surprising nor regrettable that in 1856 the Treasury triumphed so far as to win back the banking business of the Commissariat.[4]

In any case so small a measure as the transfer of the Commissariat would obviously neither satisfy Parliament and the public nor solve the practical problems of military administration. As the new parliamentary session approached and the disappointing situation in the Crimea began to be known, Lord John began again to urge a comprehensive plan upon Aberdeen. As usual, however, Lord John seemed to have ulterior motives: this time to put himself in Aberdeen's place and Palmerston in Newcastle's, while getting rid of Herbert's altogether. First he told Aberdeen that the House would insist on the abolition of the War Office, then that the House could be fobbed off with mere promises of consolidation provided there was 'a Minister of War of vigour and authority'

[1] Public Record Office, War Office, 43/98, 156222.

[2] Gladstone to Trevelyan, 13 January 1855, Add. MS. 44530, fo. 12.

[3] See, for example, 3 *Hansard*, cxxxvi, cols. 1067–114 (29 January 1855), cxxxviii, cols. 755–61 (18 May 1855), and cxxxix, cols. 1558–64 (31 July 1855).

[4] Memoranda of Trevelyan and W. Anderson, 13 October 1855, W.O. 43/99; *P.P.*, 1860, vii. i, questions 85–97.

and with a seat in the Commons.[1] When Aberdeen resolutely maintained that Newcastle already possessed 'all the authority with which any person could properly be invested', Lord John threatened the 'thunderstruck' Cabinet with his resignation unless they agreed to a six-member Army Board with the Secretary of State at its head, absorbing the Ordnance and the War Office and 'controuling the whole civil management of our military force'.[2] Yet when Palmerston (who began his official life as Secretary at War) asserted that it was essential to preserve the War Office, and the Cabinet turned down this plan,[3] Lord John lamely remarked that Panmure had convinced him that the time was inappropriate for such sweeping measures, and turned to trouble-making in other quarters.[4]

Meanwhile, however, the Peelites, pragmatic as ever, were succeeding in actually establishing an Army Board of their own kind. They — and especially the vigorous Sidney Herbert — had always believed that what was required was not consolidation but one supervising authority. From the first days of the Aberdeen Coalition in December 1852 (when the country was in the middle of a French invasion scare), Palmerston, Graham, Herbert and Hardinge, Raglan and Burgoyne had met at the Home Office, and sometimes at the Ordnance, to deal with coastal defences.[5] These meetings had proved suc-

---

[1] Lord John Russell to Aberdeen, 3, 18 and 28 November 1854, Add. MS. 43068, fos. 161, 179–83, 198–205.

[2] Aberdeen to Lord John Russell, 30 November 1854, ibid., fo. 211; Memorandum of Lord John Russell, 2 December 1854, P.R.O. 30/22/11; Memorandum by the Prince, 4 December 1854, RA A84/15.

[3] Palmerston to Russell, 3 December 1854, P.R.O. 30/22/11 (partly printed in G. P. Gooch, *The Later Correspondence of Lord John Russell* (1925), ii. 176–8); Aberdeen to the Queen, 7 December 1854, Add. MS. 43050, fo. 44.

[4] Memorandum by Prince Albert, 9 December 1854, *Letters of Queen Victoria*, iii. 74; Aberdeen to the Queen, 15 December 1854, Add. MS. 43050, fo. 55.

[5] The 'Defence Committee' of the 1850s and 1860s was this specialized inter-departmental coastal-defence committee, which was not, of course,

cessful, and it was natural that in the worsening situation at the end of 1854 both Palmerston and Sidney Herbert, apparently quite independently, suggested to Newcastle that similar meetings should regularly be held of the heads of the military departments at his office.[1] Herbert indeed hoped to secure the presence of a Lord of the Admiralty in order to secure administrative co-ordination between naval and military departments as well, but this Graham vetoed as a threat to that 'central superintendance and authority of the First Lord' which he was always so jealous to preserve.[2] The Board which began its weekly meetings on 3 January was a purely military one, consisting of the Commander-in-Chief, Secretary at War and Lieutenant-General and Clerk of the Ordnance, with the Secretary of State for War.[3] It met again on the 10th, 17th and 20th, its minutes being sent to the Queen at her request by Newcastle.[4] In this way the consultations under a supervising authority which Herbert had urged from the beginning became, briefly, a formal *fait accompli*.

Towards the end of January 1855 it became known that another parliamentary attack was imminent from the indefatigable Lord Grey. At once the Peelites through Sidney Herbert produced for the Cabinet a draft Order in Council making obligatory these weekly Board meetings. This the Queen was quite ready to accept, although she wanted the militia to be

---

a Cabinet committee. *A fortiori* the Defence Committee was not the same committee as the War Committee of the Cabinet, as supposed by Mackintosh, op. cit., p. 138.

[1] Palmerston to Newcastle, 4 December 1854, Newcastle MSS. Ne C 10044; *P.P.*, 1854–5, IX. i, question 20159. Informal meetings had already been held for some time (3 *Hansard*, cxxxvi, col. 1194, 29 January 1855).

[2] Graham to Aberdeen, 27 December 1854, Add. MS. 43191, fo. 281.

[3] *P.P.*, 1854–5, IX. i, question 19177; 3 *Hansard*, cxxxvi, col. 994, (Sidney Herbert, 26 January 1855).

[4] Newcastle to the Queen, 22 January 1855, Newcastle MSS. Ne C 9786, fo. 36. Two sets of minutes are to be found in ibid., Ne C 10858 and 10859 (Meetings of 10 and 20 January 1855).

transferred to the War Department and the powers of the Commander-in-Chief to be clearly defined.[1] Herbert's Board was to be purely advisory, in no way encroaching on the sphere of the Secretary of State or the Cabinet, and represented a limited step already proved to be practicable and useful. Inevitably this provoked from Lord John a far more sweeping counter-proposition, for a true administrative Board, with six members, and substantial powers, including those of the Ordnance Board, which was to be immediately abolished.[2] Consolidation and simplification, not practical usefulness, remained Lord John's watchwords. The very next day (23 January), however, his sudden resignation precipitated that prolonged ministerial crisis in the course of which Palmerston emerged as Prime Minister and both Lord John and the Peelites irreparably damaged their political reputations. With their decline their rival schemes for an Army Board sank from view and the newly begun weekly meetings at the War Department came to an end.

It was thus left to Palmerston and the man whom he at once chose as War Minister, Fox Maule, second Lord Panmure, to ride the storm which was raging by then. In February 1855 military administration was the question of the day as never before or since. Floods of pamphlets and newspaper articles left no doubt that what most people wanted was consolidation under one 'real War Minister'. Discussion and piecemeal reform would be tolerated no longer; decision and accomplished fact were necessary, and moreover along the lines of popular clamour. This may well have had something to do with Palmerston's choice of Panmure for the key post, 'an honest good fellow but by no means of the calibre for such an office

[1] Aberdeen to the Queen, 20 January 1855, Add. MS. 43050, fo. 123; The Queen to Aberdeen, 22 January 1855, ibid., fo. 128; Herbert to Graham, 22 January 1855 and Graham to Herbert, same day, Graham Papers, Microfilm 45. The document in question is printed in *P.P.*, 1854–5, IX, i, p. 58.

[2] Memorandum on Army Departments by Lord John Russell, 22 January 1855, Add. MS. 43068, fo. 271.

at such a moment'[1]— although the fact that he was a Whig (he was a close associate of Lord John's) was also relevant. For Panmure had long been known as a convinced believer in consolidation. Only a few days before Palmerston offered him the War Department, he had written to Prince Albert: 'The lamentable results which have attended our present expedition . . . are solely to be attributed to the want of proper control by a single Minister of every department of the Army.'[2] Moreover it might be hoped that he would be able to soothe the most likely sources of opposition: he was trusted by the Prince,[3] had himself served in the Army between 1819 and 1831, and had been Secretary at War between 1846 and 1852. He had defects of temperament and capacity which were to prove serious drawbacks; but in February 1855 his record made him the obvious man for the job, and his stipulation for 'powers to amalgamate the War Office' cannot have been unexpected.[4] Nor can it have been unexpected that the next day the able Deputy Secretary at War, Sir Benjamin Hawes, submitted a long memorandum pointing out the confusion which consolidation would create.[5] But by the time Palmerston's Cabinet met for the first time it was already obvious that their only chance of defeating Roebuck's alarming motion for a Select Committee to enquire into the state of the Army was to persuade Parliament and the public that they would immediately take the very steps which a Select Committee might recommend after months of enquiry. Panmure was therefore instructed to prepare a scheme for dividing the Ordnance between the Commander-in-Chief and the War De-

[1] Clarendon to Palmerston, 4 February 1855, Broadlands MSS.

[2] *The Panmure Papers*, ed. Sir G. Douglas and Sir G. D. Ramsay (1908), i. 47.

[3] The Prince sent his 'Paper on the organisation of the Army' to Panmure for his opinion in January 1855 (Panmure to Lord John Russell, 31 January 1855, P.R.O. 30/22/12).

[4] Panmure to Lord John Russell, 7 February 1855, P.R.O. 30/22/12.

[5] Memorandum by Sir Benjamin Hawes, 8 February 1855, Scottish Record Office, Edinburgh, Dalhousie Muniments, 8/316.

partment, a separate Transport Board was to be set up under the Admiralty, and the Secretaryship at War was to be kept vacant as proof that consolidation of the War Office and War Department was being closely considered. Changes in the staff and in the medical arrangements in the Crimea would also be announced.[1] All of this the Queen approved as 'very judicious'[2] and when the House reassembled on 16 February 1855 after its emergency adjournment for a week these were the measures which Palmerston announced in his disastrous 'I will be your committee' speech.[3] The House was not to be thus placated: Roebuck's Select Committee was appointed, the Peelites resigned again in protest and the Government was left committed to large administrative changes decided upon as a political manœuvre. Nearly three months elapsed before detailed arrangements were suddenly announced in the House as part of another parliamentary manœuvre of Palmerston's, intended to spoil the effect of the motions for administrative reform which Lord Ellenborough and A. H. Layard had put down in each House.[4] But the plan itself had been maturely considered. Panmure drew up a first memorandum on 17 February; two months later a more complete memorandum was ready for Palmerston's eye. At the beginning of May both

[1] Connell, op. cit., p. 166, quoting Palmerston to the Queen, 10 February 1855. As recently as 3 December 1854 Palmerston had said that the War Office must be retained (Palmerston to Lord John Russell, P.R.O. 30/22/11). The militia was also transferred from the Home Office to the War Department — another change of attitude on Palmerston's part.

[2] Connell, op. cit., p. 168, quoting the Queen to Palmerston, 12 February 1855. It was not upon consolidation of the civil administration of the Army that the Crown felt strongly, but upon the relationship of the *command* of the Army to a political officer. By 1861 the Queen believed the Admiralty should be remodelled on the lines of the consolidated War Office (Connell, op. cit., p. 299).

[3] 3 *Hansard*, cxxxvi, col. 1424. Gladstone's assertion that these measures had not been before the Cabinet (Memorandum of 21 February 1855, Add. MS. 44745, fo. 140) is difficult to understand.

[4] 3 *Hansard*, cxxxviii, col. 428 (11 May 1855); *Leaves from the Diary of Henry Greville*, p. 218.

were printed for the consideration of the Cabinet, which to Panmure's surprise did not amend his proposals, and on 10 May submitted to the Queen.[1] Thus although the Government's plan was sprung on the Commons, it was certainly not a hasty expedient. There followed the Order in Council of 6 June, the Ordnance Board Bill in August, and on 2 July 1855, after several reminders from the Queen, minutes regarding the relations of the Sovereign and the consolidated War Department were drawn up.[2]

Yet despite these substantial measures of consolidation, criticism of the country's military administration continued, though with less hysteria and exaggeration than during the political crisis of the spring. Even at the end of the war the opinion prevailed that 'whatever the military authorities do *seems* ill done, and generally is so'.[3] Why did the changes of 1855 prove so unsatisfactory? The chaos in the new War Department lasted too long to be merely the inevitable result of reorganization.[4] Two other factors were at work. One was mediocrity at the top, that lack of 'the right man in the right place' which afflicted every department of English public life during the Crimean War. Panmure, 'the Bison', had a dogged, stolid self-confidence which although it made him a good choice to initiate consolidation, unfitted him for the personal co-operation, systematic organization and flexible attention to

[1] Memoranda of 17 February and 2 May 1855, Dalhousie Muniments, 8/316 (also in W.O. 33/1/321–5); Palmerston to Panmure, 15 April 1855, *Panmure Papers*, i. 149; Panmure to the Queen, 10 May 1855, ibid. i. 194.

[2] Ibid. i. 267.

[3] R. Monckton Milnes to C. J. McCarthy, 21 February 1856, in T. Wemyss Reid, *The Life, Letters and Friendships of Richard Monckton Milnes, first Lord Houghton* (1890), ii. 3.

[4] In February 1856 G. R. Gleig complained of 'utter anarchy' there (Public Record Office, Ellenborough Papers, P.R.O. 30/12/18) and the Queen more moderately of 'confusion' (*Panmure Papers*, i. 488), and such complaints persisted (e.g. Sir Charles Trevelyan's denunciation in December 1858, printed in J. Hart, 'Sir Charles Trevelyan at the Treasury', *English Historical Review*, lxxv (1960), 105).

detail which its implementation required.[1] Panmure never questioned the wisdom of what he had accomplished in 1855, despite the crowd of doubting Thomases around him. But in fact even an administrative genius would have been severely taxed to make the system of 1855 work satisfactorily. The whole process had been disastrously piecemeal, and a really comprehensive definition of duties was only undertaken after many arrangements 'scarcely in harmony with the whole scheme of central control', as Hawes himself admitted, had already been sanctioned.[2] Moreover each of the three main original criticisms made when the plan was announced in Parliament proved all too well founded. The Secretary of State was overwhelmed by the concentration of authority without due division of labour; military expenditure had been deprived of its historic financial check (this was the criticism which a few years later permeated C. M. Clode's learned attack in his great tract, *The Military Forces of the Crown*), and the professional military element was dangerously absent from the Cabinet and from the War Department itself.[3] Subsequent experience was to make the divided responsibility of the War Department and the Horse Guards the most notorious fault of all; but this, it must be admitted, was rather the result of the Duke of Cambridge's appointment as Commander-in-Chief in July 1856 and of the Royal Warrant of 11 October 1861, than of the much-cited supplementary patent of 18 May

---

[1] Even the tolerant Palmerston found Panmure's obstinacy in acting 'off his own hook' or not at all, as he pleased, difficult to bear (e.g. Palmerston to Panmure, 27 June 1855, Broadlands Archives, and Public Record Office, Cowley Papers, Clarendon to Cowley, 30 May 1856, F.O. 519/171).

[2] Hawes to Grey, 20 December 1855, Grey MSS. To contemporaries moreover the sheer size of the new establishment seemed unworkable.

[3] 3 *Hansard*, cxxxviii, cols. 751–8 (18 May 1855), and cxxxix, cols. 1559–63 (31 July 1855). The Master-Generalship of the Ordnance had often been a Cabinet post in the past. However, this complaint (a favourite one of Ellenborough's, see P.R.O. 30/12/18) was less impressive than it seemed, since no Master-General of the Ordnance had sat in any Cabinet since Peel's of December 1834.

1855. This, with its phrase 'subject to the responsibility of the Secretary of State' should surely have made the subordinate position of the Commander-in-Chief clear, especially with the gloss provided by Panmure's official statement in the Lords on 21 February 1856.[1] For the next fifty years enquiries into military administration succeeded each other at ominously short intervals. The Select Committee appointed in 1858 to enquire into the effects of the alterations of 1855 urged instead the Peelite scheme of regular meetings of the Secretary of State with professional advisers[2] — not surprisingly since the Committee was chaired first by Herbert and then by Graham — and this theme of the need to delegate more to subordinate departmental heads remained a significantly constant one for the next fifty years. Indeed, Cardwell's War Office Act of 1870 and the Army Council which emerged at the beginning of the twentieth century might well be regarded as a belated vindication of the Peelite plan of January 1855 and thus a condemnation of the cult of unalleviated concentration under a single minister which triumphed in the crisis of the Crimean War.

The experiences of the Crimean War did indeed spotlight faults in the British system of military administration. But these faults had long been familiar commonplaces among the well-informed. What the war accomplished was not the revelation of unsuspected defects, but the creation of a political atmosphere in which decisions could no longer be postponed. When hysteria gripped the British public, the politicians found themselves unable even to choose between rival plans for administrative improvement; only one course was open to them, to adopt the plan of ministerial consolidation which had become identified with the salvation of the troops besieging Sebastopol. Division and delegation in any shape or form were the unclean thing. In this department of government the ancient principle, and still more ancient practice, of checks and balances were completely jettisoned. Administrative wisdom

[1] 3 *Hansard*, cxl, col. 1041.   [2] *P.P.*, 1860, vii. i, p. xviii.

was quite submerged beneath political necessity. Thus the Crimean War did indeed accomplish long overdue alterations in Britain's military organization: but the history of the next fifty years lends all too much support to the suspicion that the institutional changes produced in democratic governments by the strains of war rarely correspond with a country's real needs.[1]

In the naughty world of the Civil Service, the Admiralty shone out like a good deed during the Crimean War. With one exception, the smugness with which British naval administration had been regarded since its reorganization in 1832 was undisturbed. Graham as First Lord continued to bask in congratulations from all sides upon his perfection as an administrator.[2] It is doubtful whether this reputation was altogether deserved. Prince Albert, who was a good judge, believed towards the end of the war that 'the *system* of not only the War Office but of the Admiralty was infinitely inferior to the French'.[3] Yet only one branch of naval administration became notorious: that of transport. The Admiralty's incapacity in getting transports for reinforcements in November and December 1854 was certainly a prime cause of the state of affairs in the Crimea and ministers knew well that the outcry in Parliament and the Press against the transport service was quite as well founded as the much more spectacular and far-ranging outcry against the military departments at home and the supply services and staff in the Crimea. Palmerston's original programme submitted to the first Cabinet he ever

[1] Since the present discussion is concerned only with constitutional ideas and the machinery of government during the Crimean War, the important topics of military education, purchase and promotion, as well as the actual functioning of military administration in the Crimea, are excluded from consideration.

[2] See, for example, C. S. Parker, *Life and Letters of Sir James Graham* (1907), ii. 274, 275, 277.

[3] Lord E. Fitzmaurice, *The Life of Granville George Leveson Gower, second Earl Granville* (1905), i. 140.

presided over included the re-establishment of a separate Transport Board under the Admiralty. As he explained to the Queen, transport by sea had hitherto been 'not very well directed by the department employed in victualling the navy, a department which had too much business of its own to do to be able properly to attend to the transport service'.[1] Graham himself had already decided upon this step and rejected the idea of creating an additional naval Lord of the Admiralty to be responsible for transport, deterred (or so he later rather inconsistently said) by the evils inherent in all administration by boards, including the Admiralty Board.[2] Thus the old Transport Board reappeared upon the scene. The immediate results, however, were small, largely because Panmure failed to insist that all requisitions for transport should be made through the War Department alone, as Graham had intended.[3] Thus the phobia against Boards during the Crimean War had led in very different directions in naval and military administration — in the former, to the ancient practice of subdivision and specialization, in the latter, to unprecedented consolidation under a single minister — but with equally unimpressive results in each case.

[1] Palmerston to the Queen, 10 February 1855, printed in Connell, op. cit., p. 166.

[2] 3 *Hansard*, cxxxvi, cols. 1194, 1426 (29 January and 16 February 1855); *P.P.*, 1854–5, ix. i, question 21189.

[3] Sir Charles Wood to Panmure, 5 June 1855, Dalhousie Muniments, 14/689.

F

CHAPTER TWO

The Role of Publicity and Discussion in time of War

SOON after the beginning of the war *The Times* declared: 'There is only one rule for improvement and success, whether in peace or in war, and that is to be found in publicity and discussion.'[1] This might be discounted as merely an obviously biased editorial opinion. But in the 1850s few assertions commanded more widespread acceptance than the view that liberty was the chief source of strength and improvement, for society and the individual alike.

At that very time John Stuart Mill was expressing the same conviction, almost in the same words, in his first draft of the *Essay on Liberty* — 'crying Fire! in Noah's flood', as Macaulay put it.[2] It had long been platitudinous that a free Press was one of the best defences against despotism, and by the middle of the century this had broadened into the belief that 'history' showed that states which enjoyed the free expression of public opinion through the Press, public meetings and a representative assembly, possessed greater 'fertility of resources and pertinacity of purpose'[3] than those which did not. There could be no doubt that Britain in the 1850s was such a state. Did the country in the Crimean War reap the benefits which were confidently expected? 'When we are told, we are now to see whether a great war can be effectively carried on in the face of a free public opinion, an unfettered press, and absolute

[1] 10 June 1854.
[2] Quoted in R. P. Anschutz, *The Philosophy of John Stuart Mill* (Oxford, 1953), p. 25.
[3] *Saturday Review*, 1 December 1855.

publicity,' boasted *The Times* on 5 November 1855, 'we can
now reply triumphantly that not only can such a war be
carried on under these circumstances, but that such nations
as England and France could not carry on such a war under
other circumstances. We do not worship our Sovereigns as
demi-gods. . . . We are intelligent and self-respecting races,
and require to have our interest and sympathy fed and sustained by constant participation in the history and even the
conduct of the war.' But was this complacency justified?
Certainly the Press made 'constant participation' very easy
for any literate citizen. The conduct of the war was subjected
to unprecedented publicity and discussion. The modern war
photographer and special correspondent at the front were each
a creation of the Crimean War. Above all one correspondent,
W. H. Russell, and one newspaper, *The Times*, secured a
phenomenal amount of attention for their treatment of the
war. In 1855 *The Times* had a daily print order of 61,000, as
against its rivals' 3,000–6,000, and circulated in ordinary
middle-class homes in every part of the country. 'Even the
most sensible Englishmen (unless they are professional
politicians and belong to a particular party) are nothing more
than 100,000 echoes of *The Times*,' discovered the German
novelist Fontane when he visited England in that year. The
author Kinglake said the same thing rather more succinctly
when he wrote that during the war 'women and practical men
simply spoke of *The Times*', instead of referring to public
opinion.[1] It may well be doubted whether *The Times* influenced
the actual course of events as much as its contemporary readers
believed or its twentieth-century historians have claimed. To
assert, as the official history of the paper does, that it 'made
the war; it had been largely responsible for the Crimean
campaign, that had brought victory in the end; it had saved
the remnant of an army; it had destroyed one Ministry and
forced important changes in another; and it had caused the

[1] T. Fontane, *Journeys to England in Victoria's early days* (1939),
p. 115; A. W. Kinglake, *The Invasion of the Crimea* (1863), ii. 84.

removal of a commander-in-chief,' among other great things,[1] is obviously to exploit the official historian's licence. Yet in 1855 these claims would not have seemed grotesque to most practical men outside the inner circle of politicians. To them the thunderings of *The Times* and the public's response were among the wonders of the age. The other organs of the daily and periodical press, public meetings and associations, even parliamentary debates, were all dwarfed almost into insignificance in their eyes by the immensely more striking role of *The Times*. It follows that in considering the effect of the war upon contemporary convictions of the supreme value of publicity and discussion, it is the public's reaction to the conduct of that journal which deserves pride of place. To them it provided the great test case of the benefits of free discussion in time of war.

Only in the most responsible quarters did *The Times*'s detailed reports of events at the seat of war very quickly suggest what now seems an obvious qualification: that the military and political aspects of the freedom of the Press must be distinguished, and some control imposed on the former. Commanding officers and Cabinet ministers exclaimed with dismay upon the valuable information unwittingly disclosed to the enemy by special correspondents. 'If *we* could get such information or a tithe of it, it would be worth thousands to us,' Lord Clarendon at the Foreign Office repeatedly lamented.[2] At the request of the Commander-in-Chief in the Crimea, the Secretary of State for War circulated all editors of the daily press in London, pointing out the dangers of publishing military information in war correspondents' letters and expressing his confidence that 'I have only to appeal to your patriotism to ensure a rigid supervision of all such

---

[1] *The History of The Times*, vol. ii, *The Tradition Established (1841–84)* (1939), pp. 191–2.

[2] e.g. Clarendon to Stratford Canning, F.O. 352/42, 1 January 1855. However, after the war the Russians claimed that *The Times* never old them anything they did not know already.

letters'.[1] The editor of *The Times*, the renowned Delane, at once offered to go further and 'suppress the much more important items of intelligence which appear under the *Naval and Military* head'.[2] But the business was left to the editors' discretion, and Delane at least was quite unfitted by habit and outlook for the function of censor. Newcastle's circular and the complaints of the military men so strongly made between November 1854 and March 1855 thus seem to have had little effect. To the modern mind it is extraordinary how limited was the control thus envisaged and how half-hearted its enforcement. Nevertheless it is untrue to say that press censorship was unknown and unthought of during the Crimean War. The principle that the Press should not disclose information of military value was enunciated by the Government and accepted by the Press, although its application was left to the patriotism of individual editors and correspondents in a way thoroughly characteristic of that generation.[3] Even to a somewhat unconventional thinker like George Warde Norman, 'to impose any legal restrictions on the Press could hardly be thought of'.[4] It is indisputable, however, that no military necessity to control the whole field of intelligence was ever perceived. The notorious war correspondents were not in reality the only offenders, although they alone were condemned. Letters from both the troops and the many sightseers at the front arrived quite uncensored and were freely quoted and printed, or worked up for publication in book form. Even the House of

[1] Newcastle to certain editors, 6 December 1854, printed in *The History of The Times*, ii. 576. W. H. Russell claimed that he had offered to submit his letters to the censorship of Raglan's headquarters in the Crimea, but been ignored (J. B. Atkins, *Life of W. H. Russell* (1911), i. 93).

[2] Delane to Layard, 16 February 1855, British Museum, Layard Papers, Add. MS. 38983, fo. 16.

[3] The claim that the government acted thus through fear of *The Times* (*History of The Times*, ii. 187, 201) is unconvincing.

[4] Letter to the Press dated 11 May 1855, reprinted in his *Papers on Various Subjects* (n.d.), Pamphlet Collection, British Library of Political and Economic Science.

Commons was not free from indiscretion: when the former Secretary of State for War gave evidence on Allied strategy before the Sebastopol Committee his evidence was published and the sitting held in public, despite the fact that the military situation he referred to was still in existence.[1] No clear evidence of Russian exploitation of press information ever emerged to shake this indifference. Thus it was upon the political functions alone of full publicity and free comment that the attention of the lay public continued to concentrate, political functions which at the beginning of the war were assumed to be an essential part of the country's prized constitution.

To the articulate mid-Victorian public these political functions in war-time could be reduced to two: first, to purvey full and speedy news of events and thus stimulate patriotism, sacrifice and endeavour by enabling the public to identify themselves with the war effort; and secondly, to subject the Government to continual public criticism or encouragement according to its deserts. Only with the cosmopolitan upper classes and with ministers themselves did a third function loom large: that of maintaining the country's prestige abroad by discretion in publicizing defeats and moderation in criticism of the country's leaders. The great insular middle class neither appreciated the repercussions abroad of unbridled publicity, nor thought them very significant. To them the function of the Press was the domestic and political one of making constitutional government militarily more effective through informing and therefore inspiring the public, and through bringing enlightened public opinion to bear upon the authorities.

By the end of the war many people found it much less easy to assume that untrammelled publicity would indeed achieve these ends. As soon as the condition of the troops before Sebastopol became a public obsession the sophisticated began to point out the impossibility of entirely distinguishing fact from opinion in even the best war correspondent's reports.

[1] The British Ambassador in Paris noted this with horror (Cowley to Clarendon, 25 April 1855, F.O. 519/171).

Very many more people thought that the class bitterness and hysterical despair which almost engulfed the nation in the first months of 1855 were exploited and very largely created by the Press, above all *The Times.* Clarendon, for example, on 26 January 1855 told Stratford that *The Times* 'through exciting the people almost to madness' was responsible for the ministerial crisis.[1] This was not altogether fair. Social tension had always been very near the surface, and to discuss public affairs in a tone of censure or despondency was already a well-established popular English habit. To a large extent the Press was not guiding public opinion, but reflecting it, as indeed it had done for the last fifty years, much to its profit.[2] Nevertheless the unique prestige which *The Times* enjoyed with its enormous middle-class public allowed it greatly to intensify and prolong the movements of opinion. Above all it was able to disseminate a stereotyped explanation of the country's difficulties and disasters by reiterating a few neat censures and solutions. 'The System' (the ancestor of 'the Establishment'), 'the cold shade of Aristocracy', 'routine' and bureaucratic failings, Raglan and his staff officers, Aberdeen and the Peelites, Lord John Russell when his turn came — *The Times* always had a plausible scapegoat. Very often the news was presented in such a way as perforce to illustrate the paper's current theme. By the spring of 1855 no one could still suppose that the Press was fostering national unity or individual sacrifice. It had obviously ceased to aspire to this role as soon as the excitement of the first engagements in the Crimea had given way to the prolonged anti-climax of the siege of Sebastopol. 'All attacks on the Government are perfectly legitimate,' protested Clarendon to his friend Reeve, a frequent leader-writer for *The Times*, 'but the country, the institutions, the upper classes, all have been run down by *The Times* latterly, and the feeling thereby created abroad — at home too, I believe — is that we are in a state of helpless confusion, and

[1] Bodleian Library, Clarendon deposit, c. 131/385.
[2] A. Aspinall, *Politics and the Press, 1780–1850* (1949), p. 380.

drifting to revolution.'[1] Only if *The Times* was correct in its analysis of the situation could its attacks on people, policies and institutions be regarded as justified, and its stridency and overwhelming predominance hailed as blessings in disguise. Those who believed this — and the ordinary middle-class citizen was remarkably credulous about *The Times* — would have approved Kinglake's later description of that journal as 'the Patriot King of 1855.' But did it in reality deserve such a title, or was the 'leading journal' the '*mis*leading journal', as by the autumn of 1855 it was fashionable to claim?

No doubt the attack upon *The Times* in 1855 by preachers and fashionable society, as well as politicians, radicals and intellectuals, was more virulent than it deserved. By October there was talk of forming an 'Anti-*Times* League' (the men of the 1850s were still inveterate formers of associations).[2] Sermons and pamphlets multiplied accusing *The Times* of tyranny and malice. The religious press early joined the chorus. W. H. Russell's very first reports from the Crimea suggested to the High Church *Guardian*[3] the danger of the public demand for news, and the *Churchman* and the *Record* were soon denouncing exaggeration and continual fault-finding. The Evangelical *Record* in particular had long been out of sympathy with *The Times* and was among the first to claim that its autocracy threatened to undermine the English constitution.[4] To F. D. Maurice the Press was killing what was to him the greatest good, the nation's mystic unity: *The Times* was 'horribly wicked', he confided to Charles Kingsley.[5] More worldly critics conceded that in many ways the public and not

---

[1] J. K. Laughton, *Memoirs of the Life and Correspondence of Henry Reeve* (1898), i. 330.

[2] The Queen to Palmerston, 6 October 1855, Connell, op. cit., p. 186. *The History of The Times* has a not altogether convincing chapter on 'The second "war with *The Times*"', ii. 193–215.

[3] The *Guardian*, 27 December 1854.

[4] The *Record*, 29 January 1855.

[5] 3 January 1855, *The Life of F. D. Maurice*, ed. F. Maurice (1884), ii. 250.

The Times was to blame for the evils which they lamented. Several years later Kinglake made a sensible point which was not sufficiently appreciated at the time, when he drew attention to 'the want of proportion between the skill of the public writer and the judicial competence of his readers'.[1] Yet it was not simply that *The Times* possessed a team of writers whose verve and fluent cocksureness impressed their largely unsophisticated public. As Charles Greville remarked, it was also 'the extreme mediocrity or coarse vulgarity of its rivals' which gave *The Times* its long ascendancy.[2] Its own faults of taste and policy were sometimes very glaring; but its rivals' faults were worse. The embittered former chief contributor to the moribund *Morning Chronicle* was not far wrong when he declared at the end of the war that not a single journal had made the British public acquainted with the real state of affairs abroad or displayed much common sense.[3] Moreover the habit of publishing anonymous articles, the editorial 'we', bestowed upon *The Times* an almost living personality, and one which its somewhat gullible public freely credited with all knowledge and all wisdom. If articles had been signed by their various and frequently varying authors, their tone might have been less presumptuous and their statements reduced in the eyes of the public to their proper value! By the end of the war the abandonment of anonymity was often urged.[4] Such a step would have allowed more readers to suspect what only the initiated knew, that those who wrote for the Press, even for *The Times* itself, had no special qualifications and often not much experience. More often than not they were merely young professional men, especially barristers, in need of money.

The Times was not 'making the railroad of a democratic

[1] Op. cit. ii. 76.

[2] Greville to Reeve, 19 October 1855, *The Letters of Charles Greville and Henry Reeve, 1836–65*, ed. A. H. Johnson (1924), p. 248.

[3] A. Hayward to Gladstone, 2 January 1856, Add. MS. 44207, fo. 17.

[4] For example, James Douglas of Cavers, *Passing Thoughts*, part ii (1856), p. 193.

revolution', as Lord John Russell in his bitterness believed.[1] Palmerston knew better when he dismissed that paper's conduct as merely its accustomed astute exploitation of a temporarily paying line.[2] Moreover much of the run against *The Times* was the work of men whose own interests or reputations had been jeopardized by that journal. The circle around Lord John Russell which discussed at the end of 1855 setting up a new daily newspaper specifically to challenge *The Times* was inspired by that paper's repeated criticisms of Lord John's conduct. The *Saturday Review*, whose first number appeared on 3 November 1855 and which explicitly set out to deflate *The Times*, inherited the editor and attitudes of an old opponent of that journal which had just collapsed, the Peelite *Morning Chronicle.* A much-discussed essay on 'The Newspaper Press' published in the very influential *Edinburgh Review* in October 1855, was the work of a former *Times* leader writer who had quarrelled with the paper.[3] In short, much of the indignation against *The Times* was inspired by strictly personal motives or was the expression of social, religious or intellectual outlooks entirely opposed to those championed by that paper in the excitement of 1854–5. Finally, in England there was always a shrewd minority which refused to take *The Times* seriously.

On the Continent, however, this was not so, and it might well be argued that by far the greatest practical importance of the conduct of the English Press during the war was its effect upon continental ideas of English military power and English institutions. Foreigners under the spell of *The Times*'s prestige and ignorant alike of the commercial pressures upon the English Press and of the Englishman's fondness for conducting political debate in an exaggerated tone of censure and gloom,

[1] Lord John Russell to Clarendon, 6 October 1855, Clarendon deposit, c. 31, fo. 449.

[2] Palmerston to the Queen, 9 October 1861, Connell, op. cit., p. 187.

[3] H. R. Fox Bourne, *English Newspapers* (1887), ii. 233; *History of The Times,* ii. 232.

took everything they read in *The Times* as truth. The views of the silent and the moderate were as always overlooked. The results were particularly lamentable in those neutral states whose attitude was being closely watched by the Foreign Office, and also in France, where the French were always on the alert to discern the familiar features of perfidious Albion beneath the new look of their unaccustomed British allies. The Foreign Secretary's private correspondence is full of despair over the effect abroad from the moment in December 1854 when *The Times* began its revelations. 'If ever a man deserved the title of "Enemy of his Country" it is Mr. Delane,' exploded Clarendon to the British Ambassador in Paris on 24 January 1855. 'I wish you would write him a few facts as to the extent of the injury that *The Times* has done to England in France.'[1] It was the disastrous effects upon British popularity in Germany which particularly impressed the Queen, and when peace came to be made she would not agree with her Prime Minister that the injuries done by free speech had been more than counterbalanced by its advantages.[2]

British travellers abroad were disgusted by the decline in their country's reputation. That minor literary hostess and writer Mrs. Sarah Austin while travelling abroad in 1855 reported to George Cornewall Lewis soon after he became Chancellor of the Exchequer that 'the conduct of our press disgusts all Europe', and sent Lord Ellesmere a cutting from the *Volkszeitung* in which a liberal journalist declared that after reading *The Times* he began to wonder whether the liberty of the Press was a curse.[3] Far graver doubts were

[1] F.O. 519/171.

[2] The Queen to Panmure, 11 March 1856, *Panmure Papers*, ii. 150; E. Longford, op. cit., p. 255.

[3] Mrs. S. Austin to Sir G. Lewis, 21 February 1855. National Library of Wales, Harpton Court MSS., c. 824. Bonapartists felt that the harm done in England by the unlimited freedom of the Press proved how fortunate France was to have got rid of it under Napoleon III (Walewski to the French Foreign Ministry, 23 January 1855, quoted in *The History of The Times*, ii. 203).

expressed in weightier quarters. The great Tocqueville, preoccupied though he was at that moment with the writing of his *Ancien Régime*, warned his English friends that the reports he read of the state of England reminded him uncomfortably of France in 1847. 'Your people seem, as was the case with ours, to have become tired of their public men, and to be losing faith in their institutions. What else do these complaints of what is called "the system" mean?' A little earlier Tocqueville had given warning that in Germany and France England was now thought utterly devoid of military talent. 'Since I was a child I never heard such language. You are believed to be absolutely dependent on us.'[1] V. E. D'Azeglio, then in London as the Sardinian envoy, found England 'un assez triste spectacle', for 'la critique est dans toutes les bouches au moment où il s'agirait le plus d'obéir et d'agir avec ensemble'.[2] No doubt the bare facts of the country's difficulty in recruiting enough men and incompetent military administration would have lowered British prestige however discreet its Press. But the lurid accounts and charges in British newspapers undoubtedly vastly increased their impact abroad, since on the Continent military strength was regarded as an indispensable element in national greatness. By the end of 1855 it was common on the Continent to think England moribund. There it had been all too often believed that 'les Anglais peints par eux-mêmes in *The Times must* be true', and Clarendon had good reason to write in October 1855: 'That Paper is the worst enemy that England has to contend against. It labours unremittingly to prove that we are powerless.'[3] It was at this juncture that the distinguished French liberal Catholic,

[1] Tocqueville to Senior, 22 January 1855, and conversation of 2 March 1855, *Correspondence and Conversations of Alexis de Tocqueville with Nassau Senior, 1834–59*, ed. M. C. M. Simpson (1872), ii. 91, 98.

[2] D'Azeglio to Cavour, 21 February 1855, *Cavour e l'Inghilterra*, Carteggio con V. E. D'Azeglio a cura della commissione reale editrice (Bologna, 1933), i. 43.

[3] Clarendon to Lord John Russell, 6 March and 4 October 1855, P.R.O. 30/22/12.

Montalembert, published his *De l'Avenir politique de l'Angle-terre* in an attempt to refute these continental prophets of doom. His book, though a great success, was far from being altogether convincing.[1] Auguste Comte for once was in agree-ment with a widely held view when he expressed his contempt for England as a country incapable of war, with a weak govern-ment which allowed itself to be dragged along by public opinion.[2]

Were these evil effects abroad counterbalanced by advan-tages at home?/Contemporary preoccupation with the great *Times* question seems to have diverted attention from really fundamental issues. The experience of the war might well have suggested that a commercial Press, dependent upon advertis-ing revenue and therefore upon circulation figures for its profits, could hardly be relied upon, when left to its own counsels, either to stimulate civilian morale or to conduct a prolonged Socratic debate upon public affairs. Thus the political value of a free Press in war-time might well have seemed to call for re-examination, even if the challenge was not extended to the basic mid-Victorian assumptions that full knowledge was desirable and wisdom obtainable from public debate. To contemporaries, however, neither the desirability nor the practicability of the general principles of publicity and discussion seemed to need reappraisal, for those who believed that publicity had not accomplished all it should have done during the war found their scapegoat in the over-whelming pre-eminence of a single journal or in the manner in which that journal was conducted. The more reflective at once pointed out that in the existing state of affairs it was not true variety of opinion which was secured by the freedom of the Press, but the dominance of one attitude alone, that of *The Times*, slavishly echoed or as slavishly contradicted by its

[1] It first appeared in parts in *Le Correspondant* and then in book form, when it went through five editions in a few months according to R. P. Lecanuet, *Montalembert* (1902), iii. 151.
[2] A. Comte, *Lettres à Richard Congreve* (Paris, 1889), p. 18.

competitors. Thus it could be claimed that it was only a travesty of the liberty of the Press which had been tried and found wanting during the war.[1] Above all, many who were convinced that something was wrong with the official conduct of the war, if not as much as *The Times* asserted, doubted whether these faults could have been effectively brought home without the clamour of a loud-mouthed journal backed by a huge circulation. If *The Times* had usurped the functions of other branches of the Press, of public meetings and associations, above all of Parliament itself, had it not been obliged to do so by the shortcomings of these other channels of opinion? In this case — unless all claim to liberal institutions was to be renounced — it could only be accused of excessive zeal in well-doing. This was the argument which seemed particularly telling to all those who were discontented with the institutional framework of the country and believed that political life should be more broadly based than it had yet become. It impressed even the moderates who had no wish to extend the social basis of English politics, and believed *The Times*'s violence and exaggerations had harmed a good cause already won. Thus to understand the war-time activities of the newspaper press and the very restricted lessons contemporaries drew from them, it is necessary to consider how far other channels for the expression of public opinion were adequate, or felt to be so.

One formerly much-used medium which had lost most of its usefulness was the pamphlet. By the 1850s lengthy pamphlets or hard-cover books were no longer the chief vehicles of political controversy, as they had been, for example, in the debate on the French Revolution. Short pamphlets continued to appear, but more often than not they were reprints of articles or letters which had originally appeared in some newspaper, or of papers or speeches made to a society or associa-

[1] See, for example, C. E. Kennaway, *The War and the Newspapers*, a lecture delivered to the members of the Literary Institute at Otley St. Mary (1856).

tion.[1] Army questions do seem to have inspired the composition of a large number of pamphlets during the Crimean War,
but they had a specialized audience, and their rarity today
suggests that their original circulation was limited. Two best-
selling pamphlets on the conduct of the war — W. R. Greg's
The Way Out and *The One Thing Needful* — were certainly
written in that form, but it is difficult to think of other widely
read examples. The *Edinburgh* was as usual right when it
declared: 'Pamphlets rarely sell more than a few hundred
copies. Few authors, therefore, now resort to them,' unless
debarred access to the reviews and newspapers.[2] In fact it was
extremely easy to publish in the Press. Very large numbers
of newspapers of various kinds were in existence, and they
printed readers' letters — or even a series of lengthy letters,
in all but form a set of articles — in their columns with great
readiness. It is not surprising that the pamphlet had lost its
earlier place in political controversy.

One medium, however, which might have rivalled the newspaper press in the formulation and expression of public opinion
during the Crimean War was that of the public meeting, a
method of demonstration very popular with mid-Victorians
of all classes. The custom of a large platform gave an opportunity to lure lukewarm notables into more active sympathy
by placing them thereon while the leading spirits displayed at
length their powers of oratory. At the end a few resolutions
were customarily passed, or a petition resolved upon. Yet
only two significant series of public meetings and demonstrations were provoked by the events of the war, both in 1855:
those of David Urquhart and his supporters held in the
North-East and Midlands in the late summer and autumn,
and an earlier series in May and June in London and most
other 'principal towns and cities' inspired by the activities of
the Administrative Reform Association. (A National and

---

[1] This, for example, was the case with many of David Urquhart's
well-known pamphlets.

[2] *Edinburgh Review*, cii (October 1855), 475.

Constitutional Association sponsored by the *Morning Advertiser* in March and a State Reform Association in July failed to come to anything.) These meetings heard speeches, passed resolutions, collected funds and drew up petitions in the usual way. But Urquhart's activities never affected more than a small and both socially and geographically restricted section of the public, namely, the superior artisans and lower-middle class of the North and Midlands, and his own obvious megalomania as well as his limited following deprived his activities of much importance in the eyes of governing circles and the serious Press. The Administrative Reform Movement, however, was for a few weeks the great topic of the day. In May and June 1855, when a climax was reached with two mass gatherings at Drury Lane Theatre, it did indeed serve, with its string of meetings throughout the country, as an outlet for public feeling which had to be taken into account by the Government. But not for long. Weaknesses of leadership and confusion of aim soon discredited the movement. In any case it was already true, as the late Victorian historian of public oratory admitted in 1892, that 'a great deal of the power of the Platform is dependent on the Press'.[1] Much of the Administrative Reform Movement's original success was the result of its good press (Charles Dickens brought to its support *Household Words* and other mass-circulation periodicals), and Urquhart was consistently supported by the *Morning Advertiser* (the daily with the largest circulation after *The Times*: though the gulf was enormous), as well as by the *Sheffield Free Press* and after October 1855 his London *Free Press*. The fact remains that although very many citizens of weight supported the Administrative Reform Movement for a time (that is, by their presence at meetings; few became subscribing members of the Association), they did so only briefly. In short, public meetings failed to provide a lastingly satisfactory or effective outlet during the trials of the war for the feelings of those 'within the pale of the constitution'.

[1] H. Jephson, *The Platform* (1892), p. 603.

What of Parliament, still regarded primarily as 'the grand inquest of the nation'? It is undeniable that during the war something of a gulf existed between Parliament and nation. Yet according to traditional constitutional theory it was through the House of Commons that public opinion should be expressed and thus make its contribution to the conduct of affairs. Many members of the public doubted whether a House so out of touch with public feeling as that elected in 1852 could either perform this function or itself act as a sound critic of government errors in the conduct of the war. The two issues on which the General Election of July 1852 had concentrated — Free Trade and Protestantism — had quickly sunk into the background, and the all-important Eastern Question appeared in a very different light to those within and those without the doors of St. Stephen's. Inside the Commons the enthusiasm, indignation and, finally, despair which the conduct of the war excited, were little felt. It was notorious that the war was 'the People's War', and not the war of the governing class. Twice in 1855 the House of Commons found the pressure of public opinion irresistible — when it swung over to the belief that a committee of enquiry into the reasons for the state of affairs in the Crimea must actually be held and not threatened as a mere manœuvre to oust the Aberdeen Coalition, and when it denounced Lord John Russell's willingness to make substantial concessions to Russia during the Vienna negotiations in the spring of 1855. But as a general rule, parliamentary debates seemed to furnish evidence only of Parliament's unresponsiveness to public opinion and lack of sympathy with public preoccupations. Triviality, lack of realism and preoccupation with petty personalities and factious manœuvres were charges for which the conduct of the House, and particularly of its front-benchers, furnished even more evidence than usual during the war. Factious combinations of extremes — Derbyites, Peelites, Radicals — troubled the executive repeatedly. When the Bill guaranteeing the second Turkish loan, for example, was passed by only

G

three votes on 22 July 1855, the House appeared to be ready to play fast and loose with a measure regarded by the public as essential to the war effort. It is not surprising that, as soon as Sebastopol fell, the Cabinet contemplated a dissolution, in the firm belief that 'the conduct of the House last session in multiplying votes of censure, and on the Turkish loan' would justify such a step.[1] At the height of the ministerial crisis in February 1855, the Commons wasted time upon a petty dispute centred around a distant connexion by marriage of Lord John Russell. In December 1854, when Parliament met especially to pass an urgent Foreign Enlistment Bill, a prolonged opposition was mounted, based less upon the practical objections which might well have been made (that it was unlikely to attract many men and very likely to provoke disputes with neutral powers) than upon an unrealistic rehearsal of constitutional myths and nationalistic sentiments. The ineffectiveness of the badly run Sebastopol Committee was something of a last straw. 'While the country deliberates, the Legislature does not,' thundered *The Times* as the administrative reform agitation began, and again a month later: 'It has power which it uses to do nothing, speech which it employs to perplex, counsel and influence which it seems determined to throw into no scale.' The young Layard of Nineveh, then trying to make a political career as a radical, was loudly cheered when he declared at an Administrative Reform Association meeting that the motion he had just put down in the House should have been, 'not "That this House views with deep concern the state of the nation" but "That the nation views with deep concern the state of this House." '[2]

Altogether the war-time role of the House of Commons was not a distinguished one. Far from acting as a safety valve for public opinion, its unresponsiveness and apparent irresponsi-

---

[1] Sir George Cornewall Lewis to Palmerston, 18 September 1855, Broadlands MSS.

[2] *The Times*, 25 April and 24 May 1855; 15 June 1855 (report of Layard's speech on 13 June at Drury Lane Theatre).

bility contributed much to that mood of impatient frustration which sparked off the string of meetings agitating for state reform (for that was the wide meaning contemporaries attached to the phrase 'administrative reform') and encouraged grandiose conceptions of the function of the Press. 'Journalism is not the instrument by which the various divisions of the ruling classes express themselves,' declared the *Edinburgh* in a much-discussed article in October 1855, 'it is rather the instrument by means of which the aggregate intelligence of the nation criticizes and controls them all. It is indeed the "Fourth Estate" of the Realm,' it concluded triumphantly, 'not merely the written counterpart and voice of the speaking "Third".' It followed that the Press was not merely the guardian of free institutions; it was itself a part of the representation of the country and its power made a violent measure of parliamentary reform unnecessary, despite Parliament's defects. The Whig *Edinburgh Review* could make such remarks without expressing dismay; an old Tory like John Wilson Croker found only cause for lamentation when 'newspapers assume that they represent public opinion in a more direct and authoritative manner than even the House of Commons'. But the *Edinburgh* knew where the fault lay. 'If the authority of Parliament has sometimes allowed itself to be usurped by the press . . . the House of Commons is alone to blame,' its contributor wrote.[1]

It is indeed difficult to believe that if the level of parliamentary debate had been more impressive *The Times* could in December 1854, for example, plausibly have described itself as 'a perpetual Committee of the Legislature', whose existence made retrospective debates on the war after a recess quite unnecessary. Nor would it have felt able to claim that 'nearly every speaker [in Parliament] merely re-iterates what has been given to the world weeks before in these columns.'[2] Clearly the Crimean War marked a definite stage in the de-

[1] *Edinburgh Review*, cii (October 1855), 487; Croker to Brougham, 21 July 1855, *The Croker Papers*, iii. 340.

[2] *The Times*, 14 December 1854 and 15 October 1855.

cline of the prestige of Parliament. For years Conservatives had been lamenting the growing power of public opinion. What happened during the war convinced even the most obtuse that this power was not being exercised through the House of Commons as traditional constitutional theory demanded it should be. Some were now prepared to argue that if middle-class influence had increased in the last generation, this was not because since 1832 the House had come to represent a wider section of the community (in effect it had not), but because public interest in politics had increased and the competence of the Press to feed and express it had grown with it.[1] In other words, it could be claimed that if the British constitution was 'popular', it was so not because of its parliamentary institutions, but because of the efficiency of other channels in expressing an increasingly enlightened public opinion. Quite obviously after the experiences of 1854–5 the Press appeared to be much the most important of these channels.

Nevertheless this dethronement of the House of Commons in reality involved loss of prestige, not of power. Many people used language which suggested a swing towards direct democracy, but the realities of power had changed far less than they supposed. 'The House of Commons has no choice between giving expression to the deeply felt sentiment of the nation and making way for some other organ through which that sentiment can find articulate expression,' declared *The Times* on 5 May 1855. In fact no such dilemma existed. Although few people seem to have realized it, public opinion outside Parliament rarely made much difference to ministerial decisions, whereas the temper of the House of Commons was a constant concern of governments. The *Westminster Review* was wildly inaccurate when it claimed in October 1855 'the government is governed by public opinion acting through *The Times*', and Lord John Russell also when he asserted that Palmerston's

[1] An article on 'Representative Reform' in the *Edinburgh Review*, cvi (July 1857), 270–1, argues effectively along these lines.

government 'rests on *The Times*'.[1] In fact Palmerston frequently acted in ways sharply criticized by Press and public in his first few months as Prime Minister, and his predecessor Aberdeen had been notoriously unresponsive to public opinion. As far as Cabinet decisions were concerned, it was the attitudes of their colleagues and of Parliament and their supporters that concerned the Queen's ministers, not those of the general public. At the highest level of decision-making, the highly articulate excitement of the public during the war had little more than nuisance value, despite contemporary claims to the contrary, except when it infected Parliament.

What lessons were drawn from the defective functioning of British constitutional institutions during the war? Publicity and freedom of discussion had certainly failed to secure nationwide unity and perseverance, and the wisdom of the criticisms so energetically expressed of the conduct of the war remained a matter for dispute (markedly along lines of social class). Nevertheless, very many people were able to rest unshaken in their belief that in war as in peace free and full discussion could do only good. They were able to do so either because they blamed the excesses of *The Times* for the gloom and bitterness and extreme counsels which had prevailed, or because they honestly believed gloom and bitterness to have been fully warranted and extreme counsels essential for the nation's salvation. On the other hand, the doubts with which at the beginning of the war the nation had regarded its legislature and executive had been vastly strengthened. In 1854 the Cabinet had fiddled while Rome burned, and the War Committee of 1855 too tardily made amends. The administrative departments had appeared to be riddled with out-of-date routine and inefficiency and to have taken an unconscionable time to begin to put their house in order. As a crowning blow, in the midst of military disasters and national

---

[1] *Westminster Review*, N.S., viii (October 1855), 520; Lord John Russell to Minto, 22 July 1855, P.R.O. 30/22/12.

despair, the legislature had deprived the country of a government for nearly two weeks and displayed a scale of values which seemed to prove it unfit either to represent the nation or to be heard by the Queen's ministers.

It is thus not surprising that the war provoked much talk of representative institutions having been shown to be unfitted for war, if not for peace. Those eccentrics who had long denounced a parliamentary régime found a responsive English audience at last. In the gloomy hysteria of the spring of 1855, it became fashionable to say that the country needed some kind of dictator, that there was never anything equal to a despotic government in carrying on war. At best it might be admitted that 'a democracy may carry on war successfully, but it can never carry on war democratically with success'.[1] Richard Congreve (an Oxford don then on the brink of declaring himself a disciple of Auguste Comte) addressed the Edinburgh Philosophical Society on the unsuitability of constitutional government for modern European countries. 'It has ever failed ... it is failing you now, in the presence of real dangers and war,' he declared.[2] This theme was a common one even in Britain, and abroad there were many more who were delighted to observe the discredit of English parliamentary institutions — Comte himself in France, the disillusioned radical Lothar Bucher in Germany (his *Der Parlamentarismus wie er ist* was published in 1855), as well as very many on the Right. But in England, although a market was found for a reprint of Carlyle's attacks on Parliament and Downing Street under the title *Prophecy for 1855* and many agreed with the West Country parson R. W. Barnes that 'the great blessings of our free institutions and divided responsibilities are unsuited

[1] G. W. Norman, op. cit., Letter of 9 February 1856.
[2] *The Roman Empire of the West* (1855), p. 61. According to Congreve's recollections in old age, although he hesitated to become a 'positiviste complet' until 1856, he had been 'attracted from the historical, political and social side' since 1849 (British Museum, Congreve Papers, Add. MS. 45259, fo. 13) and he resigned his Fellowship at Wadham in 1854.

to a state of war ',[1] many others maintained that this was not the correct inference to draw. 'Our constitutional government is on trial,' Prince Albert said on 9 June 1855 at the annual dinner of the Trinity Corporation, and similar phrases had long been on everyone's lips.[2] But radicals of every kind were quick to point out that as far as they were concerned representative institutions were *not* on trial, for the country did not possess them in any true sense.[3] A further extension of the franchise, some redistribution of seats or the ballot was needed before the nation's institutions could be called truly representative. Nor were representative institutions on trial in the eyes of die-hard Conservatives; to them, the nation's institutions had been so gravely tampered with in 1832 that executive weakness and legislative irresponsibility were all that could be expected in moments of crisis. But these dissentients from the view summed up by the Prince, that free institutions were undergoing a critical testing-time, were very much in a minority. The Prince had gone on to call for restraint and loyal support of the Queen's Government, so that the trial could be successfully undergone,[4] and the great majority emerged from the war still clinging to the optimistic view that his appeal implied. There was nothing wrong with the British constitution which good will and good sense could not put right. Towards the end of the war a complacent feeling

[1] T. Ballantyne, *Prophecy for 1855* (1855), a selection from *Latter Day Pamphlets*; *Public Opinion, considered in Letters between one of his Friends and R. W. Barnes, M.A., Vicar of Probus* (1855), p. 10.

[2] For example, on Lansdowne's (the doyen of Whig ministers) on 8 February 1855, in the midst of the ministerial crisis, when he went on to warn the Lords: 'If we do not procure that unanimity by patriotism, by argument, and by similarity of opinion which despotism is able at all times and in all periods to command, despotism will be too powerful for liberty' (3 *Hansard*, cxxxvi, col. 1355).

[3] Particularly effective expressions of this view appeared in *Reynolds News*, 25 February 1855, and the *Morning Advertiser*, 16 May 1855.

[4] Inevitably, as *The Examiner* predicted (23 June 1855), the Prince's speech was taken by radicals to be preaching despotism (e.g. *News of the World*, 1 July 1855).

was spreading that the flexibility of English institutions had been triumphantly demonstrated again; the shortcomings of the legislature and executive had been counterbalanced by developments in a wider field. This was the complacent view expressed by the young George Brodrick in his *Essay on Representative Government in Ancient and Modern Times*, which won the Chancellor's English Essay Prize at the University of Oxford in 1855 and much of which he read to an admiring and most distinguished throng at the Encaenia in the Sheldonian on 20 June 1855, thereby attracting so much favourable notice that he secured his entrée into journalism.[1] 'Self-government is the noblest instrument of moral elevation,' declaimed Brodrick in the conventional mid-Victorian vein. But he made it clear that he had taken into account and surmounted the doubts raised by the Crimean winter which had just been passed. 'Wealth and intelligence are outstripping our institutions,' he admitted, but 'new outlets and regulating forces' had appeared, above all 'the entire publicity of political actions, and the freedom of the press', and thus equilibrium had been restored.[2]

In the end complacency such as this was the most common attitude. The assumptions with which most people entered the war had been shaken, but only briefly. Cabinet government and the electoral system and administrative departments clearly left even more to be desired than had been supposed at the beginning of the war; but it was still believed that the power of public opinion could remedy their defects. Very many people were prepared to allow that *The Times* had gone too far and to remark upon the dangers of the despotism of one journal, but few hazarded more fundamental doubts. The abolition of the stamp duty (achieved in March 1855) would

[1] George Brodrick, *Memories and Impressions* (1900), p. 109. The distinguished Montalembert, who was receiving an honorary degree, called his Essay 'remarkable' (Lecanuet, op. cit. iii. 147). Derby, Gladstone and Tennyson were among those present.

[2] G. Brodrick, 'Representative Government in Ancient and Modern Times', in his *Political Studies* (1879), p. 45.

in any case probably solve the problem of *The Times*, by putting it at a financial disadvantage in its competition with other London journals and provincial newspapers.[1] Thus it was only on the Continent that the prestige of British political institutions remained very low. In England the gloom and doubt soon lifted. 'Doubtless freer governments are *slower* machines than absolute ones,' conceded the *Edinburgh Review* at the end of the war, 'but their ultimate means are incalculably vaster ... In the third year of the war, England — clumsy, constitutional, almost democratic, but opulent even to plethora — is only just warming to her work, whereas our autocratic ally and our despotic adversary are alike breathless and bleeding.'[2]

Despite the happy ending to the war — or rather, the feeling that the ending could have been triumphant if only France had not obliged England to make peace — confidence in the existing machinery of government had received a ruder blow than any it had yet sustained in England. A perceptible stimulus had been given to a tendency which had hitherto been very unobtrusive: the tendency away from the cult and practice of parliamentary government. It was popular influence alone which was believed to have saved the Army. Nevertheless the war did not last long enough or entail a sufficiently prolonged series of grave disasters for these developments to go very far. The shock to complacency had been very great. But it was too brief, and found too diverse and convincing an assortment of scapegoats — *The Times*, a restricted franchise, aristocratic power, unhistoric practices — for the changes in political institutions and practices to be very substantial or the doubts over constitutional shibboleths to be very lasting.

---

[1] This indeed happened to some extent, since *The Times* was considerably heavier than its competitors, and after July 1855 postage on newspapers had to be paid by weight, and only on those actually sent through the post.

[2] *Edinburgh Review*, ciii (April 1856), 571.

PART TWO

War, Radicalism and Reform

IF in strictly constitutional matters the Crimean War thus proved 'the negation of many anticipations', as one contemporary political writer promptly acknowledged,[1] this contrast was even more striking in the sphere of class relationships and attitudes to political and social institutions in general. At the beginning of the war it was widely believed that war would purge the nation of personal selfishness and social disunity. Only slightly less widespread was the conviction that concern over 'the condition of England question' would be laid aside and parliamentary discussion of domestic problems cease for the duration of hostilities. A political and social pause, made acceptable by an upsurge of patriotic emotion — this was what the war was expected to bring.[2] Radicalism and reform would be submerged beneath the nation's new preoccupations. In the event these expectations proved to have been very much mistaken. The course of the War provoked an outburst of overt class bitterness and impatience with prevailing institutions far more comprehensive and alarming than anything which had been seen since the early 1830s or was to be seen again for many years, and served to convince many continental observers that the admired English body politic was at last in decline.[3] At the same time it was accompanied by some of the most significant legislation in the field of social institutions passed between the repeal of the Corn Laws and the Second Reform Act.

Nevertheless it would be a misleading simplification merely to assert that the misfortunes of this war, like those of so

---

[1] John Wade, *England's Greatness* (1856), p. 765.

[2] See above, pp. 22–23.

[3] Cf., for example, Count Vitzthum von Eckstaedt, *St. Petersburg and London* (1887), i. 168 (to Baron von Beust, 19 May 1855), and p. 80 above.

many others before and since, administered a powerful
stimulus to radicalism and social change or (in Nathaniel
Hawthorne's phrase) gave 'a vast impulse towards democracy'.[1] English radicalism in the 1850s was far too diverse in
its origins, attitudes and ideals to respond uniformly to the
experiences of the war. While a few English radicals followed
Cobden and Bright in denouncing the war as politically unnecessary and economically disastrous, many more supported
it ardently either from sheer patriotic jingoism, or from
sympathy for 'the oppressed nationalities' crushed by the
spectre of Russian military power, or both. But this was not
the only way in which the war divided English radicals. Some
were moved by the war to extreme discontent with the *status
quo* in politics, or society, or both, and therefore to intense
activity; whereas others who were cynical or became disappointed about the nature and scope of the war, were comparatively indifferent even to its most dramatic episodes.
Certainly it cannot be assumed that those radicals who were
filled with belligerent patriotism were less inclined to attack
existing institutions than the pacifists or the disillusioned;
quite the opposite was usually the case. In short, the effects of
the war upon English radicalism were almost as varied as the
radical groups themselves.

Yet because these groups, though too distinct to co-operate
for long, were organized extremely loosely and had enough
personal and ideological links to shade off into each other, it
would be clumsy as well as difficult to trace separately the
response of each to the war. The followers of David Urquhart,
for example, though often quite literally at blows with the
Chartists, came to have much in common with them where the
diplomatic side of the war was concerned — common ground
which is well symbolized by the close and friendly relations of
Karl Marx during the war with both Urquhart and Ernest
Jones, the Chartist leader. Similarly many of Urquhart's

[1] Nathaniel Hawthorne, *The English Notebooks*, ed. Randall Stewart
(New York, 1941), p. 99, entry under '3 January 1855'.

constitutional doctrines were shared by middle-class radicals
who found his diplomatic views unconvincing and his flamboyant personality distasteful. Thus it seems more profitable
to discuss the effect of the war on English radicalism in terms
of its impact on radical ways of thinking rather than on
specific radical groups. The discussion which follows, however,
is for the sake of relevance deliberately confined to a consideration of the protests against the established order of
things in England which the war inspired, despite the fact that
very many English radicals at this time were deeply concerned
with foreign affairs and anxiously hoped that the Crimean
War might bring the struggles of Italy, Hungary and Poland
to a triumphant conclusion.[1]

Protest against the established order is inevitably most
active when that order is discredited by failure, whether
economic or military. Between the repeal of the Corn Laws in
1846 and the economic difficulties of the 1870s, moments of
crisis which impinged upon the whole community were few
and far between in England. The ruling classes largely escaped
blame for the Indian Mutiny, and although the financial and
commercial crises of 1857 and 1866 had their political repercussions, hunger politics on any large scale were unknown.
Only when the disasters of the Crimean campaign were firmly
laid at the door of 'the System' by the British Press was the
acquiescent mood of mid-Victorian politics briefly but
decisively broken. Moreover, in these noisy manifestations
during the Crimean War basic economic resentments played
only a small part, and this is typical of English radicalism as a
whole in this ambiguous period. For the two currents of
thought and emotion, continental sympathies apart, which
most often led to criticism and rejection of the established

[1] This large exclusion is not intended to imply any claim that home
policy was more important than foreign policy in keeping radicalism
alive in the fifties — the opposite was no doubt the case, as has often
been suggested (e.g. S. Maccoby, *English Radicalism 1853–1886* (1938),
p. 33, and A. Briggs, op. cit., p. 430, and 'The Crimean Centenary',
Virginia Quarterly Review, xxx (1954), 555).

order in the 1850s were in no way directly inspired by economic wants or needs.

They were currents which pulled in entirely opposite directions. One clearly expressed the new class-consciousness of both the middle- and working-classes which had been growing in intensity since the beginning of the century and which was closely connected with the pace and nature of economic change. But the other still drew heavily upon ancient constitutional ideals and a certain vision of English history, finding fresh encouragement to do so in the historical vogue which reached a peak in the 1830s but whose impetus was far from spent twenty years later. Neither current of thought and feeling was entirely peculiar to any one radical group. Indeed it is striking how much the very group which might have been expected to feel least sympathetic to historical perspectives — the successful, ambitious business and professional men — in fact responded to the vision of 'the ancient constitution' as much as to class feeling. These two aspects of radical psychology, each so important in the deceptively unspectacular history of social protest in mid-nineteenth-century England, thus cut across many lines of division. Each was stirred into activity by the war, and together they inspired an outburst of protest strong enough for a while to provoke fears and hopes that 1855 would prove England's long-expected year of revolution, or at least a turning-point in the structure of English politics and society. It is their history which will be discussed in the following chapters.

CHAPTER THREE

The Effect of the Crimean War upon Class-consciousness

THE national unity which was so confidently anticipated at the beginning of the war was expected to spring chiefly from an outburst of patriotic excitement great enough to sweep away the selfish materialism commonly blamed for discontent with the established order of things. But many people also predicted that feelings of resentment would be stilled as war demonstrated once again that only the aristocratic spirit and aristocratic leadership could guide a nation and an army to victory. Unity of purpose, warmth of sentiment and keenness of action — these were the qualities commonly identified with an aristocracy and thought to be conspicuously lacking in a liberal and industrial state. The war would put a premium upon these virtues, and vindicate aristocratic institutions accordingly. That this could so often be suggested reveals how vigorously the old concept of war as primarily an affair of personal heroism flourished at the outset. Only a minority, though an able one, believed from the start that a new era of warfare was beginning, one in which technical knowledge, specialized experience and powers of organization would be all important and the personal qualities of the officer and the gentleman of correspondingly small account. Most people were prepared to concede that the nation needed the aristocratic virtues to purge it of the spirit of selfish calculation repeatedly associated in these months with the middle class, and that the Army needed the dash of born leaders to carry it to victory. Thus in reality the outbreak of the war greatly increased the vulnerability of the whole range of aristocratic institutions. For the more the defence of

H

the aristocracy was associated with its military usefulness, and the more the conduct of the war and above all of the spectacular Crimean expedition was associated with that one class, the more inevitable it became that any military setbacks would transform this very defence into a potent weapon of attack.

With contemporaries it was a commonplace that England still possessed an aristocratic social and political structure. The extent to which the foundations of this structure had already been undermined was scarcely appreciated. The military appointments and promotions made in 1854 (which seemed to overlook socially undistinguished officers with unfashionable Indian experience), and the system of purchasing commissions, combined with many other circumstances to make the Army seem even more of an aristocratic preserve than it really was. At the same time the prolonged airing in 1854 of the Northcote–Trevelyan plan for recruiting Government officials by open competitive examination publicized still further the familiar picture of a country governed by aristocratic influence and favouritism. On the Continent, too, England was widely regarded as the last refuge of aristocracy. Aristocracy, wrote Léon Faucher in his *Études sur l'Angleterre*, 'qui n'est plus même à l'état de tradition sur le continent, demeure chez ce peuple à l'état d'institution'.[1] According to a militant radical like Ledru-Rollin, England had wasted empires, devastated continents and pillaged the world to maintain the prodigalities of her lords.[2] On the other hand, since the 1820s moderate Liberals had been finding in aristocratic leadership of English society and English local government the secret of the country's much admired political and social stability.[3] During his visit to America in 1831, Alexis de

[1] *Études sur l'Angleterre* (Paris, 1845), p. xxxi.
[2] A. A. Ledru-Rollin, *De la Décadence de l'Angleterre* (Paris, 1850), pp. 10–11.
[3] For examples, see Theodore Zeldin, 'English ideals in French politics during the nineteenth century', *Historical Journal*, ii (1959).

Tocqueville with his companion Charles de Beaumont came to see England as the last stronghold of aristocracy in a world advancing inevitably towards the evils and dangers of democracy,[1] and the immense success of his *Democracy in America* diffused his views very widely indeed on both sides of the Channel. Thus at the beginning of 1854 both at home and abroad many moderate Liberals were ready to hope, and many advanced radicals to fear, that the coming war would demonstrate beyond dispute the moral and practical benefits of vigorous aristocratic institutions. As late as 7 December 1854, while the excitement of the battles of Alma, Balaklava and Inkerman still persisted and before *The Times* began its revelations, Tocqueville's self-confident friend Henry Reeve assured him that the march towards democracy was less inevitable than he feared. In England the aristocracy had never been so strong; for it had never behaved with more distinguished gallantry. Even more smugly, Reeve went on: 'il a été donné à l'aristocratie anglaise de marcher avec les temps et même de les conduire.'[2] Few people would have cared to repeat these opinions a few weeks later, and Tocqueville when he came to reply needed no great powers of perception to see that Reeve was wrong. 'Military services are not enough to preserve an aristocracy,' was his comment, 'it must also know how to govern.'[3] He might have added that by then even the military services of the English aristocracy were being criticized almost as much as their method of governing, and that they were being denounced on all sides as conspicuously behind the times, not abreast of them.

For in the spring of 1855 a significant stage was completed in the evolution of class-consciousness among the middle class, under the impetus of a dramatic shift in the British public's

[1] Seymour Drescher, *Tocqueville and England* (Cambridge, Mass., 1964), p. 32.

[2] A. de Tocqueville, *Œuvres Complètes* (Paris, 1954), ed. J.-P. Mayer, VI, i, p. 150.

[3] *Memoir, Letters and Remains of Count Alexis de Tocqueville* (1861), ii. 291.

conception of the nature of war and the conditions of victory. By then it was all too common knowledge that although the rank and file had fought doggedly, although the Light Brigade had charged — 'noble six hundred' — and the enemy been held back, yet sickness and death were decimating the Army in a long winter siege for which it was tragically unprepared. Heroism was seen to be not enough; there was more to war than fighting. As this truism gripped the British public, war began increasingly to be seen in terms of matching supply with demand, in terms of organization and administration and the manipulation of material resources, rather than of personal bravery and leadership.[1] From this economic conception of war it was but a short step to the equation of military strength with practical efficiency, and this in the 1850s was inevitably associated with the middle class and modernity, not with the aristocracy and tradition. The aristocracy thus came to appear as the living embodiment of the survival of the past into a new age — a survival which had condemned the Crimean expedition to its tragic fate. If efficiency and freedom from tradition were the twin virtues a nation at war should aspire to, there could be no doubt in the middle of the nineteenth century that these were the virtues of the English business world, and not of the English aristocracy.

From the end of December 1854 such themes were trumpeted brazenly abroad by *The Times*. They were repeated by the meteoric Administrative Reform Association — founded in May 1855, a mass movement by June, and by August quite insignificant — and developed in numerous journals and pamphlets. With men who had brought themselves to the fringe of political power and social esteem and were anxious

---

[1] 'War', wrote Gladstone in a disapproving review of Tennyson's out-dated expression of war feeling before the Crimean expedition in *Maud*, 'is now always associated with commercial enterprise' (*Quarterly Review*, cvi (1859), 10). (*Maud* was written between June and September 1854.)

to cross it, in particular, though not with the working classes or the intellectuals, they became a new gospel. Their persuasive coherence and apparent aptness focused feelings which had been in existence for some time.

In the last years of peace the inefficiency and jobbery of the aristocracy had been one of the assumptions of the Liverpool Financial Reform Association, and the superior efficiency of private businesses to government departments was already becoming a favourite claim. But until the Crimean disasters this particular phase of middle-class assertiveness, which attacked (at least ostensibly) not the privileges of the aristocracy but their incompetence and out-of-date attitudes, had not yet been fully worked out or given nation-wide expression. The two great outbursts of middle-class feeling in the previous generation — over the Reform Act of 1832 and the repeal of the Corn Laws — sprang from earlier and different phases of middle-class self-awareness. Moreover those two earlier outbursts lacked the appeal to an almost universal social emotion, whose presence in 1855 in the shape of patriotism and military pride made the movement of that year potentially so dangerous.

The nature and fortunes of these war-time ideas thus deserve analysis. Both can best be studied in that war-time movement for administrative reform which stimulated the foundation of the Administrative Reform Association, but which was, as *The Times* acknowledged, far wider than the Association.[1] That organization was preceded by the National and Constitutional Association founded in February 1855 under the auspices of the *Morning Advertiser*, a lower-middle-class affair with a blatantly anti-aristocratic bias which was soon swallowed up by the Administrative Reform Association. It was copied by the State Reform Association, a body supported by the Chartists and explicitly pledged to manhood suffrage, which barely got off the ground. But it was the

---

[1] The history of the Association is discussed in detail by the present author in *Victorian Studies*, viii (1965), 231–42.

Administrative Reform Association itself and its programme which alone appealed to the solid and successful business and professional men, the readers of *Punch* and *The Times*, and which therefore most faithfully reflects the impact of the Crimean campaign on influential middle-class feeling.[1]

The most striking thing about this middle-class attack upon the aristocracy in the Crimean War is that it was not a direct one. It did not appeal to envy of wealth or rank, or exploit traditional egalitarianism of the 'Jack's as good as his master' kind,[2] it did not even make very much play with the notion of aristocratic privilege as a type of monopoly which flouted the laws of nature and the free play of competition. It appealed to prejudices and emotions even more deeply cherished by the successful middle-class men to whom it was addressed and from whom it sprang. For it attacked privilege only when it did not spring from ability and success, when it had failed to vindicate its continued existence even in the situation from which it derived its original justification. Why were the aristocracy thought to have been found wanting, even in war? Because their habits of idleness and self-indulgence had deprived them of that initiative and toughness which had now been shown to be as important as enthusiasm and bravery; because — and this was the fault for which they were most severely castigated — they were hidebound by precedent and

[1] It never had the support of the advanced intellectuals, or of the working classes, or of course of the upper and upper-middle classes, as may be seen for example from the files of the *Leader*, *Reynolds News*, the *Morning Post* and the *Globe*. Cobden, too, refused his support, on the grounds that 'the People' were partly to blame for the state of affairs (British Museum, Cobden MSS., Add. MS. 43665, fos. 12 and 305, and 43669, fo. 15). For other middle-class critics of the Association, see below, pp. 137, 145.

[2] Although there was much of this in the publications intended for the lower-middle class which Charles Dickens, that leading spirit of the Association, either controlled or influenced. Dickens, of course, was 'continually stuffing a scarecrow under the title of aristocracy and carrying it through the streets for the people to see how ugly it is and to throw stones at it', as the German writer Theodor Fontane put it, op. cit., p. 190.

tradition and failed to realize that new military techniques, new weapons, new administrative methods were required, failed to adapt old routines and improvise new ones, even when confronted with a crisis. In short, in the Crimean War the aristocracy had committed the sin which was unforgivable in middle-class eyes in the 1850s: they had failed to be 'practical'. It was this shortcoming which had allowed the Russians to prove themselves superior in mechanical resource to the workshop of the world, contrary to all reasonable expectation,[1] and thus brought bitter humiliation upon the nation.

Thus in 1855 the ultimate historic defence of aristocracy — its supreme value in time of war — received for the first time in England an outright denial. For the first time competent administrative processes and freedom from routine ideas loomed as large as bravery or dash in action in the public's concept of military strength. This was the bridge over which the professional and business men of 1855 crossed to their claim that they and not the aristocracy, were best fitted to perform the complex functions of modern war. War was equated with a commercial undertaking or a specialized profession, not with an amateur sport or a moral crusade, and by the same token could be claimed as properly a middle-class and not an aristocratic preserve. The orators of 1855 were fond of denying charges that their movement was stirring up class antagonism.[2] Their only object, they claimed, was efficiency in the conduct of the nation's affairs. The catchword of the Administrative Reform Association was 'the Right Man in the Right Place', and they were prepared to admit that an aristocrat might in theory be as much 'the Right Man' as a man of business. But in practice, they argued, his upbringing, education and experience ('practical experience' was another key phrase of the movement) would almost certainly prevent him from being fit to govern.

[1] Cf., for example, *Daily News*, 2 August 1855.
[2] Even Dickens disclaimed the charge (*The Speeches of Charles Dickens* (Oxford, 1960), ed. K. J. Fielding, p. 203).

For if the first ingredient of this indirect attack on the
aristocracy was a new conception of the skill which war
demanded, the second was an unwavering faith in what might
well be called the mystique of business. The picture of an age
of deference prolonged well into the second half of Victoria's
long reign by timely aristocratic concession over the Corn
Laws has been too strongly drawn, and the fifties and sixties
too often seen as a golden age of social harmony, when the
aristocracy enjoyed its Indian summer and middle-class
militancy was vanquished by middle-class snobbery. No
doubt there was indeed a contrast between the *Sturm und
Drang* of the thirties and forties and the succeeding 'age of
equipoise', but that contrast was more coincidental and
precarious than is always supposed. Certainly in the Crimean
War it was the most respectable members of the middle class,
and not the workers, who led the attack on the established
order of things, and they did so under the inspiration of a
distinctive middle-class set of values which had been develop-
ing since the 1820s, although it was only given complete
conviction and widespread currency by the disasters of the
Crimean campaign. The poetry of hunting and shooting, of
county society and the London season, had had since the days
of George IV a rival in the poetry of business, and the closing
decades of the nineteenth century become unnecessarily
difficult to understand if the growing authority of commercial
and professional values and standards of behaviour in the
middle of the century is overlooked. In the crisis of the Crimean
War, the great middle-class public identified military and
political ability with commercial experience with an arrogance
and confidence which could hardly have been more complete.
Nothing could give stronger proof of the spell cast by the
poetry of business in the fifties than the assumption which
permeated the Administrative Reform movement that even
in the midst of war — indeed especially in the midst of war —
the techniques of government should be but the techniques of
commerce writ large. The crowning development — or the

reductio ad absurdum — of that English cult of commercial values which had struck so many observers since the end of the Napoleonic Wars, was surely the public clamour in 1855 for the Army and the State to be run by business men, not because of any belief in identity of interests or equality of opportunity, but simply because ability was identified *tout court* with business experience. If the Crimean War was ushered in by much admiration of knightly self-sacrifice and heroism, and frequently expressed hopes of salvation from sordid Mammon-worship, before it was half-way through it had effected a total reversal of the qualities held up for admiration, and of the class stereotypes with which they were associated. The aristocracy no longer appeared as born war leaders free from base middle-class materialism, but as out-of-date privileged bunglers who should make way for the efficient, self-reliant men of the age. Adaptability, technical skill, hard work and competence in the correlation of means with ends, had been put on a pedestal. Some of the most popular preachers of the day now assured their congregations that the war had ushered in 'the beginning of the last times when no longer ancient hierarchies but young living ability and force, God's anointed servants, shall take charge of the world'.[1] It is perhaps significant that after the Crimean War Samuel Smiles's *Self-Help* became a best-seller, although at its beginning it failed to find a publisher.[2] For despite the prestige enjoyed by 'the Idea of the Age' in the later 1840s, that idea

[1] J. Baldwin Brown, *What is to Follow the Fast? All Hands to Work, A Discourse on the Duty of all honest Englishmen at the present Crisis* (*Penny Pulpit* (June 1855), p. 231); cf. Charles Spurgeon, 'The People's Christ' (sermon preached on 25 February 1855), *Sermons delivered in Exeter Hall, Strand* (1856), p. 126.

[2] A. Smiles, *Samuel Smiles and his Surroundings* (1956), p. 88. Mrs. Craik's popular novel, *John Halifax, Gentleman* (1856), consistently relates the ideal of the gentleman to moral worth, not birth, and Thackeray's immensely successful lectures on *The Four Georges* (written in 1855 while he was actively supporting the Administrative Reform Association) ended with his famous definition of a gentleman, couched in purely moral terms.

lacked the emotional, moralizing intensity of the later cult of
the self-made professional or business man, a cult which in the
late fifties and sixties captured even the working classes.[1] The
religion of work and self-help reached its maturity only after
1854, and a landmark in its growth was the exposé of the
consequences of aristocratic frivolity and dependence upon
tradition offered by the Crimean campaign. The claim that
fitness alone should be the password to power and place had
been transformed in the excitement of war into an identification
of fitness with middle-class experience and values more explicit
and exclusive than any which had been attempted before.

The Crimean War was thus a landmark in the evolution of
an independent rationale for middle-class pride, as well as in
public concepts of the conditions of military success. Each of
these two developments strengthened the other. The large
extent to which the nature of warfare had in truth changed
gave added plausibility to the claim that military success
depended upon the permeation of government departments
and the Army by middle-class skills and values. The aura of
success which deservedly hung around British commerce and
industry made it seem all the more convincing that 'commercialize' was the proper cry to raise to remedy all evils. At
a time when 'war has become an affair of science and
machinery, of accumulated capital and skilful combination',
it did indeed seem doubly intolerable that 'this great commercial and mechanical country is governed by an official
body comparatively ignorant of commerce and the mechanical
arts'.[2] For it was increasingly plain that, as the *Edinburgh*
put it, 'We have now to do for war what we have accomplished
in the arts of peace, by machinery as applied to manufactures,
by steamships and railroads, and by gigantic associations.
We must win by skill, wealth and organization.'[3] We must

---

[1] Cf. J. F. C. Harrison, 'The Victorian gospel of success', *Victorian
Studies*, i (1957), 157.

[2] *The Times*, 31 October 1854, 1 March 1855.

[3] *Edinburgh Review*, ci (January 1855), 285.

beat Russia's huge resources 'by making the century our ally'.[1] Such arguments made it seem an obvious disaster that the standard of professional training of British Army officers was probably the lowest in Europe, and that British government departments were a haven for mediocrities with influential patrons.

Middle-class impatience with aristocratic inefficiency was far from new, and had as it happened been particularly outspoken in the years immediately before the war in the campaign for economy in government spending; but faith in 'scientific' warfare as the road to victory and then, far more important, spectacular revelations of bungling and disaster in the Crimea, gave these feelings unprecedented force and plausibility and secured them a national — indeed an international — audience for the first time. 'At this moment', wrote Nathaniel Hawthorne on 3 January 1855 in one of the notebooks he kept during his visits to England, 'it would be an absurdity in the nobles to pretend to the position which was quietly conceded to them a year ago. This one year has done the work of fifty ordinary ones; or more accurately, perhaps, it has made apparent what has long been preparing itself.'[2] Hawthorne's afterthought was a sound one; the Sebastopol revelations must not be given all the credit for these developments. The poetry of business would not have seemed so sweet if Government had not already been in such bad odour, and the mid-nineteenth-century platitude that 'government does everything badly' had many older, more important sources than the apparent bungling of an unpractical aristocracy in the Crimean War. Moreover, lukewarmness about the war on the part of Aberdeen as Prime Minister and many other members of the governing class created an emotional atmosphere of impatience and suspicion of the Government and aristocracy long before the Crimean landing.

> With faces turn'd from Battle, they went forth:
> We march't with ours set stern against the North,

[1] *The Times*, 1 December 1854.   [2] Op. cit., p. 99.

wrote Gerald Massey in his *War Waits*[1] and the same theme
was a favourite of Mr. Punch in 1854. But to the mass of
sympathizers with the Administrative Reform Movement in the
spring of 1855, the conclusive reason for damning the British
Government and all its works, was that it neither drew upon
the services of men of business nor copied business practices.

The equation of efficiency with commercial experience was
indeed monotonous among supporters of that movement.
Even A. H. Layard, for example, renowned as the discoverer
of Nineveh and an early hero of the movement, although
himself by no means of middle-class origins or outlook and
quite lacking in business experience, evidently fell under its
spell, for one of his proposals for reform was, 'That a non-
parliamentary commission of commercial men shall be
appointed to investigate the present condition of government
departments.' Upon this, his ally the radical young Viscount
Goderich was understandably driven to comment, 'Why do
you talk of a commission of practical *commercial* men?
Practical men would surely be enough.'[2] It would certainly
not have been enough for the large audience to please whom
Mr. Punch's 'Madrigal of Administrative Reform' was
written:

> No more will we be ruled by men
> Whose sole qualification
> Is not ability and ken;
> But lies in rank and station:
> None shall this land
> Henceforth command
> No men will we submit to,
> But those who business understand;
> Practical men of ditto [3]

[1] *War Waits* (1855), p. 40. This collection of war verse was written
in 1854.
[2] Layard's proposals, 'private and confidential', undated, Add.
MS. 39053, fo. 7; Goderich to Layard, 25 June 1854, ibid. 38984, fo. 78.
[3] *Punch*, 26 May 1855.

THE MEMBER FOR NINEVEH DIGS OUT THE BRITISH BULL.

(Punch, April 7, 1855)

Among even the most intelligent and serious men, the notions that public and private business were the same in kind, and that private business was currently better conducted than public, were articles of faith. The new 'Civil Service and Commerce Department' at King's College, London, was surely significantly named; the combination would have seemed eminently desirable to most middle-class men. From the beginning the Administrative Reform Association's claim that its intention was not to attack the aristocracy but to introduce business principles into government was widely praised.[1] Men who were themselves successful tycoons naturally preached these doctrines with much enthusiasm, but they were preaching to the converted. At the foundation meeting of the Association the great shipowner W. S. Lindsay was rousingly received when he offered lengthy illustrations of the achievements of English men of business in support of his motion that 'the true remedy was enlarged experience and practical ability in the service of the state'.[2] But Charles Dickens too, when he addressed a mass meeting at Drury Lane Theatre, made great play with the Exchequer's tally sticks and took it to be 'as clearly established as the existence of the sun, moon and stars . . . that our public progress is far behind our private progress'.[3] 'To bring up the public management to the level of private management in this country' was officially declared to be 'the first object' of the Association,[4] and it was entirely characteristic that when the Committee of

[1] e.g. *Illustrated London News*, 5 May 1855.

[2] Report of the meeting of 5 May in *The Times*, 7 May 1855.

[3] *Speeches*, p. 206. A more sustained development of this almost platitudinous belief can be found, for example, in the *North British Review*, xxiii (1855), 161. It had already been put forward in the *Westminster Review* (N.S. iv (1853) 55) in Herbert Spencer's famous article, 'Over-Legislation', and when Chapman reprinted this article separately early in 1854 Samuel Morley, who became President of the Association formed in 1855, took part of the edition (H. Spencer, *Autobiography* (1904), i. 423).

[4] Official papers of the Administrative Reform Association, no. 3, p. 8.

the Association finally put forward specific proposals for the reform of the Civil Service, it recommended a preliminary, open qualifying examination in provincial centres which would lead to a certificate of competence equally acceptable to private employers and to government departments. It opposed an 'irrelevant' academic syllabus, and urged the adoption of 'the common sense business practice' of holding heads of government offices responsible for their management, dismissing them if incompetent, and allowing them to dismiss their subordinates likewise.[1] Clearly to the Administrative Reform Association, though not to Sir Charles Trevelyan, Civil Service reform meant the closest possible approximation between government departments and commercial houses in methods of recruitment and promotion. The same prescription of proved practical expertise was offered to the Army. There was a good deal of feeling that the legend of the devoted aristocratic officer had been exploded by the self-indulgence and privilege to be seen in the Crimea. When Palmerston attempted to defend the aristocracy by pointing to their valour on active service, the radical journalist John Forster advised Layard in riposte to move for returns of all officers who had come home from the Crimea on leave, or with permission to retire — 'fair-weather' officers who had left the sinking ship.[2] Scientific military education became the prescription of the day. But the main brunt of the attack continued to fall upon the Civil Service. In the spring of 1855 it was useless to point out that aristocratic influence was in reality far more rife in the Army and the diplomatic service, and equally useless to show that the two most inefficient departments — the Commissariat and the Army medical service — were also notoriously

[1] Official papers of the Administrative Reform Association, nos. 6 and 8.
[2] Forster to Layard, 9 May 1855, Add. MS. 38983, fo. 379. In fact, Layard overshot his mark badly in his attacks on the Services, for he descended too much to personalities, and inaccurate ones at that. His ally Lord Goderich made a much greater impression by his sober arguments for making military command open to talent.

the least aristocratic in personnel, or that private business
had its full share of swindlers and failures. The public persisted
in believing that the panacea was to remake the Civil Service
in the image of private business.

Moreover the cry of 'commercialize' did not stop at the
recruitment and promotion of Government personnel. It
extended to methods of transacting Government business as
well. Only a few months after the war began, Layard claimed
to have 'often heard it said, why does not the Government
allow some great firm to contract for carrying on the war?'
and urged that this would be good common sense.[1] When
Parliament reassembled for the first time after the Crimean
revelations had begun, no one can have been surprised that
one of the opening shots in the debate was that 'if there had
been sense enough in the Government to leave the whole to
the management of a private commercial concern, they would
have got over that last seven miles' — the disastrous distance
between the troops and their supplies at Balaklava.[2] For the
next few months ministers were repeatedly advised to learn
their lesson from private business. In March 1855 the third
Earl Grey advised the new Secretary of State for War, Panmure, to seek advice from successful civilian engineers, 'the
Stephensons and Brunels', and not from the Corps of
Engineers — a corps where promotion went according to
seniority.[3] At the same time in the Commons the Government's
running of its small arms factory at Enfield was repeatedly
criticized (most loudly by the Member for Birmingham, the
significance of which was not lost upon the House, although it
may have been upon some of the public). Government
methods of tendering were equally found wanting, and the
tendering for some new huts at Aldershot was made a prolonged case in point by Sir Joseph Paxton. To call in civilian
contractors became a stock prescription. It is true the great

[1] 3 *Hansard*, cxxxv, col. 652 (24 July 1854).
[2] Ibid. cxxxvi, col. 1004 (26 January 1855).
[3] Ibid. cxxxvii, col. 394 (12 March 1855).

business men in the House of Commons did not agree in the detail of their advice. For example, J. L. Ricardo, the founder and chairman of the Electric and International Telegraph Company, dismissed the gospel preached by Sir Joseph Paxton and Samuel Laing (both great railway magnates) of invariably accepting the lowest bid after opening a contract to public tender, as an out-of-date relic of the days when peculation was the chief evil to be guarded against. But they united to urge the Government in general terms to pay attention to the principles of private undertakings, to utilize the experiences of the business men whose vast undertakings had so deeply impressed contemporaries, and to benefit from their huge resources by employing them to feed, equip and transport the Army.[1] When severe criticism of mismanagement and waste in the transport service obliged the Admiralty to set up a Transport Board in February, it was careful to include among its members 'a gentleman of the mercantile community'.[2] The critics were unappeased, however, and by April even that highly experienced Whig minister Sir Charles Wood admitted to their ringleader, the shipping magnate W. S. Lindsay: 'That the system of all public offices is slow and cumbrous as compared with private Establishments is too true and moreover it cannot altogether be avoided. You cannot find any adequate substitutes for the stimulus of private and individual interest.'[3] In February 1855 Alexis Soyer left the Reform Club's kitchens on his own initiative to teach the Army how to manage their catering;[4] Florence Nightingale at Scutari showed the medical service how a military hospital should be run, and Sir Joseph Paxton sent the navvies who had re-erected his Crystal Palace at Sydenham to build huts and

---

[1] 3 *Hansard*, cxxxvi. cols. 1793–4, cxxxvii, cols. 125–31, 365, 447, 451, 1424 (5, 9, 12 and 30 March 1855).

[2] Ibid. cxxxvi, col. 1971 (27 February 1855).

[3] Wood to Lindsay, 13 April 1855, Add. MS. 49562, fo. 103.

[4] H. Morris, *Portrait of a Chef* (1938), pp. 129–82; Alexis Soyer, *A Culinary Campaign* (1857), *passim*.

I

roads under contract in the Crimea.[1] But the greatest triumph
for the doctrine that only civilian expertise could win the war
was surely the building of the Balaklava railway by Sir
Thomas Peto and his navvies. Even before the cry to call in
civilian contractors reached its height, the much-maligned
Duke of Newcastle had begun to consider Peto's proposal that
his firm (Brassey and Betts) should build a railway, at cost
price. In the excitement of February 1855 the contract was
signed, and 900 navvies departed under a civilian engineer to
the Crimea, where under the disgruntled eyes of Raglan and the
Commanding Officer of the Royal Engineers 'thirty-nine miles
of line were laid to every part of the front' from the port of
Balaklava.[2] The much-publicized result was 'the only thing
in the Crimea an Englishman can think of with entire patience
and complacency', and was enthusiastically hailed as further
evidence that from the business men of London 'it is allowable
to expect almost anything'.[3] Thus the building of the world's
first military railway furnishes tangible proof of the potency
in 1855 of middle-class confidence that it was to the methods
and men of private commercial undertakings that the nation
must turn in order to win the war.

Not until Sebastopol had been captured did the nemesis in
store for this exclusive identification of military and political
ability with commercial experience begin to make itself felt.
The waspish realism of the Duke of Bedford's remark that 'the
qualities required are not to be found in the middle class, or if
found, they will not leave their profitable trades for the lottery
of politics',[4] would have commanded little public assent until
the crisis of the war was over. Nevertheless, the arrogance of
this claim had always antagonized working men, intellectuals
and governing classes, all alike thereby doomed to inferiority.

---

[1] V. Markham, *Paxton and the Bachelor Duke* (1935), pp. 258–70.

[2] Sir A. Helps, *Life and Labours of Mr. Brassey* (1872), p. 216.

[3] The *Watchman*, 9 May 1855.

[4] The seventh Duke of Bedford to Lady Hetty Russell, n.d. (c.
March 1855), P.R.O. 30/22/12.

'Cosaques ignorans voulant s'opposer à l'exploitation du chemin de fer à Balaclava' (*Le Charivari*, March 25, 1855)

Experienced politicians had promptly pointed out that the amount of talent available was always limited, from whatever class it was drawn.[1] Disillusioned administrators added that any objective criterion of fitness was a chimera,[2] and that government offices could never properly be compared with private concerns, for their political chiefs were constantly

[1] For example, Lansdowne on 14 May 1855, 3 *Hansard*, cxxxviii, col. 551.

[2] 'People seem to suppose there is some standard for measuring capacity or fitness for office, so that you can at once ascertain whether you have got "the right man"', grumbled Sir Edmund Head scornfully from his post as Governor-General of Canada to his old friend Sir George Cornewall Lewis (7 July 1855, Harpton Court MSS., c. 1541).

changing, and thus routine must always be essential in a government department.[1] More militant debaters had attempted to turn the tables on the middle class by ascribing the Army's woeful condition to the excessive economies which had been forced upon government departments by middle-class opinion in the last years of peace. Others pointed out that to speak of 'the aristocracy' as exclusive, effete and inefficient was as absurd as to see the middle class as the embodiment of all the virtues. Nepotism, for example, argued Gladstone, was to be found in all classes of society; and a favourite Right-wing device was to expose the inefficiency of some of these 'volunteer middle-class statesmen' even in the conduct of their own businesses.[2] There was plenty of proof 'how dangerous it would be to entrust military administration to trading civilians', claimed the *Morning Post*, the mouth-piece of the governing class *par excellence*, on 26 June. Its evening counterpart, the *Globe*, pointed with gusto to the current outcry about adulterated foodstuffs as proof that 'mercantile merits' had been much exaggerated.[3] Disraeli's organ, *The Press*, pointed out with truth that one of the feelings behind this attack on the Establishment was sheer impatience of war taxation and the puerile delusion that without aristocratic incompetence 'new loans might have been necessary but not new taxes'.[4] Such arguments emboldened the *Post* — though no other journal was so forth-right — to repeat calmly that in reality the aristocracy 'do the work the best', and that the administrative reformers were nothing better than 'declamatory adventurers'.[5] Church-

---

[1] Sir Stafford Northcote, 15 June 1855, 3 *Hansard*, cxxxviii, col. 2080.

[2] Ibid., cols. 2099, 2180–3 (15 and 18 June 1855).

[3] *The Globe*, 8 May 1855.

[4] *The Press*, 28 July 1855. This point was indeed made twice by W. Tite, a Deputy Chairman of the Administrative Reform Association, in his adoption speech as parliamentary candidate for Bath (reported in the *Daily News*, 28 May 1855).

[5] *Morning Post*, 7 May and 26 June 1855.

men too (though conspicuously few nonconformists) had raised their voices to remind the nation that all alike had sinned.[1] The Christian Socialist leader, F. D. Maurice, claiming to speak from the touch-lines ('We working-class and professional men are only listeners in the trial going on between merchants, manufacturers and tradesmen and aristocracy,' he told his audience at the Working Men's College on 31 May 1855) urged both sides to reverence Man, and not a Class.[2] Anti-radical politicians frequently dismissed the whole movement as a pretext to attack every kind of rule and order. Indeed Sir James Graham, embittered and out of office, persuaded himself as late as November 1855 that the continued radical enthusiasm for the war was inspired by 'the hope of wresting from the Aristocracy and the Crown the remnant of their sway by means of the clamour for Administrative Reform, and by the insolence and Predominance of the Press'.[3]

The intelligentsia, too, of the Right and of the Left, had always been scornful of this bestowal of all vice upon one class and all virtue upon another. The positivist weekly, the *Leader*, pointed out how inert the middle class had been about entering the public service and how foolish it was to fail to realize that government was 'a craft of its own', not at all the same thing as private business, and finally, with characteristically ruthless logic, declared it 'mere childishness to revile the aristocracy for taking advantage of their eminence ... If it exists, it must be what it is — a class of privileged families, whose innate claims are superior to all others.'[4] John Stuart Mill, who in 1850 had been gloomily impressed by the 'low intellectual and moral state of all classes'.[5] thought the

---

[1] e.g. The *Record*, 2 April 1855.

[2] F. D. Maurice, *Administrative Reform and its connexion with Working Men's Colleges* (1855), p. 6.

[3] Graham to Gladstone, 19 November 1855, Add. MS. 44163, fo. 206.

[4] The *Leader*, 14 April, 5 May and 6 October 1855.

[5] Mill to E. Herford, January 1850, *Letters of John Stuart Mill*, ed. H. S. R. Elliot (1910), i. 153.

Administrative Reform Association 'entirely wrong in their
assumption that the middle classes of this country possess the
eminent qualities which are wanting in the higher.' 'I am
convinced', he told a disappointed correspondent firmly, 'that
any public matter whatever, under the management of the
middle class, would be as grossly, if not more grossly, mismanaged than public affairs are now.'[1] To Carlyle the whole
situation was 'a general Balaklava' and all the talk about
administrative reforms 'very idle and worthless'.[2]

But none of these numerous retorts really went home until
the passage of time brought reassuring naval and military
successes, an almost luxuriously supplied expeditionary force
in the Crimea — and the inevitable crop of war contractors'
scandals. By the end of 1855 circumstances had changed
sufficiently for distinctions again to be drawn: distinctions
between some government departments and the rest, between
the system and the individuals who ran it, between the
possible and the ideal. The Administrative Reform Association
was by December nothing more than 'a burst bladder'. The
vagueness of its programme, the tactical errors of its leaders,
their vulgarities and inconsistencies or worse, made the
Association as a mass movement one of the first victims of
returning good times — although it lingered on as one of a
plethora of respectable, highly articulate but chronically
impoverished and unimportant middle-class pressure groups.
Just before Christmas 1855 it was even possible for the newly
founded intellectual weekly, the *Saturday Review*, to argue at
length that in reality it was for their inefficiency that large-

[1] Mill to Wentworth Holworthy, 11 July 1855, ibid. i. 185. On the
other hand, neither did Mill hold any brief for 'the English higher classes'
(Mill to his wife, 9 February 1855, F. A. Hayek, *John Stuart Mill and
Harriet Taylor* (1951), p. 221).

[2] Carlyle to Sir A. Helps, 17 May 1855, and Diary of Sir C. Duffy,
28 July 1855, quoted in D. A. Wilson, op. cit., pp. 158, 165. Carlyle
had long thought tycoons like Hudson were mere 'gamblers and paltry
adventurers' (*Latter-Day Pamphlets* (1850), no. 7, *Hudson's Statue*,
p. 11).

scale business methods in England were outstanding, since they persisted in clinging to 'that simplicity of method and large discretion which succeed only in small affairs'. By March 1856 the same journal was able to point to the patched mortars and defective boots recently revealed to have been supplied by certain civilian firms as proof of the folly of regarding business techniques as a panacea for the ills of the state. 'Suspend your Judgment' must be the moral on the question of whether all Government work should be done by contract.[1] Already attacks had been made upon even that sacred monument to entrepreneurial ability, the Balaklava railway. 'Let it [*The Times*] now do honour to its favourite contractor [Peto] by sending a correspondent to the scene of his vicarious labours, to ascertain whether the railway was in reality better arranged than the hospitals', sneered an editorial in *The Engineer*, apparently with some justice.[2] Nor was it only circumstances which had changed; an unparalleled assertion of middle-class self-confidence had been followed by a relapse into middle-class snobbery, always the reverse of the coin. Charles Dickens was too bitter at the collapse of all his hopes from the movement he had done so much for in the spring of 1855 to be fair, but there was a grain of truth in his cry of despair in October 1855: 'We have no middle class, for although we are perpetually bragging of it as our safety, it is nothing but a poor fringe on the mantle of the upper.'[3]

Dickens had some reason to despair. In the field of political organization and recruitment, the middle-class apostles of business techniques and modernity so triumphant in the Crimean War, accomplished little of lasting importance. Here,

[1] *Saturday Review*, 1 December 1855 and 22 and 29 March 1856.
[2] *The Engineer*, 18 January 1856, quoted by Michael Robbins, 'The Balaklava Railway', *Journal of Transport History*, i (1953), 40. As early as 13 August 1855 the Queen was worried because the rails had been laid only on mud (the Queen to Palmerston, 13 August 1855, Broadlands Archives).
[3] Dickens to W. Macready, 4 October 1855, *The Letters of Charles Dickens* (1882), eds. G. Hogarth and M. Dickens, iii. 405.

the spoils fell rather to their antiquarian rivals who expounded that backward-looking aspect of mid-nineteenth-century English radicalism which drew its strength from the concept of 'the ancient constitution'. As a direct political force the phase of aggressive middle-class self-consciousness which reached its climax in the Crimean War was short-lived. Its importance lay not in any immediate effects upon the distribution of political power, but in its lasting effect upon social psychology. The image of an aristocracy of born leaders confronting a middle class of pettifogging money-grubbers had been effectively blurred by the brief but spectacular superimposition of a very different vision — a vision of well-born bunglers, out of date and helpless, who had been obliged in a crisis of the very kind which they should have been best fitted to handle, to turn for salvation to the middle class, the competent, experienced self-reliant 'men of the age'. In the long run the significance of this was profound.

For the working classes, however, the Crimean War furnished no such dramatic moment of truth. Militant working men needed no revelations in the Crimea to convince them that existing social institutions must be destroyed. Nor did they need the high food prices of the last months of the war to inspire them to attack primogeniture and the concentration of agricultural land in the great aristocratic estates. True, the Government's failure to make the war one for the 'oppressed nationalities' and the resulting spate of denunciations of secret diplomacy and treason in high quarters, furnished fresh arguments for manhood suffrage as the only means of altering the course of politics. But in the mid-nineteenth century it was not class antagonism between working class and aristocracy but between working class and middle class which was of practical importance, and here the war had no decisive effect. The activities of the Administrative Reform Association served only to convince the politically alert among the working classes that bankers — 'the only class who have not hitherto come into collision with labour' — were as bad as mill-owners.[1] In its opening stages that City-led movement was praised by the London Chartists for inviting Chartist support and offering them one seat on its committee; but moneyed men were denounced as no more trustworthy than manufacturers after the 'infamous chicanery and fraud' revealed at its first public meeting, when Ernest Jones the Chartist leader was kept off the platform and working men with tickets refused admittance on the grounds that the room was full, although gentlemen were still allowed in. Thereafter the *People's Paper* repeatedly called upon its readers to wreck the Association's meetings, and poured scorn upon the idea of merely changing the 'Aristocracy of Land for one of Money'.[2]

On the other hand, for a time Ernest Jones hoped much from co-operation with the State Reform Association. Founded on 11 July, chiefly under the auspices of Jonathan Duncan, the currency reformer, Herbert Ingram, self-made proprietor of the *Illustrated London News*, and Thomas Hodgskin, the veteran Godwinian anarchist, at least four out of the twelve members of its executive committee were Chartists. Its programme was based upon manhood suffrage, but its target was wide: sub-committees were formed on Financial Reform, Colonial Government, British India, Free Trade and secret diplomacy, as well as on parliamentary reform.[3] In its early weeks the State Reform Association seemed to Jones promising and highly significant, in that it represented for the first time middle-class support for universal manhood suffrage. To him it furnished proof that working-class tactics of withholding support from all middle-class reform movements were now bearing fruit and obliging the middle class to raise their bid for working-class support. Provided the Chartists kept up their own organization, Jones

[1] *People's Paper*, 5 May 1855.
[2] Ibid. 12 and 19 May, 2 June 1855.
[3] *Morning Advertiser*, 12 July 1855.

argued, there was nothing to be lost by testing the good faith of this new auxiliary.[1] To judge from the correspondence columns of the *People's Paper*, his followers were fairly evenly divided over the wisdom of such co-operation. One stalwart reminded Jones that in fact it was in 1842, at the Sturge Conference, that members of the middle class first as a group 'came out for our principles'. Bronterre O'Brien openly opposed the alliance at meetings of the Association, and George Reynolds, the editor of the other newspaper most read by politically active workers, consistently urged his readers to have nothing to do with a movement with such a 'miserable shortcoming programme', which ignored the ballot, annual parliaments and equal constituencies.[2] In the event the State Reform Association soon petered out in the changed atmosphere after the victories on the Tchernaya and at Sebastopol, and by November 1855 the campaign to control the price of bread through the establishment of public granaries had entirely taken its place in the attention of working-class politicians. Even Jones was temporarily disillusioned. 'We have found middle-class reformers powerless', he wrote in his editorial survey of the year on 29 December 1855.[3]

This junction with the State Reform Association had, however, brought to a close that period of relentless hostility between the Chartists and middle-class reformers which began in 1842 with the failure of the Sturge Conference. With it, Jones had made his first attempt to extend his activity beyond his own supporters while at the same time trying to keep his grip on them by means of a specifically Chartist organization.[4] He had publicly defended this strategy. Thus the inspiration and occasion for the first of those Chartist experiments with reformism which Jones was to carry much further and which

[1] *People's Paper*, 4 August and 1 September 1855.
[2] *Reynolds News*, 29 July and 23 September 1855.
[3] *People's Paper*.
[4] Cf. 'Fr. de J.', 'Ernest Jones and Chartism circa 1856', *Bulletin of the Institute of Social History*, v (1950), 100.

Marx so deplored,[1] were in fact provided by the widely diffused war-time attack on established institutions in 1855. But this first experiment in reformism was not a fruitful or a lasting one. It cannot be argued that it was any more than a formal precedent for the important junction of middle- and working-class reformers which was to take place in the sixties, still less that it represents any real landmark in the growth of reformism in the British labour movement. It was sympathy with foreign nationalities which furnished the strongest bridge between middle and working classes in the fifties rather than more moderate views about the class struggle. The Crimean War was undeniably not the crusade both thought it should have been. Yet although one perceptive young radical intellectual predicted that the 'New Holy Alliance' of 1854 between Louis Napoleon, the Hapsburgs and the aristocracy of Britain might prove the undoing of the British governing classes by giving their opponents 'sufficient vitality to over-power the enormous weight, which so many respectable qualities, antiquity, and thorough skill and experience give to our upper classes', his prophecy was premature.[2] Even among those who shared a deep impatience with official policy abroad, there were significant disagreements: some blamed treason and Russian gold, some upper-class solidarity, some blind fear, and some a reasoned plan to use foreign issues to distract the workers from their grievances. Not even shared sympathies in foreign affairs could fuse lower and middle classes into a powerful political counterforce during the Crimean War.

Yet that fusion had been dimly and abortively foreshadowed. Above all, the hitching of the middle class to the aristocratic

[1] e.g. Marx to Engels, 24 November 1857, *Marx–Engels Correspondence, 1846–95* (Calcutta, 1945), p. 89. It should be noted that Jones was a fervent supporter of the war, as is shown by his war verse, published under the title of *The Emperor's Vigil and The Waves and The War* (1856).

[2] Frederick Harrison to E. S. Beesly (n.d.), London School of Economics, Harrison Papers, box 1.

constitution accomplished in 1832 had been loosened. 'Never have the wealthy and educated portions of the middle class spoken as they now speak,' exclaimed the *Atlas* on 7 April 1855, and the writer went on to foretell with confidence the union of the working and middle classes against the aristocracy. The middle class had learnt their lesson from the war — and, he might have added, acquired the self-confidence to apply it — if the working class had not; 'the merchant and manufacturer have found out that in employing an oligarchy to save them from a proletariat, they have acted as if a farmer had turned a wolf into his sheepfold to frighten the flies'. The Crimean outburst against the aristocracy was thus a turning-point in the restoration of the ancient cry of 'aristocracy versus the people', a restoration which was to allow the call for a death struggle between proletariat and *bourgeoisie* to die away after 1860. To this extent, the experiences of the Crimean War did indeed pave the way for the junction of middle- and working-class radicals, and thus for the class cooperation which distinguished the next generation in politics, industrial relations and social activities alike.

CHAPTER FOUR

The War and Radical Ideals of the Ancient Constitution

FEW mid-nineteenth-century habits of thought and speech are more striking than the taste exhibited at almost every level of society for arguments from history. 'Once theories of socialism had been grasped, men shook themselves free of the past,' it has been claimed,[1] but the process was an extremely slow and limited one, and in the 1850s 'the clutch of history on English political thought'[2] was still very powerful. Too much attention has been paid to *laissez-faire* economics and utilitarian philosophy as sources of mid-nineteenth-century ideas about the proper function of the state, and too little to concepts of English history. It is dangerously easy for the twentieth-century man, who finds it neither natural nor necessary to appeal continually to historical precedents, to dismiss mid-nineteenth-century arguments from the ancient constitution as mere verbal flourishes. But in fact these historical arguments, expressed in more or less sophisticated forms, impressed a socially very diverse audience in much the same way as the economic theories of the day, expressed with different degrees of refinement, made their impact throughout widely different levels of society. Notions of the ancient constitution were a political force in the mid-nineteenth century whose full importance can only be appreciated when the respect accorded to historical arguments

[1] Christopher Hill, 'The Norman Yoke', in *Democracy and the Labour Movement*, ed. J. Saville (1954), p. 65.
[2] J. G. A. Pocock, *The Ancient Constitution and the Feudal Law* (Cambridge, 1957), p. 127.

and allusions of every kind is remembered. The men who prided themselves on their complete emancipation from the past and refused to look for 'the lessons of history' were at that time very much in a minority. In particular, a vision of the vigorous functioning of municipal and parochial communities as always an essential part of the ancient constitution, of local self-government as the historic core of English liberties, fostered and inspired that impatience with interference by the central government and its bureaucracy which reached its height in the fifties and sixties. Too often this impatience has been described in terms of *laissez-faire* theories of the economic functions of the state, whether these theories are seen as based upon an economic argument about ways and means of maximizing wealth, or upon belief in natural law or even the direct providence of God, and thus in the folly of all human interference. It is clear, however, that its intellectual source, or rather its rationalization (for strong private interests were of course also at work), was at least as often drawn from the interpretation of the course of English history current at that time.

The first half of the nineteenth century saw a great revival of interest in Anglo-Saxon studies in England. Among scholars this was stimulated by the rehabilitation of Norse studies by Thorkelin and Grundtvig, and the work of the two Grimms in Germanic philology. Among the wider public the success of Sharon Turner's *History of the Anglo-Saxons* (1799–1805) and the stimulus given to national pride by the Napoleonic Wars contributed something, but far more important than either was that romantic enthusiasm for the past which owed so much to Sir Walter Scott. When combined with the early nineteenth-century enthusiasm for book-collecting, this movement of opinion produced between 1834 and 1848 a spate of societies and inexpensive printing clubs for the publication of early historical and literary remains and the encouragement of antiquarian research — the Camden Society, English History Society, Ælfric Society, Parker Society, Philological

Society and very many more.[1] The learned societies also, led by the Society of Antiquaries, supported the revival of Early English scholarship by their publications, some of which are not yet superseded. At the same time appreciation of the historical as distinct from the legal value of the public records grew and a *Monumenta Historica Britannica* was planned.[2] Less learned echoes followed from commercial publishers. By the 1850s faith in the Anglo-Saxon folk-moot as the origin of English political liberty — a view which dates back at least to the early seventeenth century — was more widely diffused and more impressively documented than ever before. The sceptical conclusion reached by John Millar in his *Historical View of the English Government* (1787) that the Anglo-Saxon system of government was not calculated 'in any peculiar manner to secure the liberty and the natural rights of mankind' was further than ever from winning acceptance. In 1854, for example, J. A. Langford's successful little book published 'for those of little leisure and less means', *English Democracy: Its Historical Principles*, used Sharon Turner, John Wade and J. M. Kemble himself (whose best-selling *The Saxons in England* was published in 1849) to drive home the lessons of Alfred's 'noble institutions'. The greatest of these lessons, the constitutional principle peculiar to 'Old England', was almost invariably taken to be, in Sir Francis Palgrave's words, 'the perfection of *our municipal communities*'.[3] As a result the popularizers of serious historical

---

[1] H. R. Steeves, *Learned Societies and English Literary Scholarship in Great Britain and the United States* (New York, 1913), pp. 117–20; prospectuses of these societies in the Library of the British Museum.

[2] T. P. Peardon, *The Transition in English Historical Writing, 1760–1830* (New York, 1933), pp. 299, 310. The national records were first placed in the care of the Master of the Rolls in 1837.

[3] Sir Francis Palgrave, *Conciliatory Reform* (1831), p. 5. Palgrave, knighted in 1832 for his work for the Record Commission, was probably the most successful of the men who simultaneously both popularized and promoted the serious study of medieval history in England in the generation before the Crimean War. His *Observations on the Principles to be adopted in the Establishment of new Municipal Corporations* (1832)

studies were able to connect with the ancient constitution precisely those moral values which increasingly appealed to the mid-Victorian generation. The importance both to society and the individual of activity and responsibility in personal and public affairs amounted to a mid-Victorian gospel. Its practice, it could plausibly be argued, was hampered by existing political institutions but had been fostered by the ancient constitution. The mythical free Anglo-Saxons who had gathered in their folk-moots and shire-moots were used to promulgate, and in turn appealed to, the same concept of individual self-improvement and activity in the community as can be found in such dissimilar but extremely influential works of the period as John Stuart Mill's *Essay on Liberty*, Samuel Smiles's *Self-Help*, and Thomas Carlyle's *Heroes and Hero-Worship*.

The extent to which the well-worn radical myth of the free Anglo-Saxons whose perfect institutions had been debased by succeeding generations had been given new life by the 1850s is abundantly demonstrated by the fact that in one radical quarter after another, indignation at the Crimean disasters and disappointment with the official policy of a limited war provoked a series of appeals to the ancient constitution as the source of national salvation. If one cure urged for the country's evils was the application of business experience and modern techniques to the problems of government and war, another was the restoration of the sound and healthy practices which were believed to have flourished before 1688, or 1660, or most of all, before 1066. Some men indeed urged both cures at once, without any sense of inconsistency; and the second can no more be dismissed as pure rhetoric than the first. Thus when the events of the Crimean War discredited the existing order of things, the ideal of political freedom and public well-being springing from active participation in government by

had some influence on the adoption of a resident ratepayers' franchise in the Municipal Corporations Act of 1835.

enlightened and virtuous citizens came together with the belief that its practice had been exemplified in earlier periods of English history to form a very effective radical ideology.

To contemporaries, the appeal to the ancient constitution suggested three different though connected answers to the question which the Crimean disasters made it seem so urgent to determine, the question of what was wrong with the political institutions of the day. Each became the dominant theme of a distinct radical group. To some, the root of the evil was seen as the encroachment of the central government with its attendant bureaucracy upon local self-government; and to them the remedy was to foster the public spirit of private citizens and extend the powers of municipal institutions, in short, to restore the folk-moots of the Anglo-Saxons. Others singled out the irresponsibility of ministers, their power to shelter behind collective Cabinet responsibility, collective responsibility moreover to a servile Parliament, and not to the Courts or the Crown, and urged accordingly the restoration of the supremacy of the Privy Council and the liability of ministers to impeachment, as in the days of the Stuarts. Finally, yet others believed the real fault to lie with Members of Parliament for their susceptibility to influence, their greed for favours or their enslavement by the ties of party, and if Members were thus to blame, the electors who chose them could not be exonerated. In this case, it was to the growth of corruption, the exploitation of patronage and the rise of party — again dated from the later seventeenth century — that the analysts pointed. All agreed that the ancient constitution had been deformed, almost abandoned, and that the country was reaping its reward in the untoward events of 1854–5. Local self-government had withered away, real ministerial responsibility had disappeared, and the honest independence of Members of Parliament and electors had been lost. It is the vicissitudes of these three diagnoses of the malady from which the Crimean War seemed to show the country was suffering, each based upon its own set of historical

K

arguments and with its own group of supporters, which will now be considered.

When the war began, the movement for the revitalization of local self-government, with all its undertones of vested interests and petty economy, was already well under way. As it happened, however, the chief organized expression of this movement, Joshua Toulmin Smith's Anti-Centralization Union, coincided very closely with the war (it was founded in January 1854, probably as part of the campaign against Edwin Chadwick's Board of Health,[1] and disbanded in 1857), and its course furnished his supporters with some devastatingly effective arguments.

At the very outset of the war, those who opposed 'improper government interference with private affairs' simply on grounds of vulgarized political economy, had consoled themselves with the thought that heavy war expenditure was at least likely to impose a check upon expensive meddling. One of the uncovenanted blessings of the war might thus be that 'population, wealth and knowledge would be left to develop themselves according to the natural laws of their existence', as that staunch *laissez-faire* organ, *The Economist*, put it.[2] The redoubtable Harriet Martineau was even more optimistic. She felt sure that a war with Napoleonic France against Tsarist Russia would 'lay open to us the spectacle of what those countries and people are like, in which centralization prevails',[3] and thus deter England from accepting the same fate. There was much talk of believers in government action being fit only to be subjects of the Tsar. In the event the anti-centralizers found themselves presented with a salutary spectacle of the disastrous consequences of centralization on their own doorstep. 'The government mismanaged every-

[1] This campaign is discussed in S. E. Finer, *The Life and Times of Sir Edwin Chadwick* (1952), p. 466.
[2] *The Economist*, 2 December 1854.
[3] *Daily News*, 18 November 1854.

thing that fell into their hands; he was therefore in favour of leaving the citizens to manage their own affairs,' declared one supporter of Toulmin Smith at a heated ward-meeting of Farringdon Without on 18 January 1855, thus drawing the obvious moral at a time when Balaklava and Scutari were on everyone's lips.[1] The day before, the Anti-Centralization Union at its Annual General Meeting had found Toulmin Smith's pamphlet, *A Letter to the Right Honourable Lord Viscount Palmerston, M.P. on the Home Policy which the present war-time needs*, so apt that it had resolved to send a copy to each Member of Parliament.

To exploit the Crimean situation Toulmin Smith and his supporters did not need to alter the arguments they had been urging for the last six or seven years. The war simply presented them with a series of circumstances which could be used to drive those arguments home. In the earlier, optimistic stages of the war, it was the premium placed by war upon a high moral and intellectual calibre in the country's citizens, and the claim that the war had been undertaken to defend the nation's institutions and welfare, which served their purpose. For they could accordingly argue that the continuing justification and success of the war could only be achieved by promoting that 'temper and public spirit' which alone would ensure that 'the value of the stake in question is well understood and practically appreciated by every man'; and that this in its turn was dependent upon the preservation and restoration of England's ancient institutions. In his *Home Policy which the present war-time needs*, Toulmin Smith accordingly outlined yet again the constitutional principles deduced and illustrated from the national records which he had been expounding since 1847 in pamphlets and treatises packed with argument from the law reports, the rolls of Parliament, the close rolls, Wilkins's *Anglo-Saxon Laws*, Palgrave, Kemble and many more. It was these principles which he now claimed the challenge of war had made it doubly

[1] Report in *Daily News*, 19 January 1855.

necessary the nation should apply. Only a return to local responsibility and 'mutuality', instead of the 'modern system of perpetual experimental and shifting legislation', would secure efficiency and patriotic morale.[1]

As the revelations of the Crimean disasters mounted to a crescendo, Toulmin Smith and the Anti-Centralization Union found themselves presented with an even stronger line of argument. They now claimed to have 'long since foreseen and foretold with precision, that the circumstances now existing, and which have now roused general indignation, must inevitably come, as the consequence of the violation of those principles upon which the Union takes its stand'. Nothing else was to be expected, once public neglect had allowed 'our Institutions [to be] tampered with and over-ridden . . . by a novel system entirely alien to our Constitution'.[2] To the Anti-Centralization Union, Balaklava and all it stood for was thus a blessing in disguise, since by demonstrating beyond dispute the inefficiency of bureaucracy it silenced talk of the advantages of state action, advantages in reality 'already exploded by England's 1400 years of History'. As a reviewer of Toulmin Smith's influential book, The Parish, noted in July 1855, 'functionarism' had been carrying everything before it until, a few years before, the tide turned; and 'now, the mismanagement of the war in the Crimea has suddenly roused a most serious storm against bureaucracy and redtapism. We may predict that the future will probably be characterized by greater reverence for local self-government and by measures directed against centralization long after the disasters at Balaklava have ceased to be felt.' Looking back a year after the end of the war, Toulmin Smith felt that it had

[1] *The Home Policy which the present war-time needs* (1855), pp. 4, 19. A good statement of the principles which Toulmin Smith was here applying is to be found in his *Local Self-Government and Centralization* (1851), p. 33.

[2] See the long extract from the Union's pamphlet of May 1855 against the Administrative Reform Association, reprinted in its later pamphlet, *Government and its Measures in 1857* (1857), p. 4.

indeed shown even the doubters and the blind that bureaucracy was merely a device for multiplying the loaves and
fishes, for 'taking care of the Dowbs at the public expense'.[1]

It naturally followed that with these views the Anti-
Centralization Union stood aloof from the cry for 'the right
man in the right place' which was raised by the Administrative Reform Association (an organization in which its arch-
enemy, Edwin Chadwick, was active behind the scenes[2]).
When that Association was founded in May 1855, the Union
denounced it as 'calculated to hinder rather than help what
the times most need', since it diverted attention from the real
evil, namely, the perversion and decay of the country's institutions. 'You must restore a sounder and more constitutional
action,' one of their pamphlets told the Association, 'before
any change of men will produce its fruit.' The Union therefore
concentrated all their efforts during the crisis upon wrecking
whatever legislation appeared to them to have been introduced by bureaucracy 'at the expense of constitutional
principles and the pockets and moral tone of the people'[3]
(surely the mid-Victorian Trinity). These efforts met with
great success, as Toulmin Smith was quick to claim. 'The
practical declaration by Parliament of the Principle and
Practice of Local Self Government which I succeeded in ob-
taining in 1855,' he boasted two years later, 'is beyond a
question the most important step that has been made in
Legislation and Institutional action for some two and a half
centuries in England.'[4] The measure for which he made this
impressive claim was the Nuisances Removal Act (18 and 19
Victoria C. 91), a measure which constituted the parish vestry
and not the local Boards of Guardians the basic nuisance

[1] *Eclectic Review*, N.S., x (1855), 92; J. Toulmin Smith, *Local Self-
Government Un-Mystified* (1857), pp. 32, 62.

[2] This is clear from Copy Book xx, Chadwick MSS., University College,
London, and especially Chadwick to J. Ingram Travers (Treasurer of
the Association), 28 June 1855.

[3] *Government and its Measures*, pp. 3, 5.

[4] *Local Self-Government Un-mystified*, p. 21.

authority — 'with fatal consequences to effectiveness,' in the opinion of one recent historian of public health at least.[1] Moreover the Union could draw up an impressive list of other successes: the defeat of the Police Bill of 1854, the end of Chadwick's irresponsible General Board of Health, and the establishment of the Metropolitan Board of Works, that 'definitive triumph of the vestry movement',[2] accomplished in July 1855. Thus before the crowning victory of the Local Government Act of 1858, a notable succession of victories against central government had already been won, and a growing band of converts established — converts who included among their number John Simon himself. Nor did these gains won in the war prove a mere flash in the pan. Until the end of the 1860s, local self-government and the minimization of central interference remained sacrosanct in England, in words, if not altogether in deeds.[3] No doubt these triumphs in the field of institutions would have been of greater practical benefit to the community if they had more often been applied by that 'right man in the right place' whose importance Toulmin Smith had belittled in 1855. But the fact remains that for nearly a generation after the beginning of the Crimean War, local self-government retained the stature of public orthodoxy. It had attained this stature by diverse means, some of them sinister enough (in Bentham's sense of that word), but not until the Crimean War so opportunely provided it with a favourable climate of opinion throughout the country did it grow to maturity. The lawyers, business men and engineers who for reasons of their own detested the interference of Government bodies, were furnished by the Crimean campaign with a gratuitous demonstration of administrative shortcomings far more damning and

[1] R. Lambert, *Sir John Simon, 1816–1904* (1963), p. 226.

[2] Finer, op. cit., p. 484.

[3] Cf. R. M. Gutchen, 'Local improvements and centralization in nineteenth-century England', *Historical Journal*, iv (1961), and R. Lambert, 'Central and Local relations in mid-Victorian England: the Local Government Act Office, 1858–71', *Victorian Studies*, vi. 2 (1962).

far more widely publicized than any provided by all the administrative scandals which had been unearthed in the years of peace. So undeniably black a present as that of 1855 lent the golden past an even brighter glow and made the myths of the ancient constitution irresistible. No doubt these historical arguments were very often merely fashionable rationalizations concealing murky motives; but to that historically minded generation this particular rationalization was a very acceptable one. The discredit of the existing machinery of government in the winter of 1854–5 thus played its part in the triumph of idyllic views of municipal and parochial self-sufficiency, and of judicial rather than executive procedures as mechanisms for remedying abuses. It was no coincidence that both the hey-day of the cult of the Anglo-Saxons and the golden age of the small ratepayers who aspired to be their successors, were ushered in by the Crimean revelations.

Although Toulmin Smith and the opponents of centralization very successfully exploited military disasters as supporting evidence for their own gospel, their movement owed neither its origins nor all of its success to the war. The 'National Movement' associated with David Urquhart, on the other hand, which called above all for a return to the personal responsibility of ministers to the Crown and the people, was virtually a product of the war and ebbed and flowed with the course of events. Moreover although its programme and arguments overlapped to a certain extent with those of the Anti-Centralization Union, its main objects, its tone, and the kind of person it attracted were all entirely different.

Urquhart is now remembered for his Russophobia. He has been described as 'wild and unbalanced', an exponent of 'esoteric, conspiratorial radicalism', full of 'apparently preposterous notions'.[1] Yet his views on English institutions

[1] J. H. Gleason, *The Genesis of Russophobia in Great Britain* (Cambridge, Mass., 1950), p. 153 and *passim*; Briggs, op. cit., p. 430.

were an essential part of his message, and these, although expressed with characteristic paradox and exaggeration, were in close accord with the very influential stream of mid-nineteenth-century opinion now being discussed, and drawn from the current view of English history. When it is realized that his constitutional and political, if not his diplomatic, doctrines were couched in terms which very many men then found familiar, his success becomes more intelligible than it has usually seemed. Urquhart's words and manners were undoubtedly provocative and strange, but the underlying foundations of his ideas were in the 1850s almost a series of commonplaces.

Like Toulmin Smith and so many other of his contemporaries, Urquhart drew his political arguments from English history and illustrated them freely from the national records, although he obviously lacked Toulmin Smith's scholarship and leant heavily upon the works of a few historians and legal writers of his own day, notably Palgrave and T. C. Anstey.[1] Like them, he glorified local institutions as far older than Parliament and therefore the proper agent for local business, denounced statute law, and praised the use of judicial procedures in administration. But although his gospel of salvation through the active conduct of local business by the ancient folk-moots of the Anglo-Saxons was a commonplace one, Urquhart also supported his views from one much more original source: the customs of the East. These he believed to be identical with the methods of government which had been common in medieval Europe. 'There may be points of real, as well as traces of apparent, resemblance between a divan of a

---

[1] Author of *A Guide to the History of the Laws and Constitution of England* (1845), Professor of Law and Jurisprudence at the Roman Catholic College of Prior Park, near Bath, and for a time a follower of Urquhart. Urquhart also drew upon the works of Toulmin Smith himself. For example, in his copy of *Local Self-Government Un-mystified* he underlined the passage 'History shows "the villeins" doing their business' and turned down the corner of that page (Balliol College, Oxford, Urquhart MSS. III. 126).

Moorish Sultan, and the Wittenagemotte of a Saxon King,'
he wrote; 'the Sultan publicly alleges his charges against the
governors who are removed, and the people on their part
have free access and can accuse and petition.'[1] Thus to
an orientalist like Urquhart, to restore such practices to
English political life seemed all the more a practical possi-
bility.

To the familiar doctrines of local self-government he added
other deductions from more recent English constitutional
history peculiarly his own. For Urquhart, it was the rise of the
Cabinet and the corresponding loss of executive power by the
Crown and the Privy Council under the later Stuarts which
had made the most serious breach in the ancient constitution.
Where Toulmin Smith saw the problem as one of depriving the
executive of all but its advisory functions, Urquhart wished
instead to enforce upon ministers genuine responsibility for
their actions.[2] It was the ancient rights of petitioning the
Crown and of impeachment[3] which he called upon his followers
to prepare themselves to resume. Responsibility was the
watchword of his movement, its keynote 'revolution or impeachment', and memorials and above all deputations its
favourite devices. Parliament should regard itself as merely a
trustee for the freemen of England, for 'the good old constitution of England did not send men back to make laws,
but sent men to Parliament instructed exactly what to do'.[4]
The only genuine form of universal suffrage was therefore for
every man to have a voice upon matters in a shire-moot
before they were legislated upon. Urquhart's goal was not an

[1] *The Pillars of Hercules* (1850), i. 290. Urquhart maintained that
the secret of the survival of the Turkish Empire was its respect for
local municipal institutions (*Turkey and its Resources* (1833), pp. vii,
14).

[2] Cf. the article contrasting the two in the *Sheffield Free Press*, 30
June 1855.

[3] Palmerston was, of course, the victim most often suggested, but
Graham was quite a close second. Detailed articles of impeachment
were frequently drawn up.

[4] The *Free Press*, 17 November 1855.

extended franchise, but a return to the Act of Settlement. The Cabinet should be required to sign its advice, as its predecessor, the Privy Council, had been required to do in 1701. At the beginning of every session, a minute of all Cabinet Councils held in the previous year, with the matter proposed and the names of those assenting and dissenting, should be published. Legislature and executive should be separated and ministers released from the need to sit in Parliament; they should instead explain their conduct to specialized standing Parliamentary Committees of enquiry.[1] All of this makes it clear why Urquhart once called himself a Tory of Queen Anne's reign; his heroes were the squires who made a last stand against cabinet government at the turn of the seventeenth century. The dragon he sought to slay was not Toulmin Smith's anonymous, all-powerful bureaucracy, but a much older one — 'the practical despotism of a cabal'. His weapons were to be a strengthened monarchy, the restoration of responsible conciliar government, the revival of impeachment, and, most important of all, the substitution of the informed judgment of individuals for the reign of public opinion. Early in 1855 he was encouraged by his successes to publish a lengthy work entitled *Familiar Words, as affecting the conduct of England in 1855*, which incorporated an earlier work on the pitfalls of language. In the autumn of 1855, when there was widespread concern about the role of the Press, some of this work was reprinted with the catchpenny title of *Public Opinion and its Organs*. Public opinion, Urquhart always believed, was an affair of fraud and guesswork, expressed by the anonymous, all-pervasive Press; all that

---

[1] *Constitutional Remedies, showing how the law is designed to control the acts of the Government* (1855), *passim*. This pamphlet, the fullest exposition of his views on the remedies for the political evils exposed by the war, was the result of a resolution passed on 15 March 1855 by the Newcastle Committee of his supporters that his address to them on 30 November 1854 showing 'the remedial resources which the legitimate institutions of this realm supply, be printed and published to guide the people in their present search for means of safety'.

was either worth while or constitutionally proper was the judgment of individuals, based upon real knowledge of facts.

This zeal for the ancient constitution provided Urquhart with many links with other radicals. So too did his intense hostility to Russia, which in 1854 brought him close to the Chartists and the revolutionary refugees, above all to Marx.[1] Yet the Urquhartites remained a very distinctive and unassimilable group, and this is not surprising. For although, for example, denunciations of secret diplomacy were a common radical cry, Urquhart went further and denounced not only Palmerston but Kossuth and Mazzini themselves as Russian agents. Again, to extol the virtues of local self-government was commonplace, but explicitly to dismiss the extension of the suffrage as pointless was not; similarly, to condemn the Cabinet was radical routine, but to call for a strong Monarch and an active Privy Council was extraordinary. It is indeed easy to believe that the aged Bentham had found the young Urquhart congenial.[2] 'Hunting half-truths to their consequences' was Urquhart's way as much as Bentham's, with the result that the meat he offered was too strong to appeal to any but specialized tastes in very favourable surroundings.

These favourable circumstances were provided in abundant measure by the Crimean War. Between 1839 and 1840

---

[1] Marx and Urquhart first met in February 1854. Marx's *Cahiers d'étude* show him to have been impressed by Urquhart's views of the immense effects of language and to have read much of the *Portfolio* and of Urquhart's other works throughout 1853, when he was working on the Eastern Question. It is thus not surprising that he came to share Urquhart's conclusions about Palmerston's treachery. Indeed he went further, for throughout 1856 he devoted much learning to an effort to show that English complicity in the rise of Russia dated from the beginning of the eighteenth century (Maximilien Rubel, 'Les cahiers d'étude de Karl Marx, ii, 1853–56', *International Review of Social History*, v. (1960), 76). He was a fairly frequent contributor to the Urquhartite *Free Press* until 1859.

[2] Gertrude Robinson, *David Urquhart* (Oxford, 1920), p. 27.

Urquhart had succeeded in persuading some of the Chartists that 'it was to the disloyalty of English governments to her ancient constitution and to the principles of justice, both in international and national affairs, that the present distress of the operatives was due', and in forming some Committees of Working Men to study Foreign Affairs, especially in the North.[1] This success was short-lived, however, and it was not until the outbreak of the Crimean War that he again made any headway. For of all the many radicals who could claim that the course of the war proved them right, Urquhart was able to make that claim by far the most often and in much the most detailed and striking ways. As one of his supporters said enthusiastically: 'Spoken yesterday in calm tones, but unheeded, his message now comes back, every letter illuminated by the red glare of war.'[2] His best-selling book, *The Progress of Russia in the West*, published at a fortunate moment in 1853, was in its fifth edition a few months later. The predictions made at the end of 1853 and beginning of 1854 in his letters to the Press (he constantly contributed thus to the *Morning Advertiser* and the *Morning Herald*) seemed by 1855 to have been so strikingly fulfilled that many were reprinted, either singly as a series of penny flysheets or in groups as shilling pamphlets.[3] To Urquhart, Balaklava and Scutari, which proved such heady stuff for other radicals, were small beer. It was rather the apparent half-heartedness of the Cabinet, the diplomatic alliance with Austria, the delay in despatching an expedition to the Crimea, the ineffectiveness of the Baltic expedition, above all the concessions to neutral shipping and over trade with the enemy which gave him a series of damning proofs to support his charge that Palmerston was a Russian agent and the war nothing but a sham. Even the peace itself, obviously premature and easy in its terms, and above all the Declaration of Paris which ac-

[1] Robinson, op. cit., p. 90; Gleason, op. cit., pp. 260–6.
[2] *Free Press*, 15 December 1855.
[3] They are to be found in Urquhart MSS. VIII. 2.

companied it, seemed to offer a conclusive fulfilment of his predictions of what would be the outcome of a sham war conducted by a Prime Minister bought by Russian gold. No wonder Disraeli murmured 'The Prophet!' when Urquhart's name was mentioned,[1] and no wonder many simpler souls in that eschatologically-minded age were prepared to see Urquhart in that light in sober truth.[2]

At the beginning of the war the Association for the Protection of Turkey and other Countries from Partition had massive radical support, and throughout 1854 the Government's unforthcoming attitude to the oppressed nationalities secured widespread radical agreement that the war was indeed a war of shams.[3] It was not until public attention shifted to the question of what was wrong with the country's domestic institutions that Urquhart found himself increasingly a solitary prophet, as well as a very convincing one. In February 1855 the *Morning Advertiser*, though still publishing letters from Urquhart in nearly every issue, supported Palmerston when he became Prime Minister. The National and Constitutional Association, too, which the *Morning Advertiser* promoted in March, inconsistently combined parliamentary reform with its Urquhartism. The Administrative Reform Association formed a month later was still more remote from his views, for although it shared the faith in the power of mere information, the moralizing, and the allusions to the ancient constitution then common among radicals of nearly every hue, including the Urquhartites, it was too much a movement of successful men of the world to adopt root and branch solutions. By this time too the Chartists were in active opposition to him over manhood suffrage, and G. J. Holyoake, the Secularist leader, who had felt at the beginning of the war

[1] Stewart Rolland to Urquhart, 12 July 1854, ibid. I, E 3.
[2] Urquhart's prophecies and their fulfilment continued to furnish matter for pamphlets for some time after the end of the war (e.g. *The Story of the War* (1857), *The Queen and the Premier* (2nd edn., 1857)).
[3] On 9 December 1854 even the Chartist *People's Paper* urged that the Cabinet should be impeached as traitors.

that there was 'at least as much truth in Mr. Urquhart's doctrines as in the opposite side',[1] was beginning to be dismayed by the unpractical conclusions to which Urquhart's advice to working men to use their brains fearlessly was leading them.[2] Enlightened radicals like Holyoake were repelled not simply by Urquhart's views on the suffrage, nor even by his attacks on heroes like Kossuth, Mazzini and J. A. Roebuck. They were repelled by his megalomania and lack of judgment. His movement, announced the positivist *Leader* on 17 November 1855, was 'utterly unworthy of attention', mere 'mummy-worship'. The working class, depressed by failure to secure the vote, were now being persuaded that 'to be a superficial antiquary is to be a politician'.[3] *The Leader* was being less than fair; 'mummy-worship' was after all rife on every side.[4] But Urquhart's variety of mummy-worship was more like a revivalist sect than a political movement. It was these distinctively charismatic, quasi-religious qualities which really repelled rational outsiders. They also ensured that his small band of followers were to an exceptional extent socially homogeneous, geographically concentrated and fanatically zealous. Urquhart's doctrines were a specialized taste; but once acquired they became an addiction.

The National Movement was virtually confined to the west Midlands (apart from a flourishing following in Newcastle upon Tyne) that is, to the area extending from Leeds in the north to Bath in the west, with a particularly large concentration in Sheffield and Birmingham. This was no accident. The west Midlands in the 1850s (and indeed until much later)

---

[1] *The Reasoner*, 30 April 1854.

[2] Ibid. 18 November 1855. His 'An Afternoon with Mr. Urquhart' (press cutting dated 20 April 1857 in the Holyoake Collection at the Bishopsgate Institute) shows that by this date he had decided Urquhart's influence was wholly obscurantist. A number of his own followers had by this time transferred their allegiance to Urquhart.

[3] *The Leader*, 15 December 1855.

[4] The only radical newspaper which never employed historical arguments, apart from *The Leader* itself, was *Reynolds News*.

were still the stronghold of semi-domestic, semi-craft industries, particularly of numerous small metal industries
which remained complexes of specialized workshop and out-
work production. It was among these craftsmen and small
independent masters, men who had found little in Chartism
and had scarcely been touched by trade unionism, that
Urquhart's lurid backward-looking gospel with its call, not
for class solidarity and manhood suffrage, but for individual
enquiry and ministerial responsibility to Crown and people,
won its devoted disciples. Significantly, the same area had
also produced some of the strongest supporters of anti-
centralization. In following Urquhart it only plunged further
along the same road.[1]

The twelve months after September 1854 were probably the
most active and successful of Urquhart's long life, at least
after the *Vixen* affair of 1837. Early in that month he married
one of his ablest followers, Harriet Fortescue, sister of the
Whig politician Chichester Fortescue. In September 1855 their
first child was born and they began to settle into domesticity.
But in the year between, they lived for much of the time near
Birmingham, touring the Midlands, promoting memorials to
the Crown, organizing Working Men's Committees in the
towns and villages they visited, and keeping up a spate of
letters to the Press as well as other writing. For them the
course of political events in those twelve months could hardly
have been more favourable. In the autumn of 1854 the
Coalition Government's inactivity inspired petitions and
memorials from public meetings in Newcastle, Sheffield and
Birmingham, and the creation of a 'National League'.[2] This

---

[1] Isaac Ironside, the redoubtable Sheffield rationalist and ex-Chartist
who organized Toulmin Smith's unsuccessful parliamentary candidature
for that town in 1852 (see W. H. G. Armytage, 'Sheffield and the Crimean War: Politics and Industry, 1852–57', *History Today* v (1955),
474), used his newspaper, the *Sheffield Free Press*, to support the Anti-
Centralization Union in 1854 but Urquhart in 1855, as its files show.

[2] The first meeting was held at Newcastle on 28 August (*Newcastle
Courant*, 1 September 1854) under the aegis of Charles Attwood and of

movement attracted some Tory as well as advanced Liberal
support. Disraeli at this time was not only anxious to change
his party's rural, squirearchical image, but also willing to beat
the Government with any stick he could find. His henchman,
G. A. Hamilton, was from the beginning in touch with the
leaders of the movement (Crawshay of Newcastle, Ironside of
Sheffield, and Dawson and Allday of Birmingham) through
Knox of the *Morning Herald*.[1] The movement, Hamilton assured Disraeli, was 'quite irrespective of ordinary politics —
and *British* and constitutional', and a private meeting with its
leaders would be well worth while.[2] The meeting duly took
place in London.[3] Urquhart himself hoped much from Disraeli
at this point,[4] and was not disillusioned until Disraeli turned
to a peace policy towards the end of the war.[5]

Even without Tory support, however, the movement was
strikingly successful in 1855. Its strongest rival, the Administrative Reform Association, was always too blatant an
expression of middle-class pride to have much appeal for the
small independent workmen of the west Midlands, and as the
impression spread that the Association was not in earnest and
would accomplish nothing, indignation over the conduct of
the war helped to inflate the National League instead. In
June, Urquhart was active in Newcastle and at 'Hudders-
field, Birmingham, Sheffield, Leeds, &c. &c. . . .', as his ener-

---

George Crawshay of Gateshead — to Cobden's indignation, for 'he
[Crawshay] was one of my most devoted free trade allies' (Cobden to H.
Richards, 8 September 1854, Add. MS. 43657, fo. 232). It spread to
Sheffield in October (*Sheffield Free Press*, 21 October 1854), and received
a fresh impetus from the alarming war news of December (cf. ibid.,
6 January 1855).

[1] The *Herald* was a Tory paper which regularly published letters from
Urquhart, though less frequently than the radical *Morning Advertiser*.

[2] Hughenden Papers, B XX 98, G. A. Hamilton to Disraeli, 6 December 1854; cf. ibid., 8 September 1854.

[3] Ironside to Gladstone, 5 July 1855, Add. MS. 44383, fo. 58.

[4] M. C. Bishop, *A Memoir of Mrs. Urquhart* (1897), pp. 122, 129.

[5] Cf. the article, 'Is Mr. Disraeli still alive?', in the *Free Press*, 8
March 1856.

getic wife reported, for, she added, 'the field is so promising it must be sown'. In July he was in Birmingham, and then in Coventry, Kidderminster, Worcester, Bath, Bristol, Gloucester, Stroud, Cheltenham — everywhere meeting with some success as well as with Chartist heckling. 'In each place a Committee is formed and at work,' enthused his wife.[1] 'What a strange state of things we are brought to when that madman can have thousands to look up to him as a saviour!' was Cobden's gloomy comment.[2] In August a conference of delegates from all the Working Men's Committees thus set up was held in Birmingham, which submitted its work to two public meetings, the first reported as attended by 10,000 persons, the second by 16,000[3] — no doubt most of them merely curious. The growth of the movement was rapid enough to attract comment throughout the national press and even abroad.[4]

Although other exponents of radical feeling flagged after the fall of Sebastopol, Urquhart continued to fulminate that 'catastrophe hangs over England', and to urge his henchmen to 'qualify yourselves to become teachers of your fellow-citizens, and thereby the directors of a soon-to-be infuriated

[1] *Newcastle Courant*, 8 June 1855; Bishop, op. cit., pp. 132–3; *Morning Advertiser*, 20 August 1855. Members paid one shilling quarterly in advance — a significant difference from the annual subscription of £1 paid by members of the Anti-Centralization Union and the Administrative Reform Association.

[2] Cobden to Joseph Sturge, 6 July 1855, Sturge Papers, British Museum, Add. MS. 43722, fo. 72.

[3] *Free Press*, 3 November 1855. The circulation of the weekly *Sheffield Free Press* on 29 September 1855 was only 2,400.

[4] Possibly the articles in the *Aachener Zeitung* quoted by the *Morning Advertiser*, 26 July 1855, and *Free Press*, 5 April 1856 were the work of Lothar Bucher, who fell under Urquhart's spell while a refugee in England after 1848 and was at this time writing Urquhartite articles in the German Press (Robinson, op. cit., p. 130, n. 1). Bucher's *Der Parlamentarismus wie er ist* (1855) closely echoes Urquhart's views, with its ascription of the Aberdeen Ministry's failures to the corruption of ancient constitutional practices which had taken place in England since 1660.

L

people'.[1] Soon events again seemed to justify his attitude. In October he was confident enough to publish a single sheet London version at twopence of the fourpenny *Sheffield Free Press*, with the local news left out and the emphasis upon foreign affairs. Increasing public impatience with neutral profiteering from Britain's relaxation of maritime rights made his call for the full resumption of the right of search highly topical, while the shortage of grain and the drain of gold abroad at the end of the year both furnished yet more proofs of Palmerston's treachery. On 30 January 1856 the last great public meeting of the war was held in London to protest against the fall of Kars, and this very varied gathering of radicals demanded the impeachment of ministers in the best Urquhartite style.[2] In March the peace itself, together with the Declaration of Paris renouncing British maritime rights, provided Urquhart with the most cogent proof of all of ministerial treachery. It 'openly gazettes Britain as a province of Russia', he exclaimed, and to the end of his life he campaigned for its abrogation and 'the restoration of British naval power'.[3]

It has been calculated that 145 of Urquhart's small but devoted Working-men's Committees were in existence immediately after the war.[4] This success was only partly due to the spontaneous influence of one town's example upon

---

[1] Urquhart to A. Dalzell, secretary of the Birmingham Working Men's Committee, 1 November 1855, printed in the *Free Press*, 3 November 1855. Many members of the original Committee had resigned in September, however, after Urquhart's public outbursts against the Press and against Kossuth and Mazzini (J. A. Langford, *Modern Birmingham and its Institutions* (Birmingham, 1877), II. 8).

[2] *Free Press*, 2 February 1856.

[3] Cf. Urquhart's *Answer to Mr. Cobden on the Assimilation of War and Peace* (1862) and *Naval Power suppressed by the Maritime States* (1873), *inter alia*.

[4] A. Briggs, 'David Urquhart and the West Riding Foreign Affairs Committees,' *Bradford Antiquary*, N.S., xxxix (1958). 200. Some of these Committees survived for over twenty years, despite Urquhart's altered interests and departure to Switzerland.

another, as Urquhart liked to claim.[1] From the autumn of
1854 a carefully controlled organization was also built up.
His tactful and energetic wife supervised a devoted band of
missionaries in the manner typical of mid-nineteenth-century
agitators. Thomas Johnson of Newcastle in Birmingham, then
Richard Hart of Birmingham in Worcester, for example,
worked hard to get a foothold through speaking at administrative reform meetings or making contacts in reading rooms or
commercial hotels, before organizing meetings of their own
in order to prepare the way for Urquhart's arrival.[2] As soon as
Urquhart had made his visit and Committees had been set up,
they were organized into Districts, and monthly or quarterly
meetings arranged in the District centre.[3] The most promising
Committee members were summoned to attend a gruelling
course of self-improvement (lectures on the Law of Nations
and the Constitution of England for eight hours a day, followed by two hours of discussion in the evening).[4] Moreover
for Urquhart everything about the war had worked together
for good. Not only were his diplomatic and political views
apparently substantiated to the hilt, but his fundamental outlook was shown to be in accordance with some of the strongest
contemporary trends of opinion. Strategy, diplomacy, financial and commercial policy all followed the course he had
predicted and made his highly coloured and exacting har-
angues acceptable to the unsophisticated small craftsmen
among whom he found his most rewarding audiences. At the
same time his idealized interpretation of English history and
the duties of the citizen was far more acceptable than the
materialism and the impatient and gloomy view of the past
offered by the Chartists with whom his followers had so many
disputes. His fondness for claiming to be neither a Tory
nor a Radical (though he was often called both) but an
Englishman,[5] and his denunciations of party and impatience

[1] Urquhart MSS. I, G 18. [2] Ibid. I, G 1. [3] Robinson, op. cit., p. 136.
[4] Urquhart to Le Play (n.d.), quoted in ibid., pp. 125–6.
[5] Cf. *Free Press*, 8 and 15 December 1855.

with Parliament, accorded equally well with the times. The combination of a lofty call to the individual to acquire and use civic knowledge, together with a patriotic, backward-looking constitutionalism, was a peculiarly apt one for that generation. Altogether it is hardly surprising that, given the abundant proofs of ministerial treason apparently furnished by the war, Urquhart's peculiar doctrines for a few brief months captured large audiences throughout the Midlands and the North and won a small band of lifelong exponents.

Another essential component of the myth of the ancient constitution, in addition to those already discussed, had always been the independent enlightened freeholder, who returned to Parliament independent enlightened Members. His extinction or frailty had long been lamented. In the mid-nineteenth century it was no longer the Crown which was seen as exerting the fatal pressure to which this independent freeholder had succumbed, but the landed aristocracy and (though this was an exclusively middle-class perception) organized party. 'Feudalism' as the antagonist of 'the nation' thus continued to form part of the language of radical politics. Indeed after 1815 a new explanation was unearthed of the unhealthy growth of aristocratic influence, and characteristically a fiscal one. It became a popular radical claim that by their 'infamous bargain struck with Charles II' in the Feudal Tenures Act the aristocracy 'relieved themselves from all their feudal services, and threw the weight of taxation upon the people', thus putting themselves in a position to embark upon continental wars, the establishment of the National Debt, and the enslavement of the House of Commons.[1]

This cry that the constitution had been perverted to oligarchical forms was still so much a part of popular radical thought that it was inevitable that it should be raised again

[1] John Hampden, Junior [William Howitt], *The Aristocracy of England* (1846).

when the Crimean disasters provoked acute national heart-searching. 'The canker worm in the British constitution is the corruption of the representative system which has . . . completely unsettled the balance of the three estates, and centred all legislative and executive power in the hands of a few great families',[1] repeatedly declared the *Morning Advertiser*, the 'most popular and extensively read of all the daily Papers',[2] in 1855. Amateur constitutional historians offered a variety of fatal dates — 1066, 1215, 1660, 1688 — but they agreed that it was the development of oligarchy which had ruined administration, deprived the people of their rights, and curtailed the prerogative of Parliament. 'We do not possess a constitutional government, but a landocracy', was a familiar lower-middle- and working-class theme, which inevitably rose to a crescendo in the general outburst against 'the Families' which characterized the first half of 1855. In these months the popular Press (except the Chartist *People's Paper*) was full of historical arguments to show how the perversion of the country's former institutions had brought about a modern decline into oligarchy. A favourite claim was that only thirty constituencies were then free from aristocratic influence, and that eighty-seven magnates returned more than three-quarters of the House of Commons. 'We have allowed the peers and their hangers-on to creep into hundreds of constituencies by our own corruptness.'[3] One of the five points of the National and Constitutional Association's programme was severe penal laws against bribery (presumably the Act of 1854 was already regarded as inadequate), and one of the two great themes of its publicity was the need for vigilance over elections.[4] Then too, the working-class xenophobia which

[1] *Morning Advertiser*, 13 November 1855.

[2] Sir Charles Trevelyan to Gladstone, 9 March 1854, Add. MS 44333, fo. 251. Every member of the Licensed Victuallers' Association took in this paper. (No doubt Trevelyan was tacitly excluding *The Times* as not 'popular' in his sense.)

[3] *Morning Advertiser*, 16 May, 3 August and 26 February 1855.

[4] Ibid. 3 April 1855.

the war encouraged, stimulated denunciations of the aristocracy as an alien race fostered since 1688 by a line of foreign
kings, and now allowing the spread of German influence in
high places. It was this transference of xenophobia to the
aristocracy which was exploited by Urquhart in his ostentati-
ously 'British and National' movement, with such advice as
that he gave to his audience in Newcastle: 'to act and feel as
if the whole of the classes above you were a foreign occupation,
from whom you had to emancipate the Commonwealth.'[1] It
was expressed too in the recurring attacks from much humbler
quarters upon Prince Albert and German influence as the
cause of British defeats — a theme of many Crimean War
street ballads.[2] Even more well-worn radical cries that the
aristocracy had enslaved the native English freeman by the
vast territorial power they had built up through primogeniture and strict settlement, also received a fresh lease of life.[3]

But side by side with these familiar denunciations there
was offered increasingly in the Crimean War a moralizing call
to individual duty: by forswearing all corrupt inducements at
parliamentary elections, the electors themselves could undermine the political influence of the aristocracy and restore the
ancient vigour of the constitution. The Chartists naturally
had no patience with a remedy which so completely evaded
the issue of organic electoral reform. But to the old labour
aristocracy and the lower-middle class, purity proved an
attractive specific against the disease of oligarchical influence,
the source of the perversion of the constitution and so of the
country's misfortunes. The ideal of the alert and critical
elector who would be a force for Members to reckon with after

---

[1] D. Urquhart, *Constitutional Remedies*, p. 44.

[2] For example, the ballad quoted by Fontane, op. cit., p. 100:

> 'Bad luck they say both night and day
> To the Cobugs and the humbugs,
> The Wirtembugs, the Scarembugs,
> And all the German horse-rugs . . .'

[3] For example, *Morning Advertiser*, 29 May 1855.

as well as during their election, was as much a part of the programme of the small men who supported the National and Constitutional Association, the State Reform Association, and Urquhart's National Movement, as it was of the more solidly middle-class followers of Toulmin Smith. All of these, however, combined the moral call to purity and watchfulness with a programme either of some kind of organic parliamentary reform (whether extension of the franchise, the ballot, or redistribution of seats), or, in the case of Toulmin Smith and Urquhart, with a call for institutional changes in the field of local self-government. The far more cautious, successful middle-class men who led the Administrative Reform Association were determined to confine their official sponsorship of institutional change to methods of staffing the Civil Service, which they argued affected education, efficiency and the independence of Parliament alike;[1] and this very caution over officially committing themselves to any wider programme of change in political institutions may have encouraged the orators among them to call still more loudly for the eradication of influence and corruption by the individual moral effort of existing electors. The Administrative Reform Association never ceased officially to insist that if, when they chose their parliamentary representatives, electors would do so from public motives alone and subsequently refrain from exerting any pressure upon them to seek Government favours, then at one stroke the golden age of independent electors and independent Members of Parliament would return. In this vein Samuel Morley, the Association's chairman, told the foundation meeting on 5 May 1855 that 'the first advance towards the effectual remedy of the existing evils must spring from a thorough change in public opinion as to the relations between Members of Parliament and their constituents'; and he repeated from the chair on 13 June that 'the real evil lay with the people themselves'. What was needed was 'a hundred independent Members' — a traditional theme that was taken

[1] Samuel Morley to Edwin Chadwick, 1 July 1854, Chadwick MSS.

up by other speakers and repeated yet again from the chair a few days later.[1]

But the Administrative Reform Association, unlike working-class radical movements, also claimed that the golden age of independence had been ended not only by the insidious influence of jobbery and servility, but also by the recent development of party organization through the clubs and the party agents. These, it urged, were new and malign constitutional growths which should be made to wither away by not being allowed to function. In its Committee's words, 'The candidates sent down from the Clubs are chosen with the constant object of upholding, whether in or out of office, the fixed Ministerial cliques . . . It is an essential step in administrative reform, that the Constituencies should shake off the Clubs and their Agents.' Similarly in their next address the Committee urged: 'Let there be an end of having candidates thrust upon you either by great neighbours or great clubs, for mere personal or party ends.'[2] Members of the Association were also told that the elector had a final, more continuous duty: to watch closely the conduct of his representatives after they had been elected. He should study their record in parliamentary divisions, and treat them accordingly when they stood for re-election, for 'the constituencies are the primary constitutional judges of the acts of their representatives'.[3] To give practical assistance to members in this duty the Association's Statistical Secretary analysed the division lists of 1854–5 and later of 1855–6 and circulated his findings.[4]

A backward-looking vision of a body of independent freeholders, alert to the public interest and informed upon public affairs, choosing Members of Parliament who at Westminster followed not the dictates of party organization nor of patron-

---

[1] *The Times*, 7 May and 14 and 28 June 1855.

[2] Official Paper of the Administrative Reform Association, no. 1, p. 8, and no. 8, p. 9.

[3] Ibid., no. 7.

[4] J. P. Gassiot, *Four Letters to J. A. Roebuck, Esquire* (1856–7), *passim*.

age and influence but the wishes of their constituents, was as essential a part of the Association's programme as it was, *mutatis mutandis*, of the other radical movements which flourished in the tension of 1855. Such a vision was widely acceptable and almost ubiquitous in the domestic crisis inspired by the Crimean War, partly because of the cult of individual responsibility and moral earnestness and disillusionment with parliamentary government characteristic of the 1850s, but even more because of the vitality of the traditional rhetoric of the ancient constitution. Indeed that rhetoric played an even greater part in giving emotional force to this idea of the independent citizen free alike from the pressures of social deference and of party, than it did in bringing to life those other ideals of local self-government and direct ministerial responsibility which have already been discussed. The peroration of the shipping magnate and would-be popular orator W. S. Lindsay at the foundation of the Administrative Reform Association may stand for many similar appeals to the men of 1855 to save the ancient constitution from the total ruin which the difficulties and scandals of the Crimean War seemed for a while to have made imminent. They were all attached to their ancient constitution, Lindsay said,

they were proud of that noble constitutional tree under whose protecting shadow the exiled monarchs of Europe had found a happy shelter and a quiet refuge. Its umbrageous leaves still bloomed fair, but beneath the foliage there lurked some rotten branches. If those who had the power did not remove those diseased excrescences in time, the tree might wither and die; or (which was an equal evil), if those who venerated its kindly shade, and had something at stake in its preservation, did not themselves lop off the rank growth, some more rash and relentless hands might seize the axe, and, by the inconsiderate violence of their blows, cut into the stem and whelm both trunk and branch in one common ruin. (Cheers.)[1]

Among the upper-middle and intellectual classes, however, there were many who regarded the aristocracy's strength not

[1] *The Times*, 7 May 1855.

as a perversion but as the historic secret of England's stability
and freedom, and therefore viewed with dismay these Crimean attacks on contemporary English institutions. For
those who agreed that only the survival of an active aristocracy and of habits of deference had saved England from
government despotism or the tyranny of democratic majorities, Alexis de Tocqueville was a chief source of inspiration.
Like many other continental observers, Tocqueville was
struck not by the decay of local self-government in England,
but by the extent to which it still flourished there, and this
he associated with the continued existence of a powerful
aristocracy closely linked to the land, residing on its estates
for most of the year and shouldering much of the work of
administration. His epoch-making *Democracy in America* had
been a prime source of the emphasis laid by so many liberals
and radical intellectuals since the 1830s upon the active self-
assertion of the individual as an integrated part of the community.[1] Very many of the leading ideas which Tocqueville
then threw out had become part and parcel of that highly
variegated movement for local self-government which (as has
been frequently stressed) was so important in the 1850s. His
passionate belief that political activity was inseparable from
civic liberty made him as hostile to bureaucratic domination
and centralization as any follower of Toulmin Smith (who was
in fact a great admirer of Tocqueville).[2] During the whole of
the Crimean War, Tocqueville was engrossed in the writing of
his last and greatest attack on centralization, *L'Ancien
Régime en France*,[3] in which he stressed the disastrous results
of the disappearance of parish meetings and provincial as-

[1] Tocqueville's influence on J. S. Mill is well known (J. S. Mill, *Autobiography* (World's Classics edn., Oxford, 1924), pp. 162–4).

[2] Both Tocqueville and Montalembert figure in the 'List of Principal
Authorities' in the second edition of Smith's *The Parish* (1857) and
were quoted by him as supporters of his equation of freedom with the
habitual practice of self-government (pp. 5–7).

[3] Begun in January 1854 and published in June 1856 (R. Herr,
Tocqueville and the Old Regime (Princeton, 1962), pp. 26–28).

semblies in France, and the value of the sense of community which he believed flourished in England. He inevitably saw the events of the war in the light of these preoccupations. The Crimean disasters filled him with fear that England would be tempted by this apparent demonstration of the advantages of centralization in time of war, and that the example of the French Army would make English soldiers clamour for a military career open to talent.[1] Towards the end of the domestic crisis provoked by the war, he confided to his old friend Nassau Senior: 'All that has passed in England since the beginning of the war grieves me deeply.' He went on to lament the 'frightfully revolutionary appearance' of recent outbursts, and the damage done to English institutions by the attacks on the aristocracy and by the introduction of competitive examination as the method of recruitment for the Civil Service,[2] a change widely criticized by continental liberals as a dangerous step towards bureaucracy and levelling uniformity. For Tocqueville, England's aristocratic institutions were the basis, not the enemy, of her continued local self-government and freedom from class tension, and thus of her strength and well being.

But Tocqueville's indirect eulogy of existing English institutions and rebuke to radical attacks upon them in L'Ancien Régime was not published until after the end of the war. In November and December 1855, however, another distinguished French liberal Anglophil, the Comte de Montalembert, published his De l'Avenir politique de l'Angleterre, which Tocqueville hailed as a perfect description of his own sentiments.[3] The book was an immediate success in the atmosphere

[1] Tocqueville to Mrs. Grote, 24 February 1855, Memoir, Letters and Remains, p. 290.
[2] Tocqueville to Senior, 25 July 1855, ibid., pp. 305, 297, 265; Tocqueville to Sir George Lewis, 18 November 1855, Œuvres complètes d'Alexis de Tocqueville, publiées par Madame de Tocqueville (Paris, 1866), vii. 379–80.
[3] Tocqueville to Montalembert, 10 July 1856, Œuvres complètes (1866 edn.), vii. 390.

of reviving confidence which characterized the winter of 1855–6.
'Everyone is running about asking for it,' wrote Abraham
Hayward on Christmas Eve.[1] Montalembert's work was the
product of his own strong prejudices working upon his observations when he spent two months in England during the
Crimean crisis, receiving an honorary Oxford D.Litt. at the
Sheldonian, paying numerous aristocratic visits, and listening
to parliamentary debates and going to the meetings of the
Administrative Reform Association. Like Tocqueville, he believed that England during the crisis was plunging down the
dangerous slope towards democracy and bureaucracy, dangerous not only as an instrument of despotism, but also because
it created 'le désir universel et immodéré des emplois publics'
which 'répand dans tout le corps de la nation une humeur
vénale et servile'.[2] Montalembert, however, was confident that
England possessed adequate safeguards against these perils,
and the main tenor of the book was gratifyingly reassuring.
If the standards of contemporary Europe or America were
applied, after the worst shocks of the war had passed, it was
still possible for liberal intellectuals to believe that aristocracy, diversity and local participation in administration
would be preserved in their last stronghold.

Few Englishmen with radical sympathies, however, syste-
matically and knowledgeably compared their own country's
social and political institutions with those of other countries.
Their standard of judgment was not Jacksonian democracy
or the Second Empire but the myth of the ancient constitution or its rival, the myth of business efficiency. Their conclusions were therefore very different from those of such men
as Tocqueville and Montalembert, who used English experience in order indirectly to criticize their own régime.[3] To

[1] Hayward to Montalembert, 24 December 1855, *The Correspondence
of Abraham Hayward*, ed. H. E. Carlisle (1886), i. 258.

[2] C. de Montalembert, *De l'avenir politique de l'Angleterre* (Paris,
1856), p. 74.

[3] Charles de Rémusat similarly used his article on the administrative
reform movement to criticize the second Empire ('La réforme adminis-

them the radical outburst of the Crimean War seemed less an outbreak of the revolutionary and ultra-democratic spirit than a perfectly defensible attempt to supply the deficiencies of contemporary social and political institutions.[1]

'Today you can only make progress by going backwards.'[2] The phrase is an Urquhartite one, but its echoes can be heard even in radical camps so opposed as the Anti-Centralization Union and the Administrative Reform Association. The emotional potency and widespread appeal of the ancient constitution during the Crimean War never ceases to surprise, until the extent to which mid-Victorian culture as a whole drew its inspiration from a vision of the past is remembered. Painting, architecture, poetry, even the successful novels of the day, all reflect in various degrees a vision of a future, good because it had restored the historic past. Nor was that vision always mere retrospective utopianism, least of all for those who applied it to political institutions. It was a vision often very painstakingly reconstructed with the aid of the learning available to that generation, as well as the inspiration of imaginative sympathy. It is thus not in reality surprising that when the Crimean War demonstrated that something was profoundly amiss with the nation's political and social organization, Englishmen quite as often sought a remedy by urging the restoration of past practices and institutions, as by denouncing their obsolete survivals in a society to which they were no longer relevant. But in the 1850s respect for the past was (for once) fairly evenly balanced with confidence in the future. English radicalism in the mid-nineteenth century thus presents a Janus face, with on the one side archaic notions of

---

trative en Angleterre', *Revue des Deux Mondes*, nouvelle période, deuxième série, xii (1855), 241–84).

[1] Cf. the criticisms of *De l'Avenir politique de l'Angleterre* in the *Westminster Review*, lxvi (1856). 188.

[2] [W. Cyples], 'Is Mr. Urquhart a Tory or a Radical?', *Free Press*, 15 December 1855.

the independent freeholder, and on the other newly developed class pride of a highly specialized and self-conscious kind. In the shocks and upheavals of the Crimean War it wore both masks at once, looking backward as well as forward, and thus revealed itself for what it was, a potentially explosive mixture of opposites, firmly embedded in some of the deepest emotional and intellectual currents of that time.

CHAPTER FIVE

Legislative Progress during the
Crimean War

AFTER the Napoleonic Wars it became a commonplace
that all war inevitably checked domestic progress, and
in 1854 it was assumed that the Crimean War would
prove no exception. It is true there were a few who argued
that war made reform all the more essential in order to ensure
the willing and loyal co-operation of the humblest citizens; but
most people acquiesced in the prospect of a war-time mora-
torium upon domestic questions. Those who opposed the war
naturally exploited these expectations to the full. From the
beginning pacifists and Manchester School radicals continually
emphasized the cost of war in terms of arrested domestic
progress. The latter almost invariably appeared to be referring
to economic progress, and thus made themselves easy targets
for charges of Mammon-worship, but as the war went on
pacifists of a different hue made much of the cost of the war
in terms of arrested social legislation. One such man was the
Somerset writer and landowner, Sir Arthur Elton, who from
the beginning of 1855 until the end of the war published a
series of sixty-seven penny *Tracts for the Present Crisis.* These
repeated again and again that since the original *casus belli* had
been removed, a mere war of intervention was now being
waged, 'at the expense of increased suffering to the Poorer
classes'. In one of his longer pamphlets, Elton listed half a
dozen measures 'necessary for the comfort of the working
classes' — sanitary improvements, increased facilities for
education, alteration of the law of settlement and removal,
improvement in the law of partnership, increased facility in
the transfer of land and house property, the extension of the

163

jurisdiction of the County Courts — and claimed that they
were being 'put from us, for a war neither necessary nor just'.[1]
After the end of the war, as the Cobdenite interpretation of
the war as an unnecessary blunder rapidly gained acceptance,
so too did the Cobdenite corollary that it had checked domestic progress. The stereotyped late-Victorian interpretation of
the Crimean War — 'a CRIME', as Bright told his young son —
involved the claim not only that the war settled nothing
abroad, but also that it brought heavy financial burdens and
stagnation at home. In recent years the diplomatic side of this
interpretation of the Crimean War has repeatedly been challenged. Moreover it is obvious enough that in some ways (most
strikingly through the incentive given to Bessemer to work on
his process for producing steel) the Crimean War administered
the kind of erratic economic stimulus which the strains of war
so often provide. It is now proposed to argue that the war did
not in reality bring legislative progress to a halt, nor distract
public attention from domestic issues for its whole duration.
Indeed the Crimean revelations focused public attention upon
certain special aspects of domestic issues in a peculiarly intensive way.

It is true enough that in the first year of the war public
opinion concentrated upon events abroad. These were the
months when the Press continually remarked that domestic
issues unconnected with the war could not expect to receive
attention, and the public still found this obvious common
sense. In the parliamentary session of 1854 a substantial
number of public Bills brought in both by the Government
and by private members failed to reach the statute book. The
reasons for this, however (despite face-saving Government
pleas to the contrary), were almost entirely unconnected with
the war. Moreover even this first session of the war, although unsatisfactory, was by no means so barren legislatively as Disraeli,
with his unfailing eye for a good debating point, liked to claim.

---

[1] *An inquiry into the alleged necessity and justice of the war with Russia*
(1855), p. 102. Cf. Elton's *Where are we Drifting?* (1855).

When Parliament assembled on 31 January 1854, the Queen's Speech promised the introduction of eight large measures; at its Prorogation on 12 August, three of these had been withdrawn and one had never been introduced at all. But not one of these four major measures failed because of the war. Although the ostensible reason for the withdrawal of Lord John Russell's Parliamentary Reform Bill was the inappropriateness of so controversial a subject in time of war, in reality there were the strongest political reasons for dropping it. Cabinet as well as Parliament were deeply divided upon this question. As Palmerston (who had himself briefly resigned in December 1853 in protest against the Bill) warned Aberdeen, Lord John's Bill was not only 'an Error in Statesmanship' but also 'at variance with the plainest principles of Parliamentary Tactics', since it would unite the opposition and give the waverers among the Government's supporters a pretext to desert.[1] There is no reason to suppose that, if the war had not broken out, this Bill would have had a different fate from the three other abortive Reform Bills introduced in this decade. Somewhat similarly, the Bill for the reform of the Civil Service was never even introduced because of the intense opposition to the principles of the Northcote–Trevelyan report from the Whig section of the Cabinet, the clubs and the heads of departments. The Settlement and Removal Bill was withdrawn when the House of Commons objected to a measure which related to the English poor alone, to await the report of a Select Committee upon the state of the law upon the removal of the Scottish and Irish poor.[2] As for the last of the four, the promised Testamentary and Matrimonial Causes Bill, the course of legal reform was always determined far less by outside events and pressures than by the attitudes of the legal profession. In Dickens's age as in Oliver Cromwell's, the ramparts of the law were the most difficult of all to breach.

[1] Palmerston to Aberdeen, 12 February 1854, Add. MS. 43069, fo. 212.

[2] 3 *Hansard*, cxxxii, col. 1185 (2 May 1854).

M

In the Crimean Parliament, moreover, there were two reasons why progress in this field was peculiarly difficult. In the first place, that Parliament had an exceptionally high number of lawyers in the Commons. 'It is a curious fact', noted Lord Campbell (accurately for once) in his diary at the end of this session, 'that the Lords have become more rational and more liberal on all subjects of law reform than the Commons. That House is now much infested with lawyers.' Campbell went on to claim that the number of lawyers in the Commons had trebled since 1832 (a modern scholar puts their number at 102), and that the Parliament of 1852 was a 'parliamentum doctissimum'.[1] The lawyers' lobby was a very powerful one indeed in that House of Commons. Secondly (though this was a difficulty whose importance was probably exaggerated by contemporary gossip), the Chancellor and the Law Officers throughout the Crimean War formed a most inharmonious team. Lord Cranworth, the Chancellor, was universally popular — 'a good creature' but, as his Attorney General privately confided to Lord Broughton, 'no statesman and no lawyer'.[2] Unluckily his Tory predecessor, St. Leonards, had shown outstanding vigour in law reform, and it was bad tactics, to say the least, when the ineffectual Cranworth attempted to rival him. Sir Alexander Cockburn and Sir Richard Bethell, the Attorney- and Solicitor-General, rarely agreed either with him or each other. Bethell indeed was one of the most arrogant and sarcastic of all mid-nineteenth-century lawyers. Over the unlucky Testamentary Jurisdiction Bill introduced in 1854 he for once agreed with Cranworth, but Cockburn did not support their scheme to make Chancery a court of administration as well as a court of construction and allow it to pronounce on both the validity and the interpretation of a will. Even more fatal, the whole of Doctors' Commons opposed the Bill, and

---

[1] 12 August 1854, *The Life of John, Lord Campbell*, ed. M. S. Hard-castle (1881), ii. 325; J. A. Thomas, *The House of Commons, 1832–1901* (Cardiff, 1939), pp. 4–7.

[2] Lord Broughton's Diary, 19 April 1856, Add. MS. 43759, fo. 93.

not a single expert in the old Probate practice would assist in drafting it.[1] Finally, no Bill which gave fresh business to Chancery in this way had any chance of acceptance without doors, where Dickens's unfair and out-of-date caricature of that court continued to grip the public imagination. Thus the fate of this Bill had even less to do with the outbreak of war than that of the other three. In short, the Aberdeen Coalition made the mistake of announcing far too ambitious a programme in their second Queen's Speech, and these four casualties were the consequence. A good many lesser Government measures and private members' bills also failed, but not an exceptionally high number; and in each case it was the opposition of some well-organized lobby or of some well-entrenched prejudice which was fatal, not the war.[2]

Casualties like these occurred in considerable numbers in every session during this period. When Lord John Russell told his colleagues in October 1854 that 'no one would wish to see, still less to take part in, a repetition of the session of 1854. The numerous defeats sustained by the Government, the rejection or withdrawal of measures of great importance mentioned in the Queen's speech, could not happen again without great injury to Parliamentary government', his extreme sensitivity about his parliamentary reputation — Lord John always regarded the Commons as 'his own dung-hill'[3] — and his chronic state of grievance as a member of Aberdeen's Coalition were provoking him to obvious exaggeration. The explanation he went on to offer for these ministerial defects could equally well have been called into service in a post-mortem upon almost any other mid-nineteenth-century session of Parliament. The weakness of executive

---

[1] J. B. Atlay, *The Victorian Chancellors* (1908), p. 70; T. A. Nash, *Life of Richard, Lord Westbury* (1888), p. 150.

[2] This was the case, for example, over Palmerston's Rural Police Bill, as well as a Medical Practitioners Bill imposing registration on all doctors and a proposed extension of Ewart's Public Libraries and Museums Act.

[3] Edward Ellice to Lord Grey, 8 October 1854, Grey MSS.

control over the House of Commons in the 1850s is, and was, well known. The effects of the disintegration of party were as much a favourite theme among contemporaries as among historians today. As Lord John himself pointed out, Government supporters were as conspicuous for their 'extreme divergence of views' as the Opposition, and the House of Commons was obstinately determined 'to decide for itself on matters of legislation'.[1] He himself 'never at any time well brigaded his followers'.[2] Two other perennial mid-nineteenth-century parliamentary problems also made themselves strongly felt in 1854; the archaism of parliamentary procedure and the strength of sectarian religious feeling. In 1852 and 1853 some alterations had been made in the cumbersome forms of the House following the recommendations of the Select Committee on Procedure established in 1848; but the waste of parliamentary time was still so obvious that another Select Committee was set up in 1854. Unfortunately the radicals on this Committee were outvoted, and its proposals, although promptly incorporated into standing orders, were comparatively minor.[3] Finally this session was dogged by that particularly violent anti-Catholic feeling provoked by the 'Papal Aggression' in 1850, and by a dread of Puseyism much increased because the Peelites, with their Puseyite reputation, were in office. Several of the lesser Government defeats in this session must be laid at the door of these feelings.[4]

But in any case, when judged by the standards of other sessions in the 1850s and not by those of the ambitious programme rashly announced in the Queen's Speech, the legislative record of 1854 was not a poor one. In sheer volume of statutes passed, it was one of the three most productive sessions of the decade. Four out of the one hundred and

[1] Memorandum of Lord John Russell, 18 October 1854, P.R.O. 30/22/11.
[2] J. L. Parkes to Lord Grey, 15 July 1854, Grey MSS.
[3] J. Redlich, *The Procedure of the House of Commons* (1908), i. 88.
[4] Conspicuously in the case of the Oaths Bill.

twenty-five public Acts passed in 1854 — the four promised in the Queen's Speech which succeeded in reaching the statute book — were of major importance. The Common Law Procedure Act (17 & 18 Vict. c. 125) it was agreed on all sides embodied 'improvements as great and as valuable as any introduced almost since the period in which our statutes had been in existence'.[1] In the Commons only one amendment was made to this measure, the deletion of the clause waiving unanimity of juries. Thus one legal measure of fundamental importance, embodying principles contended for by law reformers for twenty or thirty years, was finally accomplished in 1854. Another statute of real importance in its own field was the stringent Bribery and Corruption at Elections Act (17 & 18 Vict. c. 102), admitted by one Cabinet minister to be 'the result of the two parties rivalling each other in professions of purity'[2] and indisputably the principal Act on the subject all through this period.[3] By providing a much more exact and complete definition of bribery than ever before, and setting up auditors of election expenses to whom all Bills were to be sent and through whom all payments were to be made, it went about as far as it was possible to go in attacking corruption by means of discovering and punishing it, as opposed to attempting to prevent the offence from ever being committed. Of more lasting importance was the Act for the Reform of Oxford University (c. 81), which made the first great breach in the Anglican monopoly of the two ancient universities by freeing matriculation and degrees (except in the faculty of theology) from religious tests, and which went far to create a new academic atmosphere and administrative framework in

[1] 3 *Hansard*, cxxxiii, col. 1154 (30 May 1854).

[2] Sir Charles Wood to Lord Grey, 29 July 1854, Grey MSS.

[3] Sir W. Holdsworth, *History of English Law*, xiv, ed. A. L. Goodhart and H. G. Hanbury (1964), p. 162. It had, however, considerable defects in practice (cf., e.g., C. Seymour, *Electoral Reform in England and Wales* (New Haven, 1915), p. 231). These weaknesses had always been foreseen by electioneering experts (cf. Joseph Parkes to Lord Grey, 1 August 1854, Grey MSS).

the university. Finally two substantial changes were made in the legislative framework of the country's economic life with the passing of Edward Cardwell's most celebrated measures as President of the Board of Trade: the Merchant Shipping and the Railway and Canal Traffic Acts (cc. 5, 31). The former, a vast consolidating act, remained substantially the authority until the twentieth century;[1] the latter, although badly mauled by the railway interest in debate, established for the first time the duty of the railway companies to give reasonable facilities for traffic and to refrain from undue discrimination, and appointed a court where redress could be obtained.[2] Judged by the low standards of nineteenth-century railway legislation, this achievement was considerable.

At least four other measures of domestic reform passed in this session were important enough to deserve mention, particularly Palmerston's Youthful Offenders Act, which first gave official sanction to the principle that juvenile delinquents needed not punishment but education in schools specially adapted to their needs. This was a measure which Charles Adderley, the Birmingham philanthropist and politician, had tried to get accepted in 1852 and 1853 in vain.[3] With the passage of an Act establishing the direct control of the House of Commons over charges incurred in the collection of the Revenue, a change was accomplished in public finance which, in the words of the Queen's Speech proroguing Parliament, gave 'more complete effect to an important principle of our constitution, and [promoted] simplicity and regularity in our system of public accounts'.[4] Finally, after thirty years of spasmodic debate, the usury laws were at last repealed, and a useful change made in the procedure of the Ecclesiastical

[1] Cf. R. Prouty, *The Transformation of the Board of Trade*, (1957), pp. 42, 96.

[2] E. Cleveland-Stevens, *English Railways: Their Development and their Relation to the State* (1915), pp. 191–4.

[3] W. S. Childe-Pemberton, *Life of Lord Norton* (1909), pp. 127, 136, 140.

[4] 3 *Hansard*, cxxxv, col. 1552 (12 August 1854).

Courts by an Act empowering them to introduce viva voce examinations of witnesses.[1] Thus, despite the rhetoric of opposition politicians and of pacifist propagandists, the session of 1854 was by the standards of that decade a reasonably fruitful one.

It was in the succeeding session far more than in 1854 that the influence of the war unmistakably made itself felt. Yet that influence was very far from being a stultifying one. One of the most striking characteristics of the national heart-searching of the early spring and summer of 1855 was its concentration upon domestic institutions, both political and social, as the explanation of the disasters. Technical difficulties, personal faults, accidents and coincidences, the weather — factors like these received scant attention, and grandiose arraignments of parliamentary government, centralizing bureaucracy and aristocratic privilege were the rule. Inside Parliament, a vast amount of time was taken up by hysterical attacks upon the Government's conduct of the war and by generalized discussion of aristocratic privilege in the Army and the civil departments, as well as by the mass of additional legislative business entailed by the war, far greater than in 1854. Yet the volume of legislation passed in this session was the second highest of the decade. Although it included only one really important controversial measure of reform, a very substantial number of lesser measures were achieved. Some of these were a response to the outburst of radicalism outdoors, while the Order in Council of 21 May, conceding limited competition as the method of recruitment to most Government departments, was obviously carefully timed to outmanœuvre those who were campaigning for recruitment by open competition alone both inside and outside Parliament. By the autumn of 1855 radicals who supported the war (naturally the pacifists did not agree) were able to argue that far from introducing a period of quiescence in domestic affairs, the war had acted as a stimulus to change. They had always claimed that

[1] These four Acts are 17 & 18 Vict., cc. 86, 94, 90, 47.

there was no *need* for war to end social progress. Towards the end of 1854 Harriet Martineau wrote in her column in the *Daily News*: 'When, a year ago, the Peace Party and *The Times* newspaper [which opposed war in the autumn of 1853] were groaning over the state of barbarism we should be reduced to when our science, arts, literature and social reforms should all be depressed and neglected for the sake of war, we exhibited more than once historical proofs of the great progress made in all these respects even during the fearful and engrossing war of the early part of the century. . . . There need be no fear that our domestic sufferers will be less cared for, because the national heart is warmed, and everyone's hand opened, on behalf of human right and welfare on a broader scale.'[1] A year later more exacting radical commentators than Harriet Martineau found abundant proof that the war had indeed benefited their cause, and in more tangible ways than these, not only in the field of opinion, but in the field of statute law itself.

The repeal of compulsory stamp duties on newspapers in March 1855 was regarded as a major triumph by radicals of every hue, and its final accomplishment was clearly the result of the intense public hunger for cheap daily war news after the landing of British troops in the Crimea. 'The Holy War of the unstamped press' was one of the many highly moral, almost quasi-religious campaigns of the period whose substructure of sectional interest received judiciously little publicity. From 1853 onwards the repeal of the compulsory newspaper stamp duty was presented to Parliament and the country as a great educational measure, a 'war against political and religious ignorance' by the Manchester men, Chartists, secularists and Urquhartites who ran the campaign.[2] The Crimean winter of 1854–5 presented them with telling new arguments and powerful new allies. The growing demand for a continuous flow of cheap war news after the battle of the Alma prompted

---

[1] *Daily News*, 18 November 1854.
[2] G. J. Holyoake, *Sixty Years of an Agitator's Life* (1906), p. 283.

the appearance of a shoal of provincial penny war-sheets as other men in the trade followed the lead given by the astute editor of the *Edinburgh Guardian*, J. W. Finlay. Their legal position was ambiguous enough to harass the already vexed Revenue authorities still further, but their immediate success roused the influential owners of the provincial weeklies to action. Most of these penny war-sheets soon ceased publication on the threat of legal proceedings, but not before they had won mass support for the movement and proved beyond all doubt that penny dailies were what the public wanted. No London dailies then sold at less than fivepence, but with penny news-sheets, as C. D. Collett, the secretary of the campaign, saw, 'they got more in proportion for their money and had only one day instead of seven to wait for their news'.[1] The campaigners for repeal were enabled to draw affecting pictures of wives, sweethearts and aged parents deprived by the Stamp Duty of the speedy news whose comfort and support they most wanted. Quite as decisive with the governing class was the irresistible cogency given by the activities of *The Times* during that winter to the argument that the range and ownership of the Press must be widened. The monopoly of the London daily press, above all of the bulky *Times*, had undeniably been built upon the competitive advantage given by the compulsory stamp, with its accompanying right to unlimited postal transmission regardless of weight. In the spring of 1855 it appeared to many influential people that to end that competitive advantage would be to strike a real blow against the tyranny of *The Times*.[2] Nor were these expectations mistaken, despite the fact that the measure actually passed was something of a compromise, since it introduced a special cheap rate allowing four ounces of printed

[1] C. D. Collett, *The History of the Taxes on Knowledge* (1899), ii. 4–17; cf. Holyoake, op. cit., p. 289.

[2] The official historian of *The Times* sees the whole campaign as in reality a political move directed at *The Times* (*History of The Times*, ii. 193–215).

matter to be sent through the post for one penny. *The Times*, however, alone of the London dailies, weighed more than this. Thus the repeal of the Stamp Duties did indeed usher in the heyday of the provincial press, the beginning of the decline of *The Times* as the circulation leader of the daily newspapers, and the appearance of the first national penny daily, the *Daily Telegraph*, on 29 June 1855. By 1860 over a thousand newspapers were in existence. The immediate political results of the change were not what the Tories had feared or the radicals had hoped. 'Inconvenience, trouble and loss have been the result for us', acknowledged the *People's Paper* after a few months' experience,[1] and it was not long before astute politicians discovered the Tory potentialities of a cheap daily press.[2] But the mechanics of founding and managing a news-paper had been vastly eased — 'news was no longer criminal and editors were no longer a criminal class who had to give heavy bail for their good behaviour', as Holyoake rejoiced[3] — and the radical and lower-middle-class element in the com-position of public opinion had been decisively increased.

Another radical triumph of lasting importance whose accom-plishment was much assisted by the Crimean scandals, was the victory for local self-government represented by the Nuisances Removal Act and the Metropolis Local Manage-ment Act, a turning-point in the sanitary history and admini-strative evolution of London.[4] The triumph of the vestry movement and the peculiar constitution of the Metropolitan Board of Works to which the administration of London was thereby entrusted may indeed in the event have condemned metropolis and provinces alike to anarchy and unwise economy for more than a generation. Nevertheless both measures were welcomed by the radicals of the day as 'the commencement

---

[1] *People's Paper*, 18 August 1855.

[2] Cf. S. Maccoby, 'Newspaper Politics: A footnote to nineteenth-century history', *Politica*, i (1934), 213–14.

[3] Op. cit., p. 296.

[4] H. Jephson, *The Sanitary Evolution of London* (1907), pp. 82–89; cf. the comments in A. Briggs, *Victorian Cities* (1963), p. 333.

of a series of measures for giving to the different localities of the country self-government in matters that belong to them'.[1] The same attitude ensured a radical welcome for the Acts giving a constitution to New South Wales and Victoria, by which 'the finishing stroke has been given to the self-government of the Australian colonies'.[2] To working-class radicals the Friendly Societies Act even more obviously deserved a welcome, and their judgment was right, for it proved satisfactory enough to remain in force for twenty years, longer than any other piece of legislation in this much legislated-for field. Among other provisions, it abolished all fees for registration and permitted societies which did not wish to register to gain legal recognition by merely depositing a copy of their rules with the Registrar. Disputes were to go before the County Courts instead of the Registrar, although this was not to interfere with the right of a society to settle its disputes in accordance with its own rules where they made provision for doing so — an important point for the powerful affiliated orders.[3] Another Act which fully proved its value to the provident and self-improving worker was the Public Libraries Act of 1855, which went a good deal further than the first Act of 1850 since it brought towns with a population of only 5,000 within its scope, doubled the rate which could be levied, and for the first time authorized the expenditure of this revenue upon the purchase of books and newspapers.[4]

A measure which despite its brief life was important as breaking a deadlock and preparing the ground for a fuller measure was the Act to confer Limited Liability by Registration, which went some way to meet the public demand for improvement of the law of partnership. Familiar arguments that the existing law was an obstacle to philanthropy and checked local improvements and attempts at workers' co-

[1] *The Leader*, 11 August 1855. Cf. above, pp. 137–8.   [2] Ibid.

[3] P. H. J. H. Gosden, *The Friendly Societies in England* (Manchester, 1961), p. 182.

[4] A. Redford, *A History of Local Government in Manchester* (1940), ii. 228, shows the importance of this Act in Manchester.

operation, were reinforced by the argument that it bestowed unfair privilege upon rich and powerful companies — an argument powerful enough in the atmosphere of 1855 to precipitate a great leap forward towards the general limited liability which came in 1856. The radical press welcomed the Act of 1855 with enthusiasm — indeed the Government was accused of rushing the Act through at the end of the session in order to pander to public opinion.[1] 'It cannot fail to affect the condition of small capitalists very advantage-ously,' wrote *The Leader* on 11 August, and pointed out how valuable to the co-operative movement was Goderich's suc-cessful amendment, bringing the minimum capital and mini-mum amount of each share of a registered company down to the figures of £250 and £10 respectively (as against £20,000 and £25). Limited liability had thus been made very much more accessible, and the Act of 1855, although repealed by the Joint Stock Companies Act a year later, represents an im-portant breakthrough in a field where since 1844 there had been much discussion and very little else. With these develop-ments in company law the conditions had been created for the modern era of public investment.

Among lesser measures, the powers of the Charity Commis-sioners were usefully extended, an improved Coal Mines In-spection Bill was passed, and the statutes prohibiting Anglican worship in any unlicensed place in the presence of more than twenty persons at last repealed, though only after a struggle with the bishops and conservatives in the Lords. Lord Shaftesbury[2] had thus enabled the Established Church to rival nonconformity in multiplying prayer meetings, Bible Classes, and Missions to the working classes. In the field of law reform, the opposition of the lawyers and bishops brought disappointments again. No Bill on matrimonial cases was even

[1] H. A. Shannon, 'The coming of general limited liability', *Economic History*, ii (1931), 289.

[2] E. Hodder, *The Life and Work of the seventh Earl of Shaftesbury* (1887), p. 511.

introduced, and a Testamentary Jurisdiction Bill was lost
once more. Nevertheless a number of small legal reforms were
successfully carried, the most important of which were
Brougham's two Acts giving summary jurisdiction to magis-
trates for small offences and summary process to creditors
upon bills of exchange,[1] and one giving some protection to
purchasers by providing that incumbrances on estates should
be registered (though Cranworth's larger Bill for the Registration of Deeds was lost because of Bethell's preference for the
registration of title).[2] In the field of education likewise, although none of the three major measures introduced was
carried, this was not the fault of the war but of permanent
obstacles to legislation, in this case those created by religious
feeling. One of these bills (Sir John Pakington's) was at least
a landmark in educational thought, if not in educational
policy, with its acknowledgement that the voluntary system
had broken down and its attempt to introduce 'National
Education' paid for by an education rate. Even here one much
smaller step was accomplished — an Act for securing the
education of pauper children by allowing Boards of Guardians
to grant sums for the education of their children to parents
receiving outdoor relief. Lastly, although very many more
years were to pass before conservatism over parliamentary
procedure could be overcome — an obviously useful proposal
that re-election should not be necessary for ministers who
simply changed office was lost, for example, though only by
four votes[3] — provision was made for the first time for the
performance of the Speaker's duties in his absence.[4] Under the
Deputy-Speaker Act the functioning of the House at last
ceased to be entirely dependent on the health of one man.
Many working-class radicals, however, attached more importance to two negative episodes than to any of these achieve-

---

[1] Cf. John McGilchrist, *Life of Henry, Lord Brougham* (1868), p. 215.
[2] Atlay, op. cit., p. 72; 3 *Hansard*, cxxxix, col. 1190 (20 July 1855).
[3] 3 *Hansard*, cxxxvii, col. 1279 (28 March 1855).
[4] Redlich, op. cit., ii. 170.

ments: the repeal of the Act passed in 1854 for the regulation of the sale of beer on the Lord's Day, and the withdrawal of Lord Robert Grosvenor's Bill prohibiting Sunday trading in the metropolis. Sabbatarian measures like these were obviously class measures, and radicals regarded them as barely disguised class-victimization. Their withdrawal was the direct result of large-scale mobbing of the carriages of the well-to-do in Hyde Park on three successive Sundays.[1] As a consequence, licensing hours were restored to their previous limits, and shopping continued to be possible on Sunday — a genuinely important working-class consideration.

These anti-Sabbatarian victories provide a good illustration of the alteration the Crimean disasters made in the prevailing climate of opinion in matters quite unconnected with the war, through the stimulus they gave to criticism of established institutions in general, whether political, social or religious. It is indeed striking how many people felt confident at the end of 1855 that two years of war had done more for equality in England than twenty years of discussion. 'La guerre en ce moment en Angleterre est un grand instrument d'égalité ou de nivellement', the *Journal des Débats* remarked in a passage eagerly seized upon by George Holyoake.[2] This secularist crusader's favourite platform theme at the end of 1855 and beginning of 1856 was the revolutionary effects of the war on English politics and theology.[3] Its liberalizing effect upon the religious atmosphere was a point which Holyoake in his addresses to secularist societies naturally exploited to the utmost; but few people in 1855 would have disputed that the British public's zeal for victory had also succeeded in overcoming that social deference and political traditionalism for which the British were renowned. 'John Bull loves his lords,

[1] Cf. 3 *Hansard*, cxxxix, cols. 183, 1607 (26 June, 31 July 1855).

[2] The *Reasoner*, 6 January 1856; *Journal des Débats politiques et littéraires*, 25 December 1855.

[3] See the handbills advertising his lectures pasted into his Diaries at the Bishopsgate Institute, 18 November 1855, 13 and 17 January, 11 and 23 February 1856.

but he loves beating his enemy more,' as *The Reasoner* put it.[1] In 1855 it could well be claimed that the aristocracy were the real insurgents, with their exhibition of gross incapacity. Holyoake liked to exclaim that the Aberdeen Coalition had made half a dozen revolutions by revealing the inadequacies of existing domestic institutions. 'The middle class', he was optimistically declaiming in the winter of 1855–6, 'have been called to power', and 'new prospects have opened out for the people.' The recruiting sergeants had been turned into reformers. It was indeed true that the poor physique and illiteracy of the recruits who enlisted for the Crimea had shocked many thoughtful people into a new concern for elementary education and public health, particularly in the rural districts which were the Army's traditional catchment area. Holyoake went on to congratulate his audiences that 'their health, leisure and holidays were at last cared for',[2] and the sanitary measures, housing and public libraries Acts of the session, together with the check administered to Sabbatarian legislation, gave substance to his claim.

Reflections like these upon the political and social impact of the war were commonplace enough. Holyoake was much more of a *rara avis* in his claim that the war had also done something to undermine the Anglican supremacy and popular theological beliefs in England. To him as a militant secularist this was the greatest benefit of all the many benefits the war bestowed; and indeed the dominant evangelicalism of the day was so generally assumed to be the buttress of the *status quo*, that the small circle of secularists were not alone in predicting increased radical strength as a result of the impatience with certain aspects of evangelical theology which the war encouraged. Scepticism about the wisdom of passive acquiescence in the divine will and appreciation of the need for practical human effort, for example, had become much more explicit.

[1] *The Reasoner*, 18 March 1855.
[2] Précis of Lecture on 'The beneficial results of the war upon the liberties and opinions of England', Diary, 11 February 1856.

The public estimated Florence Nightingale more highly than all the chaplains with the Army. Proselytizing among the troops had been forbidden and for the first time a general regulation had been made providing for the payment of Roman Catholic and Presbyterian in the same way as Anglican chaplains. Most significant of all, the Government's injudicious use of Days of Fasting, Humiliation and Prayer had provoked much impatience.[1] Admittedly in the optimism of the first few weeks of war, the Proclamation of a Fast on April 26 had been received with acquiescence, even enthusiasm.[2] But in the totally different atmosphere of March 1855, when a second 'Public Day of Solemn Fast, Humiliation and Prayer' was proclaimed 'in order to obtain pardon of our sins', there was open disorder in the streets, scanty attendance at divine service, widely expressed doubt about the justice of depriving the labouring poor of a day's wages, and an almost universal feeling that it was not the nation, but ministers and officials who needed to humble themselves, before man as well as God. Without a doubt in succumbing to evangelical pressure to proclaim this Fast,[3] Palmerston simply revealed once more how completely he had failed to grasp the intensity of the country's response to the Crimean revelations. His apparent attempt to exploit the widespread theological interpretation of the war as a divine punishment for national sin was too provocative to be borne in silence. Even in the pulpits human misdeeds were often pungently censured;[4] and in the radical press the perennial cry that the Established Church was merely the buttress of the governing class grew much louder.

---

[1] This subject is more fully discussed by the present author in *Journal of Ecclesiastical History*, xvi (1965).

[2] Newspaper reports unanimously give this impression, e.g. *Morning Chronicle*, 26 and 27 April 1854.

[3] Shaftesbury's conversion of the Archbishop of Canterbury was decisive (Broadlands Archives, The Queen to Palmerston, 16 February 1855, and Hodder, op. cit., p. 503).

[4] See the press reports of popular preachers' Fast Day Sermons, for example in *The Nonconformist*, 28 March 1855.

The impression that the Fast Day was resorted to simply as a safe and costless way of soothing an angry public — 'Try fasting to get you out of this mess!' as Dickens's *Household Words* put it[1] — was a very widespread one indeed. Even among the devout, the argument and criticism that this step provoked (particularly among voluntaryists and nonconformists) contributed much to that deep impatience with the Establishment in Church as well as State which distinguished 1855, and made it inevitable that the Sabbatarian legislation projected in that year should be successfully denounced as yet another piece of pious humbug and class hypocrisy. At least it was certain that in future such proclamations would be used with more caution. 'Instead of a new prayer by the Archbishop of Canterbury for the success of our failing arms in the Crimea, we had a Committee of Inquiry,' Holyoake congratulated the readers of *The Reasoner* as the year 1856 opened.[2]

Thus radical gains from that storm of resentment against aristocratic privilege, bureaucracy and bungling which somewhat irrationally gripped the British public in 1855 were substantial, and they were not achieved at the expense of other kinds of domestic progress. By the end of the year a substantial instalment of the reforms which Sir Arthur Elton had claimed the war was preventing,[3] had in fact been accomplished. Such setbacks as there undoubtedly were found a pretext, but no more, in the war, and they were more than counterbalanced by the stimulus it gave to such major steps as the repeal of the stamp duties on newspapers and the recruitment of the Civil Service by competitive examination, as well as a host of lesser measures.

The Crimean War, like so many others whose course took a very different turn from any that had been expected, thus brought not social solidarity and domestic stagnation, but a violent explosion of class feeling and a varied series of attacks on existing institutions, liberalism and a free government

[1] 24 March 1855.   [2] 6 January 1856.   [3] See above, p. 164.

N

notwithstanding. Its conduct gave those who made these attacks a vast amount of gratuitous ammunition, in the shape both of telling arguments and deep public indignation and concern. Admittedly the revolution so widely hailed in 1855 proved to be a totally bloodless affair which to all appearances had collapsed long before peace was signed. But in reality this short-lived radical outburst profoundly affected the course of English history in the later nineteenth century. By vastly increasing middle-class self-confidence and the attraction of middle-class ideals of efficiency, hard work and self-help, it promoted the emergence of that well-integrated class culture which permitted the peaceful transition to democracy accomplished in later Victorian England. For at least a generation, a broadly similar moral outlook permeated those just below as well as those just above the middle classes. It was in this groundwork of cultural unity that the co-operation between middle- and working-class political movements so striking in the post-Crimean generation took root and flourished, often under the patronage of the governing classes, until the withering winds of economic change began to blow in the later 1870s. Secondly, the public disgrace of the state machine during the Crimean War won a decisive victory for a powerful movement which was already gathering momentum — the movement which put backward-looking theories of local self-government and non-interference by the central departments of the state before programmes of public welfare. In the third quarter of the nineteenth century, the development of state control and of national uniformity may have crept inexorably on, but it did so far more slowly and in an immensely more indirect and illogical way than it would otherwise have done, because of the victory of the anti-centralizers and the myths of the ancient constitution to which the Crimean disasters contributed the final push. The radicalism whose triumph the Crimean War promoted in England was a radicalism of a petty bourgeois, pseudo-antiquarian kind. It was thus a limited and specialized triumph; but its results persisted for over a generation.

PART THREE

The Economic Policies
of the Crimean War

I F the performance of Britain's unique political institutions in the Crimean War seemed to place contemporary patterns of public life on trial, the performance of the country's equally unique economic institutions was as often regarded as testing the capacity of economic liberalism to meet the strain of war. In the fields of public finance, foreign trade, currency and credit alike, Britain since 1815 had evolved distinctive policies which had provoked bitter controversies among contemporaries, controversies which the advent of the war fanned into new life. Later generations have turned to the Crimean War even more compulsively for dramatic illustrations of a theme — the dominance of economic liberalism in the mid-nineteenth century. It has become a time-honoured habit to find in its economic policies striking proof of the hold of *laissez-faire* ideas upon both government and public in Britain, and accordingly to exclaim upon their dissimilarity from the policies pursued in former wars. Thus the Crimean episode has habitually been regarded as exhibiting the triumph of political economy at the expense of patriotism, or at the least of a really strenuous war effort. 'Never had war been fought with more deference to the requirements of trade', writes one standard authority on the period, and goes on to describe Britain's substantial abandonment of her belligerent rights at sea, culminating in her signature of the Declaration of Paris at the end of the war.[1] The admirers of Gladstonian finance and Manchester School ideas of public expenditure have singled it out for praise as 'the best financed of our great wars',[2] and later scholars have repeatedly made the point

[1] R. C. Binkley, *Realism and Nationalism, 1852–71* (New York, 1935), p. 176.

[2] F. W. Hirst, *The Political Economy of War* (1915), p. 143. Similarly, S. Buxton, *Mr. Gladstone as Chancellor of the Exchequer* (1901), p. 19, and C. F. Bastable, *Public Finance* (1st edn., 1892), p. 637.

that this was a war financed without strain by an increased income tax, and distinguished by the absence of government borrowing.[1] Similarly, those concerned to expound the internationalism of finance capital in the nineteenth century, and the freedom of currency and credit from government interference, have also turned to the Crimean War for support. In particular, 'the curious case of the loan floated for Russia in London in the midst of the Crimean War' — a purely imaginary event — has reappeared in one standard work after another with dramatic effect.[2]

All of this is profoundly misleading, both as to government policies and public attitudes. The Crimean War represents neither a drastic departure from the economic policies of former wars, nor the triumph of political economy in the minds of government and public. Patriotism and the desire for victory were not submerged, either by doctrinaire economics or by the lust for wealth. In reality government policy and public opinion alike were far less dogmatic and far less novel than those who turn to the Crimean War to illustrate the themes of *laissez-faire* and economic internationalism in mid-nineteenth-century Britain usually assume. The use of government control in order to ensure the maximum exploitation of the sinews of war was more elaborately and carefully considered than it had ever been. In some cases it was exercised more than before, although in others less, or quite differently, in response to changed ideas and conditions and enemy circumstances. In short, in the Crimean War at least as much as in other wars the British Government possessed an economic policy for victory, and moreover one subject to pragmatic revision and debate.

Before embarking upon a detailed consideration of this policy, some general considerations may perhaps be noticed

---

[1] Sir John Clapham, *An Economic History of Modern Britain*, ii (1932), p. 365; A. Ramm in *The New Cambridge Modern History*, x (1960), p. 486.

[2] L. H. Jenks, *The Migration of British Capital to 1875* (New York, 1927), p. 285; A. Briggs, op. cit. (1959), p. 399; Binkley, op. cit., p. 176.

which suggest that a prima facie case exists for re-examining the familiar verdicts upon the economic side of the Crimean War. In the first place, it is now well appreciated that the classical economists disagreed over many questions of economics, and cannot be regarded without qualification as the apostles of governmental non-interference. To Nassau Senior, for example, one of the most rigid exponents of 'the dismal science', it became increasingly clear that questions of government policy could not be settled simply by general economic principles,[1] and from Adam Smith onwards defence in particular had been put before opulence. Secondly, it has recently been observed more than once that a distinguishing characteristic of the 'new men' of mid-nineteenth-century Britain was their faith in empirical observation, in statistical arguments, in 'tabular certainties'.[2] Admittedly it is also true that very often this passion for facts barely concealed an equally lively passion for dogma, and that in this as in any other age what men believed in and were concerned about, was much affected by their conception of their interests. But even so, it seems unlikely that such men should have abandoned traditional belligerent practices and policies without attempting a careful assessment of the real cost, both in purely military terms and in terms of that well-being of the whole national economy and morale upon which they well understood victory would depend in a long and costly struggle. Finally, a third, even more general consideration carries even more weight: the reflection that this was indeed 'the age of equipoise' in England, to use the phrase of one recent authority.[3] This was not the age of individualism, or *laissez-faire*, or

---

[1] M. Bowley, *Nassau Senior and Classical Economics* (1937), p. 252. For a more general discussion, see L. Robbins, *The Theory of Economic Policy* (1952), especially pp. 34–67.

[2] O. R. McGregor, 'Social Research and Social Policy in the nineteenth century', *British Journal of Sociology*, viii (1957), 146; O. MacDonagh, *A Pattern of Government Growth 1800–1860* (1961), p. 252.

[3] W. L. Burn, who first used the phrase in an article of that title in *Nineteenth Century and After*, cxlvi (1949).

Manchesterismus; it was an age distinguished by the very large number of major debates upon which opinion was pretty evenly divided and of which the outcome was perforce a compromise, an age when society possessed as many traditionalists as progressives, an age in which emotion and sentiment gathered round a rosy future in some quarters, but around a rosy past in as many others. That the Crimean War should have been 'the Free Trade War', *tout court*, is thus highly unlikely. It is now hoped to show that a detailed investigation does indeed reveal that it was nothing of the sort; and that it was not widely regarded at the time in that light, although distorted and polemical interpretations soon spread when hostilities came to an abrupt end.

Nevertheless there is one single consideration which throws so much light upon every aspect of thought about the economics of the war that it deserves notice at the outset. It is not economic liberalism in any shape or form, but the force — both by attraction and repulsion — of the nation's economic experiences during the great French wars fifty years before. It was the ghost of the Revolutionary and Napoleonic Wars which presided over British economic policies and ideas during the Crimean War, just as it haunted public expectations and anticipations at the outbreak of hostilities. The suspension of cash payments, lavish subsidies to foreign allies, a high income tax, heavy government borrowing, the control of trade through Orders in Council and licences to trade with the enemy — it was to these traumatic experiences of their grandfathers that men's minds returned when a European war was to be fought once more. That this was so was not simply a reflection of the habit of discussing public issues in historical terms, still less a proof of Nathaniel Hawthorne's acumen in exclaiming at that time upon the 'heavy and cloddish tendency of the English to cling to old ideas'.[1] The preoccupation of thoughtful Englishmen during the Crimean War with the economic experience of the previous generation

[1] Entry for 16 September, 1855, in *The English Notebooks*, p. 227.

was the product of far more than natural conservatism or the growing prestige of 'the lessons of history'. It was imposed by the whole course of economic argument since 1815. So bitterly debated had been the expedients to which the economic dislocations of the war years from 1793 to 1815 gave rise, that they formed the inevitable starting-point for the arguments of the forty years of peace. Thus when war broke out again in 1854 it merely precipitated a return to first principles in an argument which had not yet been concluded, and this was so in the fields of budgetary policy, foreign trade and currency and credit alike. To most of the disputants these earlier experiences were awful warnings, to a smaller number they were instructive examples. But together, those who condemned and those who admired were so numerous and so firmly entrenched, that even those progressives who believed that the profound changes which had occurred in English economic life and legislation since 1815 had made the past irrelevant, could not ignore it. Willy-nilly, and whether they believed it was for good or ill, in the field of war-time economic policy neither government nor public escaped the compulsion their generation felt to look backward as well as forward.

CHAPTER SIX

War Finance

IN 1854 it was still agreed that the cardinal sin of the Younger Pitt and his immediate successors in financing the Revolutionary and Napoleonic Wars was their vast expansion of the National Debt. For thirty years 'the funding system' had been the favourite target of a country convinced as never before that financial problems lay at the root of all the nation's evils. There were rival schools of thought about taxes and tariffs, currency and credit, but there was near-unanimity in condemning the National Debt. To the agriculturalists the war-swollen debt was chiefly responsible for the crushing weight of taxation which they complained they endured, and it was almost equally resented by the industrialists, because they believed it had involved a vast waste of capital and consequently retarded economic expansion. The remedies proposed did indeed vary. Among the agricultural community economy in government spending and the reduction, redemption or even repudiation of the Debt had many supporters, while industrialists often wished to rely upon promoting the rapid increase of national wealth and thus lightening the Debt burden comparatively although not absolutely. But in 1854 public and private indebtedness were almost always[1] regarded in exactly the same light, and both roundly condemned. It was still common form to assert that

---

[1] 'M. B.', The Public Debt, its influence and management considered in a different point of view from Sir H. Parnell's (1831) questions whether the Debt was harmful, and Coleridge and McCulloch argued that it stimulated production and demand and promoted the accumulation of capital, but these were not the usual views. Cf. the conclusion of B. A. Corry, Money, Saving and Investment in English Economics 1800–1850 (1962), pp. 170–1.

British taxation was exceptionally high[1] and to ascribe this and the reputed extravagance of British Governments to the Pittite habit of borrowing. The bogy of the National Debt, and not any general theory of war finance, was thus still the ordinary man's starting-point when it again became necessary to finance what was expected to be an epic struggle. Four rules for salvation from this bogy had by then long seemed clear: abstention from subsidies, loans or guarantees to foreign allies or auxiliaries; immediate resort to a high income tax; avoidance of the creation of fictitious capitals, if borrowing despite these measures became necessary; and finally, no sinking fund save that provided by whatever surplus income might arise each year, or by the use of terminable annuities.

The earliest of these cautionary rules to take shape was the denunciation of foreign loans and subsidies. £57 million had been spent thus between 1793 and 1816 with little military advantage. But this aversion from the role of paymaster of Europe had even older and more emotional roots in the ancient debate between the 'continental' strategists and the blue water school, and in 1854 and for long afterwards it remained a phobia to be reckoned with. The belief that war expenditure should be met by taxation, and particularly by an income tax, was only slightly less widely held and emerged only a little more slowly. Already in 1823 that most active publicist among the economists, J. R. McCulloch, was maintaining that if there were another war, the Government's first resort should be an income tax of 10–12%[2]. But McCulloch was a notorious zealot for taxation. Sir Henry Parnell's striking deductions from the experience of the French wars made a far more serious impression. According to a much-quoted passage in Parnell's very widely read book, *On Financial Reform*, published in

[1] Indeed the cry for Government economy had been particularly loud since 1848. G. W. Norman with his demonstration that taxation abroad was far higher than in Britain (*The Pressure of Taxation in this and other Countries* (1850)) was a voice crying in the wilderness.

[2] *Edinburgh Review*, xxxiv. 1–43.

1830, 'if an income tax of only 5% had been imposed at the beginning of the war, and then increased, the whole expenditure of the wars might have been met without loans'.[1] Sir Henry Parnell preferred a war income tax of even 15% to all other forms of taxation or borrowing, on the ground that this would interfere least with trade and industry. He was convinced that, provided economic development was encouraged to the hilt, borrowing could be entirely avoided in any future war, and his figures purporting to demonstrate the avoidability of Pitt's vast loans caught and held the public imagination.[2] Nevertheless although it was widely assumed in 1854 that the proper course was to levy a heavy income tax at the very outset, only the very optimistic or the rigidly doctrinaire believed that borrowing could be wholly avoided if the war proved at all lengthy. But even the most cautious felt confident that the expansion of the National Debt on a Pittite scale need never happen again. Pitt had been misled by 'the fraudulence of ingenious reasoning on the part of monied men', wrote Parnell, into adopting the method of funding fictitious capitals in a stock bearing a low rate of interest.[3] This had led to a vast nominal increase in the capital of the Debt, and hence to a correspondingly large increase in the permanent burden of servicing it; it had also made the peace-time reduction of interest difficult. The lesson was clear: to borrow always in real capitals, and allow the bargain to be struck only in varying rates of interest, or in *douceurs* like terminable annuities. Men familiar with the money market dismissed the former method as impracticable,[4] since stocks of

[1] p. 285.

[2] McCulloch's argument that the money which Pitt failed to collect by taxation presumably increased at compound interest and that therefore the extra cost of financing the early years of the war by borrowing was no more than £52 million (*Taxation and the Funding System* (Edinburgh, 1845), p. 421) made little impact.

[3] Op. cit., p. 297.

[4] It was however a favourite prescription of McCulloch's, urged, for example, in his very successful *Dictionary of Commerce and Commercial Navigation* (1st edn., 1832–9), s.n. 'Funds'.

such varied denominations would be unacceptable to the
dealers. (The retort was sometimes made that the Government
should in that case throw open government loans to the small
investor.) But even the most sober men were attracted by the
doctrine of borrowing in three per cents at par supplemented
by terminable annuities. Indeed, terminable annuities by the
1850s were rapidly becoming an Aladdin's lamp to make all
difficulties disappear, for they had also become the favourite
substitute for a sinking fund. In the 1820s sharp criticism and
ridicule had fastened upon both the machinery of Pitt's
sinking fund, and its underlying principle that 'war would
accelerate the redemption of the public debts, and it would do
this the more, the longer it lasted and the higher it raised the
interest of money'. It was now realized that the apparently
impressive redemption during the war of £300 million of
Debt through the sinking fund had been achieved only by
borrowing afresh on more onerous terms. The famous Fourth
Report of the Select Committee on Public Income and Expenditure, presented to the House of Commons in 1828 — a
document rivalled in impact only by Parnell's *On Financial
Reform* — secured the complete triumph of the doctrine that
Debt redemption should be attempted only through the use of
whatever real surplus income might arise each year. Eccentric
pamphleteers continued to devise schemes for special levies to
redeem the Debt, or to urge its more or less complete repudiation, but responsible opinion and official action henceforth
concentrated upon conversion — either into stocks bearing a
lower rate of interest, or into terminable annuities. Thus by
1854 terminable annuities had been widely canvassed both as
a means of gradually extinguishing the existing Debt, and as
a means of preventing fresh borrowing in any future war from
permanently increasing the National Debt.

It is clear then that the single most important source of
ideas on war finance when the war broke out was the manifold
criticisms which had been levelled against Pitt's borrowing
policy for over a generation. The framework within which the

budgetary policy of the Crimean War was developed and debated was a framework composed of four rules of thumb in war finance which had emerged in the period of unparalleled financial argument which started in the last decade of Pitt's life. But it was a framework which proved far more flimsy than most people anticipated. In the end the Crimean War was financed by many heterogeneous devices and a series of increasingly traditional compromises — devices and compromises which provoked debate at many levels but secured acceptance at most. The opinionated optimists who had expected to demonstrate to the world that it was possible to finance a major war from income tax alone, were disappointed. Those who were eager to demonstrate the magical properties of borrowing in terminable annuities were given little chance to do so. The unfashionable machinery of a sinking fund reappeared, and although foreign subsidies were avoided, foreign loans were not — and the best informed believed these were subsidies in all but name. There was no repetition of Pitt's war finance; but neither was there any demonstration of the efficacy of the new doctrines associated with Gladstone and Sir Henry Parnell. In the end the finance of the Crimean War was predominantly pragmatic, and the many-sided debate it provoked owes its interest to its comprehensiveness and often considerable sophistication, and not to any exhibition of mid-nineteenth-century devotion to a single set of doctrines.

The central issue was from the beginning the Chancellor of the Exchequer's decisions as between loans and taxes. Could and should the gospel of financing war from an income tax alone be preached and practised throughout a large-scale war of any duration? The progressively minded laymen of that day, steeped in economic vulgarizations more than ever before or since, and perpetually aware of the shadow of the Debt, were inclined to believe it could. Gladstone, who was Chancellor of the Exchequer when war broke out, in his first war-time budget speech gave powerful expression to this somewhat commonplace view, characteristically adding a strong moral argument to the more familiar historical and economic ones. 'The expenses of a war are the moral check which it has pleased the Almighty to impose upon the ambition and lust of conquest that are inherent in so many nations,' he informed the House of Commons. 'The necessity of meeting from year to year the expenditure which it entails is a salutary and whole-some check, making them feel what they are about, and making them measure the cost of the benefit upon which they may calculate.'[1] But such a very simple 'taxes only' position quickly began to be untenable at the Treasury and then unconvincing to the lay public. The City, the traditionalists and certain academic economists who had from the outset had little patience with the very commonplace 'lessons of history' with which Gladstone had associated himself, were soon joined by many moderate members of the public and the Government, including Gladstone himself — although he never cared to admit it.

For Gladstone made more use of borrowing in the Crimean War than has been realized, thanks no doubt to the evasions and sophistries to which he resorted in defending his actions. On 6 March 1854, in one of his most telling speeches, he had drawn a solemn (and in reality stale) lesson from Pitt's war finance: the whole real accumulation of permanent debt in the Revolutionary and Napoleonic Wars could have been avoided if Pitt had raised revenue by imposing heavy taxation from the very beginning of the war instead of borrowing freely in stocks far below par. But only six weeks after Gladstone had taken this emphatic stand upon financing the war by taxation, the Treasury offered for sale £6 million of Exchequer Bonds, repayable in three series of £2 million each in 1858, 1859 and 1860. Not surprisingly, he was at once attacked for incon-sistency, and also for lack of wisdom in using this particular method of borrowing (the City often thought poorly of Glad-stone's novel financial devices). He thereupon claimed that the

[1] 3 *Hansard*, cxxxi, col. 376 (6 March 1854).

Bonds were 'no loan, but a provision for the temporary raising of money', and evaded the subject as much as possible.[1] In the event his critics were justified, for these Exchequer Bonds were never redeemed. Instead they were added to the funded Debt, Gladstone himself being responsible in 1860 for remitting taxation instead of redeeming one series. Such an upshot was always so probable that it was pure disingenuousness on Gladstone's part to refuse to regard the Bonds as in any sense a loan. Nor was his use of Exchequer Bills free from the same kind of mystification and evasion. Towards the end of the first year of the war, a former Whig Chancellor of the Exchequer, Thomas Spring-Rice, first Lord Monteagle (a man with a passion for detail and one of Gladstone's sharpest critics), claimed in the House of Lords that the Exchequer Bills Bill for 1855 concealed a surreptitious abandonment of the policy of reliance upon taxes. Gladstone, he maintained, had specifically undertaken in the previous May that the £1,750,000 of Exchequer Bills for which he then asked would be paid off as soon as the proceeds of taxation came in; but by this Bill they were added to the Exchequer Bills annually renewed and so 'slipped in' to the permanent floating Debt. In the Commons a few days later Gladstone failed to make his defence really clear, but seemed to claim that although he had originally asked for these Bills merely to anticipate revenue, a few weeks later he had taken credit for them as part of the Ways and Means for the year.[2] But he had certainly never explicitly announced the change in the nature of these Bills. This half-concealed addition to the unfunded Debt,[3] together with the deficit of £2 million which had accumulated by the

[1] 3 *Hansard*, cxxxii, cols. 1074, 1176 and 1462 (1, 2 and 8 May 1854).

[2] Ibid. cxxxvii, cols. 462–7 and 826–7 (13 and 19 March 1855). See also the correspondence between Monteagle and Gladstone printed in the *Morning Post*, 13–17 March 1855.

[3] In the one year of war expenditure during which Gladstone was Chancellor the unfunded debt increased by £7,284,629. 15s. 9d. net (though the Exchequer balances also increased by £1,171,326), Return of Public Income and Expenditure, *P.P.* 1868, xxv (366), part II, pp. 116–17.

time Gladstone left office in February 1855, did much to create a strong impression of a growing discrepancy between the theory and practice of Gladstone's finance. And in fact this discrepancy was even wider than was ever publicly revealed, for in his last weeks in office Gladstone was planning a loan of some £12 million in the forthcoming financial year.[1] There was a good deal of truth in the rumours circulating throughout the winter in the City that Gladstone was contemplating indirect taxation and a large loan.[2]

But the lion's share of financing the Crimean War fell not to Gladstone, although it is with his name that British finance in this war has always been associated, but to his successor, Sir George Cornewall Lewis, a distinguished scholar with strikingly independent financial ideas. Lewis was no hot gospeller for war taxes, or indeed for any other policy. As the perceptive Bagehot put it, Lewis was 'sure to distrust, and apt to despise, a popular dogma',[3] and certainly his war finance bears this out. He did not regard the Budget in the fashion of Peel and Gladstone as a great instrument of political, economic and even moral welfare, but merely as a series of practical expedients for making ends meet from year to year. Indeed he felt convinced that 'incidental objects' ought not to be sought through taxation. To seek to use the raising of revenue for moral objects, he once noted, was 'more benevolent and well meaning than enlightened'.[4] In April 1855 it seemed obvious that he must borrow quite heavily.

---

[1] Gladstone's Memoranda of his discussions with Lewis, 3 March and 13 April 1855, Add. MS. 44778, fos. 196–8 and 203–4.

[2] G. Hamilton to Disraeli, 15 November 1854, Hughenden MSS., B XX 98.

[3] W. Bagehot, *Biographical Studies*, ed. R. H. Hutton (1881), p. 220. Contemporary gossip often credited James Wilson, the Financial Secretary to the Treasury, with the real formulation of financial policy after Lewis became Chancellor, but in fact on large issues Lewis often adopted a position with which Wilson disagreed (cf. below, pp. 209 and 236).

[4] Lewis's undated 'Notes on Taxation', Harpton Court MSS., c. 3607.

o

To him the last hundred years of British war finance offered suggestive precedents, not a cautionary tale. 'In borrowing', he told the House, 'her Majesty's Government felt that they were fortified by uniform experience and by the constant example of their predecessors' — or as the Peelite *Morning Chronicle* scornfully put it, he 'copied from some half dozen of the old PITT and PERCEVAL Budgets'.[1] It seemed to him clear that the real burden of the Debt was growing lighter as the country's wealth increased, although he also insisted on a parliamentary undertaking to establish a post-war sinking fund of £1 million a year to pay off his loan. In any case he belonged to the growing if still unfashionable school which held that heavy taxes could easily do more harm to the economy than government borrowing: 'Taxes which cripple enterprise and derange industry or interfere with the ordinary distribution of capital, are more detrimental to the community than loans effected by the Government.' He believed that war taxation had already reached this point, and drew attention in justification of this belief to the significantly smaller number of private Bills before the House.[2] Not surprisingly, Lewis soon became popular with the City (whereas Gladstone had fallen foul of it) and proceeded to raise a series of loans without any difficulty. His first and largest, raised in April 1855, was of £16 million in 3% Consols, raised to par with terminable annuities of 14s. 6d. per £100[3] — his only concession to the powerful legion of advocates of terminable annuities.[4] Many years ago Lewis, too, had been among their number, but by

[1] *Morning Chronicle*, 23 April 1855.

[2] 3 *Hansard*, cxxxvii, col. 1561 (20 April 1855). He was (typically) so unfashionable as to deplore the abolition of a fixed sinking fund in 1828 (ibid., col. 1567).

[3] Interestingly enough, in March 1854 the economist J. E. Cairnes had advised precisely such a compromise, if it became necessary to borrow, in a paper read to the Dublin Statistical Society, 'On the Best Means of raising the Supplies for a War Expenditure.'

[4] One of whom was Palmerston himself (Palmerston to the Queen, 20 April 1855, RA, A 24/43).

GREAT EXHIBITION OF STRENGTH.

P—lm—rt—n. "HE WILL NOW TAKE THE SACK BETWEEN HIS TEETH, AND WALK ROUND THE APARTMENT, NOTWITHSTANDING THE GREAT WEIGHT HE HAS TO BEAR ALREADY."

(*Punch*, April 28, 1855)

this time he felt that they 'compelled the nation to redeem on bad terms, which it might do spontaneously on better terms'.[1] In any case he was too realistic to offer the money market anything but Consols.[2] His compromise proved a successful one. 'At present there is an abundance of money, but a want of profitable investment for the purposes of trade,' he explained to a friend. 'No wild speculations are in fashion, so there is a run upon Government securities.'[3] By the New Year another, larger, loan of the order of £30 million was being contemplated,[4] but Russia's sudden acceptance of the Allied peace terms made it clear that although another year of war expenditure was unavoidable during demobilization, it would be on a diminishing scale. In February 1856 Lewis raised a loan of £5 million because the budget surplus on which he calculated in April 1855 had failed to materialize; in May he borrowed another £5 million as part of his budget for 1856–7. In both cases he borrowed entirely in the traditional Pittite way, in Consols at the market rate, and in both the loans were heavily over-subscribed.

Lewis also added considerably to the unfunded Debt. In his first Budget he asked for authority to issue £3 million of Exchequer Bills, and in August 1855 for an additional £4 million to meet the supplementary estimates he had had to lay before the House. Gladstone was quick to point out that the unfunded Debt had thus been raised in only fifteen months from £16 million to £30 million (though he refrained from

[1] Sir Edmund Head to Lewis, 15 May 1855, Harpton Court MSS. c. 1539, and Lewis's notes on the reduction of debt, ibid. c. 3466.

[2] Ibid. 3464, and George Grote to Lewis, 26, 27 and 28 March and 6 April 1855, ibid. 1360–3. Pitt's funding policy was strikingly defended on grounds of City prejudice in Newmarch's paper 'On the Loans raised by Mr. Pitt during the first French War', read on 19 February 1855 (*Journal of the London Statistical Society*, June 1855).

[3] Lewis to Sir Edmund Head, 10 June 1855, *Letters of the Right Honourable Sir George Cornewall Lewis to Various Friends*, ed. Sir G. F. Lewis (1870), p. 295.

[4] *The Greville Memoirs*, vii. 301 and *The Correspondence of Abraham Hayward*, ed. H. E. Carlisle, p. 275.

adding that he himself had been responsible for half of this increase), and that Lewis's original balance between loans and taxes had thus been still more heavily tilted towards borrowing.[1] The following February Lewis considered it necessary to fund £3 million of Exchequer Bills before attempting the annual exchange in March. This operation was successful, and Exchequer Bills rose again to par. His last application for authority to issue additional Exchequer Bonds or Bills to meet war expenses was made in May 1856, for a further £4 million, but of these only £1 million were eventually issued.

By the time peace negotiations were beginning, early in March 1856, even the Government's spokesman admitted that two-thirds of the cost of the war had been met by loans.[2] It was only the large extent to which the running-down costs of the war in 1856–7 were covered by taxation which allowed the final proportion of total war expenditure met by borrowing to fall a good deal lower. Total war expenditure may be taken as £69,277,694, and the net creation of public Debt during the war years 1854–7 as £39,715,208. On the other hand the Exchequer balances emerged at the end of the war period larger by £7,584,433. Thus net public borrowing amounted to £32,130,775 or 46% of total war expenditure. In the end, therefore, government borrowing was somewhat lighter than in any of the five previous wars (when it ranged between 50% and 95%),[3] but the credit for this must go not to government policy but to an unexpectedly early peace.

A still more striking *dénouement* is the failure to use the income tax really boldly, despite a persistent later belief to the contrary. Gladstone, it is true, at the outset raised the

[1] 3 *Hansard*, cxxxix, col. 1704 (2 August 1855).

[2] Ibid. cxl, cols. 1948–9 (6 March 1856).

[3] All these calculations are based upon the figures given in the Return of Public Income and Expenditure, loc. cit., ii. 709. These figures show that the percentage of war expenditure met by borrowing in earlier wars was 50% in 1688–97, 58% in 1702–13, 67% in 1739–48, 71% in 1756–63, 95% in 1776–85 and 51% in 1793–1815. (The increase of the Exchequer Balances has been taken into account in each case.)

rate from 7*d.* to 1*s.* 2*d.*, but Lewis added only another 2*d.*, so
that at its highest it was only £6 13*s.* 4*d.*% and never approached the rate of 1805–16 which many people expected,
namely £10%, still less that of £15% envisaged by Sir Henry
Parnell. This chariness of using the income tax is, however,
understandable. The Crimean War coincided with a period of
acute controversy over the whole structure of this form of
taxation. Both Gladstone and Lewis had to reckon with a
considerable body of opinion which condemned the existing
income tax for unfairness towards precarious professional and
business incomes as compared with secure incomes from land
or public funds. Even those who supported the existing income
tax were often not prepared to support its being levied at a
really high war-time rate, either because the poorer classes
could not be made to pay their share, or because they feared
investment would be drastically checked. Characteristically
enough, the first objection weighed more with Gladstone, the
second with Lewis. Gladstone refused to contemplate an income tax of 10% because it seemed it could not be made
socially just. He believed it was administratively impossible
to extend the income tax to incomes below £100. Even in the
£100–£150 range (which paid at a slightly lower rate — 10*d.*
as against 14*d.* in the £) the difficulties of collection were very
considerable. Yet he felt strongly that 'the educated part of
the community with £100 per annum is clearly poorer than the
less educated part of the community who may have £60, £70
or £80 per annum'. His desire to distribute the burdens of the
war 'fairly among the different classes of the community'
therefore led him in 1854 to place only two-thirds of the
burden upon the wealthier classes through the income tax,
and the other third upon all classes alike, so he claimed,
through increased indirect taxation.[1] For the same reasons he
refused to condemn the smallness of Lewis's increase of the
income tax in 1855. He had indeed himself decided against

[1] 3 *Hansard*, cxxxvii, col. 1592 (20 April 1855), and cxxxii, col.
1448 (8 May 1854).

increasing the income tax any further when he was planning
ways and means for the next financial year in November 1854,
and had been thinking in terms of an increased House Tax.
'An increase of the Income Tax might be more easily got,' he
wrote to the Deputy Chairman of the Inland Revenue Board,
'but would I incline to think be less just.'[1]

Lewis had very different reasons from Gladstone's for
failing to raise the income tax sharply. He had never felt much
enthusiasm for Parnellite doctrines of finance in general
(when he read Sir Henry Parnell's *On Financial Reform* in
1837 he found parts of it 'rather feeble and confused'), and by
1855 he thought they had been carried quite far enough. He
believed strongly that although a low income tax was a useful
source of revenue, a high rate would tend to stop investment.[2]
He also believed that a variety of small indirect taxes had
much to commend them, and that in these views he had the
support of a strong body of opinion.[3] There was, he told Lord
John Russell, who had urged him to rely upon a heavy income
tax, 'great alarm about a further increase this year, after the
doubling of the tax last year, and in case of the continuance of
this unfortunate war, it is a last resource to be relied on.'[4]
Hence his decision to avoid any considerable increase of
income tax and his reversal of Gladstone's ratio between direct
and indirect taxation with his proposal to raise £3,300,000
more from increased Customs and Excise duties, as against
only £2 million from increased direct taxation. Thus it came
about that in spite of the vastly increased yield of the income
tax — according to Lewis, his 6% tax produced virtually as
much (£14 million) as the 10% rate in the last year of the
Napoleonic War — it covered only just over a third of the
total cost of the war.

[1] Gladstone to C. Pressly, 17 November 1854, Add. MS. 44529, fo.
175.

[2] *Letters of Sir George Cornewall Lewis*, pp. 92, 307.

[3] 3 *Hansard*, cxliv, col. 652 (13 February 1857).

[4] Lewis to Lord John Russell, 3 April 1855, P.R.O. 30/22/12. See
also Lewis to Palmerston, 10 April 1855, Broadlands Archives.

Not only was there a marked failure to use the income tax really boldly, but also a significant extension of Customs and Excise duties. From the beginning there were those who predicted that the war would sooner or later make it necessary to reverse the movement towards free trade. In the very first financial debates of the war Samuel Laing, the great railway director and ardent supporter of free trade and financial reform, accused the Conservatives of deliberately building up feeling against the income tax in order to achieve precisely this.[1] Gladstone's second budget for 1854–5, with its increased duties on spirits, malt and sugar, made it seem that a retrogressive process had indeed begun. Free trade, the Conservatives claimed, had at once been proved inadequate in a national emergency, and their case was greatly strengthened when Lewis imposed further duties on spirits, sugar, coffee and tea in April 1855. They were thus able to claim that a silent fiscal *volte-face* was taking place under the financial pressure of war. The financial reformers and convinced free-traders were inclined to agree. Admittedly the influential James Wilson, Financial Secretary to the Treasury under Lewis as under Gladstone, continued to insist that even Lewis's duties met the requirements of free trade theory.[2] But Gladstone himself, freshly out of office, admitted that Lewis's duties, although not strictly speaking protective, since they were not imposed on articles of foreign production at a higher rate than on similar articles of home production, did nevertheless reverse the policy of reducing duties on the main articles of consumption. He predicted that if the war proved long, protection itself would have to be reintroduced.[3] Lewis certain-

[1] 3 *Hansard*, cxxxii, col. 106 (30 March 1854).

[2] Namely, that no Customs duty should be levied which would act as a protective duty, nor one upon raw materials; and that no Excise duty should be levied on manufactured articles or the raw materials of manufacture (*The Economist*, 21 April 1855).

[3] 3 *Hansard*, cxxxvii, col. 1801 (26 April 1855). In November 1854 Gladstone himself had been contemplating increasing the tea duty (Add. MS. 44778, fo. 1), and the following spring he favoured increasing

ly expected to increase at least the timber duties if the war continued.[1] Indeed, he must have welcomed the opportunity given by the war to call a halt to the progress of Peelite finance. He not only found the income-tax proposals put forward by the financial reformers altogether repugnant, but refused to admit that judicious indirect taxation was either costly to collect, or interfered with trade, or pressed unduly on the poorer classes.[2] 'Consumers do not object, in general, to indirect taxes; sellers complain of them, as narrowing the demand,' he once noted.[3] Retrenchment, consolidation and simplification were no part of Lewis's fiscal philosophy. His first peace-time budget in February 1857, which he introduced with a quotation from Arthur Young and a declaration in favour of a multitude of taxes pressing lightly at many points, made this clear. It roused Gladstone to denounce every detail of Lewis's finance: 'Everything in regard to finance for which we have been labouring during the last fifteen years is in principle condemned alike by the speech as by the plans of the right honourable Gentleman the Chancellor of the Exchequer.' Yet Gladstone's own Crimean War finance enabled Sir Charles Wood to deliver a well-aimed riposte. 'Why,' Wood quite correctly insisted, 'the right honourable Gentleman [Gladstone] himself in 1854 imposed taxes upon more articles than the Chancellor of the Exchequer, and, even to a greater extent than my right honourable Friend, carried out the principles of Arthur Young.'[4] Wood was perhaps not altogether fair,

---

the timber duties (Lewis to Palmerston, 10 April 1855, Broadlands MSS.).

[1] *Letters of Sir George Cornewall Lewis*, p. 299. Lewis only refrained from increasing them in April 1855 because his Cabinet colleagues feared Canadian reactions (Lewis to Palmerston, 18 April 1855, Broadlands MSS.).

[2] *Letters of Sir George Cornewall Lewis*, pp. 304, 307, 373. The article on 'The Income Tax' in the *Edinburgh Review* for April 1853 was inspired by Lewis, who himself wrote the last part of that on 'British Taxation' in ibid. January 1860.

[3] Harpton Court MSS., c. 3607.

[4] 3 *Hansard*, cxliv, cols. 986, 1138 (20 and 23 February 1857).

for Gladstone's budgetary compromises in 1854 were to him a cruel necessity, whereas Lewis in 1855 without hesitation or regret went a good deal further and much increased the elements of borrowing and indirect taxation in the country's war finance. Nevertheless, the first break in the triumphant progress of Peelite finance was made by Gladstone himself, and was only widened by Cornewall Lewis.

To the generation which lived through it, it was plain that in the event Crimean War finance did not furnish a demonstration of the feasibility or wisdom of financing war exclusively through taxation, still less by the income tax alone, despite Gladstone's brave utterances at the beginning of hostilities. Yet this 'betrayal' of liberal finance provoked remarkably little hostile reaction. At the end of 1855, when the duties on sugar and spirits were not yielding as much as had been estimated, the doctrinaire free-traders did indeed hail this as fresh proof that such duties 'crippled and embarrassed trade', and Bright in his pacifist speeches always made as much as he could of the fiscal retrogression which the war had imposed. The increase in the malt duty — always a red rag to the agricultural interest — did arouse bitter debate in the House, but as *The Times* put it, the whole discussion was 'an undertaker's job from beginning to end'.[1] Most people seem to have considered that although they had done right to travel along the free-trade road since 1842, they had now gone far enough in substituting direct for indirect taxation. Some believed it only just that the lower classes, who had always been the most ardent supporters of the war, should also help to pay for it, and it was widely held that only increased indirect taxation could make them do so. Others felt simply that the fiscal system must yield to the 'paramount necessity' of war.[2] Hence in most quarters the altered trend visible in the fiscal

---

[1] *The Times*, 16 May 1854.

[2] As for example did T. Tooke and W. Newmarch (*A History of Prices, 1792–1856* (1857), v. 447).

expedients adopted during the war was accepted without enthusiasm but also without dismay.

This acquiescence was reinforced and sometimes perhaps inspired by the conclusions reached in the wide-ranging theoretical debate these expedients provoked. The Crimean War debate on war finance has been persistently obscured by the Gladstonian legend and by the far more dramatic controversies of the Napoleonic Wars. Indeed its very existence has hardly been suspected. The whole cost of the struggle is usually dismissed as little more than half a single year's war expenditure in the last phase of the Napoleonic Wars, and it is not appreciated that this was not at all what contemporaries expected. They believed they must provide for either a very intensive or a very prolonged struggle; and indeed while it lasted the war was a much more disturbing economic factor than has usually been realized. From the point of view of the cost of each man under arms, the Crimean War was by far the most expensive war Britain had hitherto fought, and in the one year in which it was in full swing, government expenditure equalled about 92% of the declared value of British exports.[1] Thus to contemporaries the question of the best way to pay for the war was a far more urgent and important one than later writers have realized. It was equally a 'live' question from the point of view of economic theory and political feeling. It is thus not surprising that Gladstone's striking speeches in 1854 touched off a sustained discussion on war finance in the serious press and learned societies.[2]

This discussion centred around the respective effects of loans and taxes in distributing the burden of war between the

[1] J. R. T. Hughes, *Fluctuations in Trade, Industry and Finance* (Clarendon Press, Oxford, 1960), p. 24.

[2] It is only surprising that Gladstone wrote less than ten years later that he had 'never seen worked out in print . . . the general question of loans versus taxes for war purposes.' Possibly John Morley's publication of this remark (*Life of Gladstone* (1903), i. 517) fostered the idea among early twentieth-century writers that this was indeed a 'strangely neglected topic' (e.g. Hirst, op. cit., p. 151).

present generation and posterity, and between 'capital and labour'. The distinction between the money cost and the real cost of war was appreciated at that time far better than many early-twentieth-century writers supposed. *The Economist*, for example, frequently impressed upon its readers that: 'For a community, the price of war is not so much money, but the exertion, the actual sacrifice, the employment of so much labour; and how can this be thrown on any subsequent generation?'[1] Moreover it was often pointed out that the idea that by borrowing posterity could be made to bear the financial burden of war was almost as much a delusion as that it could be made to share its real cost. As the young John Elliot Cairnes, then at the beginning of his distinguished career, said in March 1854: 'It is important to remember that the question does not lie — as the received phraseology might lead us to suppose — between the advantage of raising the supplies *within the year*, and that of spreading the supplies over a *number of years*. Whatever is consumed and destroyed by the war is so much wealth taken from the country, raised by the Government in that year in which the destruction takes place.'[2] Well-informed opinion certainly did not imagine that taxation placed the burden exclusively or automatically on the present, or loans on the future, although frequent quotation of a few passages from Gladstone's speeches has given the impression that it did. It already saw the issue of loans versus taxes in the manner of the economic writers of 1914–18, as one of distribution between classes, rather than between generations.

By 1854 it was an intelligent commonplace that loans were taken from productive capital, taxes from income, and that loans were therefore paid mainly by the working class, who in addition to suffering from the high prices caused by the

[1] 9 June 1855. See also the editorials of 10 February and 14 April 1855.

[2] *On the Best Means of Raising the Supplies for a War Expenditure*, p. 6.

restriction of production, had their wages reduced. John
Stuart Mill's assertion in his widely read *Principles of Political
Economy* that loans as much as taxes were 'paid for within
the year, and that too by a tax exclusively on the labouring
classes' was very influential in spreading this view. The
diversion of productive capital to government loans, his
argument ran, inevitably diminished the Wage Fund.[1] This
view was endorsed by Gladstone in his Budget speech of 6
March 1854 when he quoted Mill and declared that with taxes
'you get a large portion of what you want out of a superfluity
of capital', but that with a loan 'you go directly to that foun-
tain head where money is supplied, upon which in a great
degree the activity of trade and the cheapness of productions
must depend'. Gladstone went on to urge next, quoting
McCulloch with approval, that only taxation could counteract
the waste of productive capital involved in war by stimulating
the industry and economy of individuals.[2] James Wilson
remained throughout the war remarkably faithful to these
ideas. Early in 1855, for example, he insisted in *The Economist*
(of which he remained the editor, while Financial Secretary to
the Treasury) that a loan would entail 'the derangement of
our money market' whereas taxes would 'preserve the trade
and industry on which the nation depends', for 'in no country
is the margin of unemployed capital smaller than in England',
and in the autumn he tried to check the drift towards borrowing by reprinting this article, word for word.[3] But there had
always been an important dissentient line of thought which
challenged this ancient belief that capital was scarce in
Britain. If Ricardo, the elder Mill and McCulloch had followed

[1] J. S. Mill, *Principles of Political Economy*, ed. W. J. Ashley (1909),
p. 873.
[2] 3 *Hansard*, cxxxi, cols. 375–6. These remarks do not altogether
tally with Gladstone's retrospective justification in 1862 of his Crimean
War taxes on the grounds that in war wages usually rise, and therefore
the working classes could stand heavy taxation better during a war than
after it (Morley, op. cit. i. 515).
[3] *The Economist*, 20 January and 13 October 1855.

Adam Smith in stressing the need to conserve capital and foster its growth,[1] Brougham, Malthus and Chalmers had preached that capital was abundant, and John Stuart Mill himself, after expounding the argument already described against government borrowing, had gone on to say that in certain circumstances his argument fell to the ground. If governments tapped 'the overflowings of capital', that is, capital which would otherwise have been invested abroad or wasted, 'then loans occasion no privation to any one at the time, except by the payment of interest, and may even be beneficial to the labouring class by employing in the direct purchase of labour funds which might otherwise have quitted the country altogether.'[2] This doctrine was consistently preached in the editorial columns of the *Morning Post*, which repeatedly urged more government borrowing in order to tap capital which would otherwise go abroad.[3] Not many people, however, were confident that capital was as superabundant as this view implied, and even fewer found it plausible that governments could in practice be so selective in their borrowing. Mill's assumption that they could was strongly denounced by Cairnes in a paper read to the Dublin Statistical Society on 20 March 1854, and Cairnes's arguments were given wider currency by G. K. Rickards in his lectures as Drummond Professor of Political Economy at Oxford delivered in the Trinity Term of 1855 and subsequently published. It would be impossible, they pointed out, to distinguish home from foreign borrowers, impossible for a government to outbid foreign borrowers without also outbidding home borrowers, impossible to use the rate of interest as an index of how far the state could go in borrowing without diminishing home investment. Rickards added that in practice government loans

[1] Cf. G. S. L. Tucker, *Progress and Profits in British Economic Thought* (Cambridge, 1960), p. 162.

[2] *Principles of Political Economy*, p. 873.

[3] See, for example, the editorials of 9 and 25 January and 1 April 1855.

would tend to attract not the speculators, but the cautious lenders so essential to domestic investment.[1] Whether or not they were familiar with these academic arguments, most people probably agreed with *The Economist* that 'Mr. Mill's plausible theory about surplus capital has no force in practice',[2] and believed that whether productive capital was scarce or not, government borrowing must inevitably encroach upon it. Few supposed that such encroachment would affect posterity alone. Most believed that it would entail low wages and high prices and thus chiefly affect the poor. The Whately Professor of Political Economy at Dublin, Richard Hussey Walsh, went so far as to urge government borrowing precisely in order to make the poor pay their share of war expenditure.[3] Thomas Chalmers' argument of twenty years before that government loans raised prices by lowering the volume of production was often reproduced in 1855. Cairnes's attack on this popular doctrine in January 1856 was an original one. When government loans diminished productive capital, he argued, a proportionate diminution of production was *not* involved, since the pressure ultimately fell chiefly on the Wage Fund; and moreover such loans diminished purchasing power in the community at large.[4] Thus Cairnes denied that government borrowing necessarily created an inflationary situation. Even Cairnes, however, admitted that it lowered wages and administered *some* check to production, and most of his contemporaries would have expected much more far-reaching consequences.

But although it was widely acknowledged that government

[1] J. E. Cairnes, *On the Best Means of Raising the Supplies for a War Expenditure*, pp. 8–10, and G. K. Rickards, *The Financial Policy of War* (1855), p. 45.

[2] *The Economist*, 14 April 1855.

[3] 'The Relative Expediency of defraying the Expense of War by Loans or by Increased Taxation, considered with reference to the present financial system of the United Kingdom' (paper read on 16 April 1855), *Journal of the Dublin Statistical Society*, i. 109.

[4] Ibid. 223–38.

borrowing involved immediate as well as long-term effects, it was also widely admitted that war taxes affected the future as well as the present. By the middle of the nineteenth century few informed people were prepared to repeat without qualification Adam Smith's dictum that war taxes were paid for from current spending on luxuries. Even the most enthusiastic believers in taxation as a stimulus to accumulative effort confessed that sudden or really heavy taxation would deter instead of promote capital accumulation, quite as much as loans. It might derange investment in many ways, or lead to private borrowing even more wasteful than public borrowing would have been. If really heavy war-expenditure had to be financed, then either way capital was bound to suffer. 'It is only very roughly true', said Rickards, a good exponent of common expert opinion, an economist who indeed never laid any claim to originality, 'that taxes are taken from income, and loans from capital'. He went on to quote with approval Chalmers's argument (the very argument soon to be denounced as fallacious by the young Cairnes) that 'it is quite the same thing whether the community shall go to market with the usual amount of money for purchases, but with prices raised to the extent of £20 million [through a government loan], or shall go to market with £20 million less of money [because of government taxes], but with the usual prices,' and few of his audience can have found this startling. Rickards did, indeed, add some commonplace qualifications to the effect that taxes encouraged effort more than loans, but caused discontent because they were involuntary. But his general conclusion was that with regard to government borrowing, political economy 'prescribes no peremptory and inflexible law'[1] and this was a conclusion which by the spring of 1855 had been reached by very many other people. It was in fact already widely realized that, as A. C. Pigou was to put it in 1921, 'the *size* of the contribution a citizen is called upon to make is a much more important factor than the *form* of it in determining

---

[1] Rickards, op. cit., Lecture II, *passim.*

whether the citizen provides it from income or expenditure'.[1]
A considerable body of informed opinion appreciated that
the antithesis between taxes and loans was artificial and misleading, and that their effects, though not identical, were
not completely dissimilar, at least if the sums raised were
large.

Perhaps an even more telling objection to the familiar
Gladstonian gospel of war finance by taxation alone was the
sheer technical difficulty of increasing taxation substantially
without 'soaking the rich' in a way unacceptable to that
generation. This difficulty, which as has been seen proved a
very real one to both Chancellors of the Exchequer concerned,
received more and more attention in public discussion as the
scale of war expenditure mounted. Only a very enthusiastic
financial reformer could seriously suppose that a 'perfect'
(that is, perfectly fairly distributed) income tax of 10%
could really be raised on all incomes above 6s. a week and
bring in vast sums.[2] The existing income tax was widely felt
among the professional and commercial classes to hit them
unfairly hard, and could certainly not be extended down-
wards to incomes below £100 without confronting unecono-
mic difficulties of collection.[3] Yet the alternative of imposing
heavy indirect taxes was contemplated with even more dis-
taste outside than inside Parliament. Practical considerations
arising out of the existing system of taxation thus did much
to make government borrowing appear inevitable as the war
proceeded.[4] The Parnellite financial reformers continued to
hope that the war might give the final push which would

[1] A. C. Pigou, *The Political Economy of War* (1921), p. 74.
[2] The argument of W. Neilson Hancock, a past holder of the Whately
Chair of Political Economy, to this effect on 18 December 1854 was
refuted by his successor Richard Hussey Walsh, on 16 April 1855
(*Journal of the Dublin Statistical Society*, i. 35–38, 106–13).
[3] These difficulties have been briefly discussed by the present author
in 'Wage-earners and Income Tax', *Public Administration* xli, (1963).
[4] The *Manchester Guardian's* editorial of 18 April 1855 furnishes a
good illustration of this movement of opinion.

P

secure sweeping income-tax reform, and *The Economist* to
the end derided fears that heavy direct taxation would
derange industry; but such opinions found little support.
Most people preferred Rickards' conclusion in his Oxford
lectures: 'Better to succeed to a mortgaged patrimony than
to an exhausted estate.' On balance the evils of borrowing came to seem less serious than those of very heavy taxation.

This conclusion was reached the more readily because it
was widely believed to be possible to minimize if not wholly
prevent permanent additions to the National Debt being made
by war borrowing. The favourite devices were not the discredited notion of a sinking fund, but borrowing at par, the
use of terminable annuities, and the opening of subscriptions
to the small investor. In the prolonged political crisis immediately before the Budget of 1855, feeling gathered especially
upon this last point. The restriction of loans to a few great
contractors through the condition that tenders must be for
the entire amount of the loan, ran altogether counter to the
clamour in those months for a broader basis in the country's
political life. Yet Lewis did no more than hint to the great
financiers that he might like to accept tenders for small portions of the loan, and gave the idea up at once when it was
made plain this would be unacceptable.[1] The loan went to
Rothschild. *The Times* was quick with its reproof. 'We
certainly were under the impression that we lived in an age of
competition,' it thundered. 'Now we are at the mercy of a
few great contractors. We think that before such a transaction
is allowed to be completed Parliament would only be doing
its duty by requiring some explanation of a course so strange
in itself, so opposed to modern experience, and to the most

[1] Cf. the *Spectator*, 21 April 1855. Denunciation of government
reliance on the great financiers, although it acquired fresh overtones
in 1855, had a very long history indeed (cf., for example, L. S. Sutherland,
'The City of London and the Devonshire–Pitt Administration, 1756–7',
Proceedings of the British Academy, xlvi (1960), 147–73).

universally admitted doctrines of economic science.'[1] The recent success of a loan raised in France by public subscription was repeatedly urged. But an English Government would not be able to draw upon a large untapped fund of 'coffee-pot savings', since in England there were far more facilities for the small investor. Pitt's Loyalty Loan was also made much of, but there was no agreement whether it had been a success or a failure. Thus in the matter of tendering, as in so much else, in the spring of 1855 Palmerston's Government was far more cautious and conservative than the public. Lewis's compromise of using terminable annuities merely to enable him to borrow in Consols at par has already been noticed. It satisfied neither the school which urged borrowing at the market rate of interest, nor the devotees of terminable annuities. His reintroduction of a sinking fund, although only a prospective post-war one of £1 million a year, is a yet more striking proof of his independence of public opinion, since this ran counter to dominant feeling in the City as well as among political economists. All the former Chancellors of the Exchequer and Presidents of the Board of Trade in the House of Commons, and most of the bankers, arose to preach from the familiar text of the Fourth Report of the Committee on Public Income and Expenditure of 1828 and to tell Lewis that 'everyone knew' that a sinking fund was little more than a 'pious fraud'.[2] Only the reluctance of the House in the critical spring of 1855 to defeat a Government yet again saved this almost universally criticized part of Lewis's budget. But in any case, sinking fund or not, the National Debt was at last coming to be regarded less and less as a bogy. The steady development of national prosperity was creating confidence that its burden would be progressively lightened. Some experts again pointed to the benefits derived from the Debt through 'the facilities which it affords to certain kinds of

[1] *The Times*, 18 April 1855.
[2] 3 *Hansard*, cxxxvii, cols. 1955–73 (30 April 1855). The Press joined in these rebukes (e.g. *The Times*, 24 April 1855).

business ',[1] and similar views were diffused through a wider public at the end of 1855 with the publication of the best-selling third and fourth volumes of Macaulay's *History of England*, in which he treated the Debt as one of the great elements of English prosperity. But by this time only a few doctrinaires remained obstinately critical of the series of pragmatic compromises by which the war was being financed.[2]

Loans, indirect taxes, even a sinking fund had thus all re-appeared as part of the financial armament of the nation against Russia, despite the denunciations heaped upon them during the long peace and renewed by Gladstone himself in an over-quoted piece of rhetoric on the very eve of hostilities. What was the upshot over the equally loudly denounced Pittite practice of foreign loans and subsidies? The method most heavily used in the past of giving outright financial assistance to European allies and auxiliaries through subsidies was not resorted to again. The private correspondence of ministers and diplomats reveals, however, that this was the result of diplomatic exigencies rather than of British financial policy. At the very beginning of the war a subsidy treaty with Sweden was given long and anxious consideration. The French had from the beginning been eager for a Swedish alliance, but the British Government was divided. Their first reaction to the proposal to pay Sweden a subsidy of £100,000 monthly jointly with France was that it was politically

---

[1] The Political Economy Club debated the extent of these benefits on 6 December 1855 at Newmarch's suggestion (*Minutes of Proceedings*, vi (1921), 72). Newmarch had in February 1855 read a striking and widely discussed paper to the London Statistical Society, 'On the Loans raised by Mr. Pitt during the first French War, 1793–1801' (*Journal*, xviii. 104–40), in which he attacked the doctrine of financing war by taxation.

[2] There was however some attempt to associate increased government borrowing with the general strain on the London money market which developed in the autumn of 1855 (*The Economist*, 9 September, 6 and 13 October 1855 and *Saturday Review*, 3 November 1855).

impossible. 'The country suffered too much from that ruinous system in the last war hastily to embark upon it again and in fact if the Government were to propose it the H.C.s [sic] would not hear of it,' Clarendon told the British Ambassador in Paris on 17 April 1854.[1] But financial and parliamentary considerations like these quickly became secondary to military and diplomatic ones. When Lord John Russell circulated a Cabinet memorandum favouring such a treaty on 20 May 1854, the objections raised by his colleagues were not financial, but diplomatic. Only Aberdeen (perhaps because of his official experience of that peak period of British subsidies, 1814–16) stressed his objection in principle to a subsidy. It would tempt other potential allies to stipulate for subsidies, he argued, and 'completely derange our financial operations and render a system of loans quite indispensable'. Other ministers, however, were far more concerned with the way in which the Swedish terms would extend the objects and scope of the war.[2] Even Gladstone himself would have been quite willing to hire Swedish troops as mere mercenaries, or alternatively to pay a French army to attack Sveaborg; what he condemned was soliciting Sweden 'to allow us to pay her for fighting *as our ally* with a view to objects *of her own*', instead of for the allies' high moral object, the vindication of public law.[3] French persistence won, however, and on 8 July 1854 the Cabinet agreed to the terms proposed.[4] It was thus only political difficulties, and not the objections of the British

[1] F.O. 519/170. Lord John Russell urged a subsidy from the beginning (Lord John to Aberdeen, 27 April 1854, P.R.O. 30/22/11 and Clarendon to Lord John, 23 April 1854, ibid.).

[2] Lord John's Memorandum, and the minutes thereon of Aberdeen, Clarendon, Gladstone, Wood, Herbert and Lansdowne, ibid. Aberdeen had already explained his objections in a letter to Lord John on 27 April 1854 (ibid.).

[3] Gladstone to Graham, 17 May 1854, Add. MS. 44163, fo. 138. Graham evidently agreed with Gladstone.

[4] Aberdeen to the Queen, 8 July 1854, ibid. 43049, fo. 181. Some ministers nevertheless remained 'vehemently opposed' to them (Clarendon to Cowley, 7 July 1854, F.O. 519/170).

Cabinet, which prevented the conclusion of a subsidy treaty with Sweden in the late summer of 1854.[1] Moreover, when a quite different treaty guaranteeing Swedish territorial integrity was actually signed on 21 November 1855, the British Government was quite prepared to pay all expenses if an expedition had to be sent to Swedish aid.[2]

Another recurring idea was that of tempting Austria with a subsidy, although the aged Lansdowne — like Aberdeen, a veteran with official experience going back to the Napoleonic Wars — preferred the idea of guaranteeing a loan.[3] Nothing came of this, since Austria was determined not to allow herself actually to come to blows with Russia. Pressing Spanish offers of a contingent of 60,000 men were turned down in the summer of 1855, partly because the subsidy which would have been necessary would have had to be left in Spain's uncontrolled possession, and this would never be acceptable in England, but also because by then Britain's need for foreign reinforcements was far less urgent.[4] In short, although financial and parliamentary objections to subsidies were always useful talking points, in reality ministers considered subsidy proposals in the light of circumstances, at least after the unrealistic first few weeks of war. These circumstances were never such as to lead to the submission of subsidy proposals to Parliament, and consequently parliamentary and public feeling on subsidies was never fully tested in the Crimean War: although at the end of 1854, when reinforcements were the

[1] The well-known article by P. Knaplund, 'Finmark in British diplomacy, 1836–55' *American Historical Review*, xxx (1925), 494, is thus somewhat misleading on this.

[2] To the indignation of some of its members and of the Queen (George Douglas Campbell, eighth Duke of Argyll, *Autobiography and Memoirs* (1906), i. 592; Clarendon to Palmerston, 23 July 1855, Broadlands MSS.).

[3] Lansdowne to Lord John Russell, 29 May 1854, P.R.O. 30/22/11 and Clarendon to Cowley, 23 May 1855, F.O. 519/170.

[4] Clarendon to Cowley, 8 August 1855, ibid., and F. A. Simpson, *Louis Napoleon and the Recovery of France, 1848–1856* (1923), p. 350.

question of the day, there is evidence of some public demand (especially in business circles) for a resort to subsidies.[1]

Two very similar financial measures — a loan to Piedmont and the guarantee of a loan raised by Turkey in 1855 — did, however, come before Parliament and the public. Reactions to these measures suggest that with the public and to a lesser extent with the House as well, it was victory and not financial shibboleths which counted, just as it did with the Government. The turning-point in this, as in nearly every other aspect of the war, came in the weeks after the battle of the Alma. Russia proved able to bring up vast reinforcements, and by the middle of November it was clear to everyone that the need for more troops was paramount, and to very many that suitable recruits would not be forthcoming at home. Emigration and high wages had from the beginning seriously reduced the pool of human scum which the British Army was accustomed to rely upon. It was this desperate need for men which led the Government to summon Parliament for a special session in December in order to pass Bills authorizing the service of militiamen overseas and the enlistment of private subjects of other states. It had already inspired thoughts of reviving the ancient practice of paying the smaller German states to supply corps of mercenaries.[2] But by the middle of the nineteenth century the development of international law made this seem very much like a breach of neutrality. None of the German states, not even Hanover, was prepared to give their consent to public recruiting of any kind within their territories, for fear of the Diet.[3] Thus foreign recruiting was necessarily unofficial, and although it was tried, and a Foreign Legion raised, it

[1] Some such evidence is to be found in the newspaper press. There is a full report on the strength of such views in Glasgow in R. Menteith to Lord John Russell, 16 December 1854, P.R.O. 30/22/11.

[2] Newcastle to Lord John Russell, 9 September 1854, P.R.O. 30/22/11, Lord John Russell to Granville, and reply, 10 October 1854, P.R.O. 30/29/23.

[3] Clarendon to Lord John Russell, 3 December 1854, 3 and 12 January 1855, P.R.O. 30/22/11.

would obviously not provide many first-rate troops, at least quickly. Moreover such unofficial touting for recruits abroad harmed British prestige. What was really wanted was, in Palmerston's words, 'some ready-made and disciplined force ... to be taken on British pay, with their own officers just as they are, but to be under the orders of our Commander-in-Chief', and for such a force Spain, Portugal, and Piedmont were the obvious possible sources.[1] It was against this background of desperation — when even conscription was being mooted in some quarters — that the Cabinet decided on 29 November 1854 to test Piedmontese reactions to the proposal that Piedmont should accede to the alliance and provide a contingent of 10,000 men for the Crimea in return for a subsidy.[2] The outcome of this proposal was determined by the diplomatic manœuvres and political struggles within Piedmont, and not by British policy, and the final upshot caused some surprise and much jubilation among British ministers. Only the financial negotiations are relevant here. From the beginning the Sardinian Government insisted upon a loan, and not a subsidy — £2 million at a rate which amounted to $3\frac{1}{4}\%$ — in return for a bait of 15,000 men, to be ready for service in less than a month.[3] It was essential to the Sardinians to be regarded as 'des alliés et non des serviteurs', and when Cavour replaced Dabormida as Minister of Foreign Affairs on 10 January 1855 he maintained this stipulation. Gladstone's objections were immediate. But although they were resented as proof of English chicanery and parsimony by the Sardinian representative, as they have been ever since by Italian writers,[4] in reality they were neither. Gladstone never objected

[1] Palmerston to Lord John Russell, 15 November 1854, P.R.O. 30/22/11.

[2] Clarendon to Aberdeen, and reply, 29 November 1854, Add. MS. 43189, fos. 255–7, Hudson to Clarendon, 15 December 1854, F.O. 62/205/173–5.

[3] Hudson to Clarendon, 15 December 1855, F.O. 62/205/175.

[4] F. Valsecchi, *Il Risorgimento e l'Europa. L'Alleanza di Crimea* (Milan, 1948), p. 453; *Cavour e l'Inghilterra*, i. 30.

to the principle of giving financial aid to Sardinia; and he would have been as ready to subsidize her as his colleagues. His objection was the characteristic one that the Sardinian provision for the arrangements to repay the loan to be settled at the end of the war made the transaction appear 'a sham Loan' and consequently made it more vulnerable to parliamentary criticism. He therefore suggested that the Loan should be raised at 4%, of which 3% should be interest and 1% go to form a sinking fund, or alternatively, that the sum involved should be clearly divided into grant and loan, and the latter be charged at a rate which would include interest and sinking fund as in his first suggestion. Clarendon at once complied.[1] A separate financial convention embodying the first proposal was drawn up, for the signature of Great Britain and Sardinia alone. It was explained to the Sardinians as entirely inspired by a desire for logic and simplicity, and to their own advantage (because of the reduction of interest from $3\frac{1}{4}$% to 3%), and signed on 26 January.[2] At that desperate moment, however, even Gladstone would in reality have been prepared to waive his objections if the Sardinians had made a stand. 'If it is clear we can get the 15,000 men immediately', he wrote privately to Clarendon, 'we must have them even upon the terms of Mr. Hudson's convention, rather than lose them.'[3]

The public was as relieved at the outcome as the Cabinet. The Press was enthusiastic about the alliance and prepared to accept the accompanying loan. But to the surprise of many,[4] when the Sardinian Loan Bill finally came before Parliament on 26 March, a good deal of opposition was voiced. To a large extent, however, this was inspired by quite irrelevant motives,

---

[1] Gladstone to Clarendon, 16 January 1855, Add. MS. 44530, fo. 13, Clarendon to Gladstone, 17 January 1855, ibid., 44133, fo. 27.

[2] D'Azeglio to Cavour, 20 January 1855, *Cavour e l'Inghilterra*, i. 33–5. A separate financial convention seems to have been the suggestion of the Foreign Office, not Gladstone (F.O. 62/206/76).

[3] Gladstone to Clarendon, 18 January 1855, Add. MS. 44530, fo. 14.

[4] Cf. D. le Marchant to Lord John Russell, 3 April 1855, P.R.O. 30/22/12.

led as it was by Disraeli, still trying to make the most of the Government's bungling of recruiting, and by an ultramontane Catholic Member, George Bowyer, who made an obviously prejudiced attack upon the unsound state of Sardinian finances. It was now Disraeli's turn to discover an awful warning in Pitt's policies, and Gladstone's to protest that he 'could not agree in the total condemnation of the subsidy system' — a neat reversal of their positions in the first financial debates of the war.[1] And in fact the Cabinet must have wished most heartily a few weeks later that the Sardinians had accepted a subsidy, since it was their determined exploitation of the fact that they were not 'stipendiée et au service d'une seule Puissance' which finally obliged Palmerston most reluctantly to concede to France equal control with England over the Sardinian contingent, despite the fact that the loan had been made by England alone.[2] Thus in order first to get troops and then to preserve the alliance, the British Government agreed to give a loan when it would have preferred a subsidy, abandoned its attempt to treat the implications of that loan as identical with those of a subsidy, and finally even gave up its effort to place those troops under the British command alone. There could hardly be stronger proof of the primacy given to the war effort in Britain at that time.

The British guarantee given to a Turkish loan in 1855 underlines this primacy yet more clearly. From the outset Turkey seemed likely to need financial assistance. But at the beginning of the war the Cabinet was entirely ruled by Gladstone on financial matters, and towards Turkey Gladstone had none of the political sympathy he felt towards Piedmont; moreover he had good reason to suspect the soundness of Turkey's credit. Gladstone insisted that the Turks' need for financial help was not established. But if it were, he thought

---

[1] 3 *Hansard*, cxxxvii, cols. 1068–109; D'Azeglio to Cavour, 27 March 1855, *Cavour e l'Inghilterra*, p. 66.

[2] D'Azeglio to Cavour, 13, 23 and 26 April 1855, ibid., pp. 78, 80, 90 and 92.

an outright gift the best plan: anything else would be 'haggling about securities which are worth nothing', as his chief, Aberdeen, phrased it. In any case, Gladstone argued in March 1854, 'The House of Commons would never consent to reward such ignorance, or obstinacy, or incurie [as the Porte's] by advancing money.'[1] At that moment Gladstone was probably correct, for as has already been shown, at the outbreak of the war the House was still dominated by the commonplaces of a generation of critics of earlier war finance. It was only the threat of a guarantee being given by France alone — with the attendant risk that France might in return secure an exclusive right to interfere with the revenues of Egypt — which drove Clarendon[2] in July to wring consent to a joint guarantee from Gladstone. But that consent was dependent upon two conditions: that it was clearly proved that the Turks were absolutely incapable of raising a loan themselves, and that the expenditure of the loan should be subject to Allied control.[3] To the surprise of all concerned, and the annoyance of the French, at the last moment the Turks secured a loan independently, on the strength of a mere 'certificate' from Clarendon that its negotiators were fully authorized and that its terms would be honoured.[4]

Thus it was not until the critical spring of 1855 that the question of guaranteeing a Turkish loan came again before the Cabinet. By then the situation had entirely changed. Various Turkish blunders had renewed all the old doubts about Turkish credit. Yet it had also become clear that the

[1] Gladstone to Clarendon, 18 March 1854, Add. MS. 44529, fo. 67, and Clarendon to Stratford, 3 April 1854, F.O. 352/40, Aberdeen to Clarendon, 6 July 1854, Add. MS. 43189, fo. 99.

[2] Clarendon to Cowley, 30 June 1854, F.O. 519/170.

[3] Gladstone to Clarendon, 6 July 1854, Add. MS. 44529, fo. 114. Gladstone's anxiety to avoid upsetting his Ways and Means arrangements at this juncture probably explains why he waived his preference for a subsidy.

[4] The beginnings of the Ottoman Public Debt are fully discussed and documented by the present author in *The Historical Journal*, VII. i (1964), 47–63.

campaign in the East would be a long and difficult business. It was intolerable that Omer Pasha's army should be melting away for want of pay. If the Allies were to get much military benefit from a Turkish loan it was obviously essential to impose a much stricter control over its expenditure than that attempted in the autumn of 1854; but it was equally obvious that a loan must be raised. The disasters in the East were creating a great revulsion of feeling against the cult of economy and indeed against the principles of Gladstonian, anti-Pittite finance in general, some of the consequences of which have already been seen in the public's welcome of the Sardinian loan and the budgetary measures of Sir George Cornewall Lewis. After the final resignation from office of Gladstone and the rest of the Peelites in February 1855, this public eagerness for victory whatever the cost was fairly accurately reflected in the Cabinet. The collapse of the Vienna negotiations in April and the extensive military operations envisaged as a result completed the conversion of the Government to the view that an Allied guarantee should be given forthwith to enable the Turks to raise a large loan without delay. The only difficulties sprang from the objections made by the French to the form of guarantee proposed. But these were quickly met by the British Government, so great was its anxiety to speed the dispatch of funds to Constantinople. 'They [the French] know by experience', Clarendon ruefully confessed, 'how much we will submit to rather than disturb the good understanding between the governments and the armies if we can possibly prevent it.'[1] It is true that there were once again unexpected parliamentary difficulties. The financial resolution authorizing the guarantee was passed on 20 July 1855 by only three votes, and two further heated debates took place. But it is quite mistaken to regard these debates as evidence of English

---

[1] Clarendon to Stratford, 2 July 1855, F.O. 352/42. The convention giving the guarantee is printed in A. du Velay, *Essai sur l'histoire financière de la Turquie* (Paris, 1903), p. 142. Successive drafts with French alterations can be studied in F.O. 78/1157.

reluctance to lend to Turkey.[1] The division of 20 July was a snap affair in a thin House, a 'plot' hatched by an ill-assorted combination of Peelites, Tories, Manchester pacifists, and doctrinaire radicals which came near to success only because of the weakness of government control at that stage of the session. Moreover their arguments were far from being purely financial. Although they made much play with the burdens of loans and subsidies and the risks of uncontrolled expenditure, they drew quite as much upon equally ancient prejudices against the French and against executive high-handedness in the conduct of foreign affairs. Gladstone himself, moreover, with his remorselessly logical mind, had moved beyond the platitudinous financial objections which had earlier occupied him to the probable diplomatic and legal implications of the terms of the guarantee—implications too complex to be appreciated either by the Government or the House.[2] Thus these highly opportunist debates give a much exaggerated impression of the extent to which Parliament still entertained old prejudices against guaranteeing loans to British allies. As a guide to the state of opinion outside Parliament they are worse than useless. To a people still almost hysterically aware of the suffering, disease and death rife among British troops in the East, the arguments put forward in Parliament — whether financial, constitutional or diplomatic — appeared to be simply irresponsible and unpatriotic quibbles. The emotional revolution which had taken place around Christmas 1854 had swept away the financial dogmatism and optimism so widespread at the beginning of the war. 'We must do that which is necessary for the present emergency,' clamoured *The Times*, and of all the leading national and provincial newspapers, the Peelite *Morning Chronicle* alone found anything to say in

[1] This is the view of Du Velay, op. cit., p. 147, and D. C. Blaisdell, *European Financial control in the Ottoman Empire* (New York, 1929), p. 52.

[2] 3 *Hansard*, cxxxix, cols. 1212–68, 1283–313, 1438–45, 1463–513 (20, 23 and 27 July 1855); Gladstone to the Solicitor-General, Add. MS. 44337, fos. 150–8.

favour of the parliamentary opposition to the loan.[1] Indeed the reputation of the Peelites and especially of Gladstone probably reached its nadir with this episode. To the public (and to the Cabinet) opposition to the guarantee seemed either mere financial pedantry or downright disloyalty, even high treason. Its near success on 20 July simply served to accentuate the failure of Parliament to reflect the views of the public at large. 'So much for the wisdom of Parliament!' was Mr. Punch's scornful comment on the affair.[2] By the Government and the country, the guarantee was accepted without hesitation, because it was plainly necessary for the vigorous prosecution of the war. The same consideration determined the English Government's attitude to the actual disbursement of the loan; it attempted some control, but not so much that the money's usefulness was impaired. From the beginning the Cabinet expected Turkey to default (in fact she did not until 1876) and was prepared to make interest payments on her behalf as part of the cost of the war, and in all this it was fully supported by British public opinion. Urgent military necessity was throughout 1855 the yardstick of judgment, and not the canons of political economy nor the lessons of history, still less any dreams of imperialist penetration or the regeneration of Turkey.

It may be objected that this interpretation of the Turkish guarantee and the Sardinian loan as a deliberate exploitation of British capital solely to achieve military victory accords very ill with the familiar claim that in 1855 a loan for Russia was actually raised in London. The difficulty, however, is an imaginary one, for no such loan was ever floated.[3] On the contrary, the Committee of the London Stock Exchange expressly forbade the quotation in their lists of each of the two

---

[1] *The Times*, 24 and 28 July 1855. Even the opposition Press found the parliamentary opposition to the loan discreditable.

[2] *Punch*, 28 July 1855.

[3] This assertion is more fully substantiated and documented by the present author in 'The Russian loan of 1855; An example of economic liberalism?' *Economica*, November 1960.

loans floated by the Russian Government in this war (in Amsterdam and Berlin, not London), thus preventing not only British subjects but also foreigners from dealing in them in the London market. In the case of the second loan (in 1855) the prohibition was extended even to dealings after peace should be restored. These bans were hailed with satisfaction in the City press.[1] Moreover the Government itself actively took steps to make it clear to British subjects throughout Europe that to subscribe to these loans would constitute high treason.[2] Most striking of all, in August 1854 a Bill was rushed through Parliament making it for the first time a statutory offence for British subjects to deal in enemy stock, whether at home or abroad. Originally a private member's Bill, the strength of feeling in the House obliged the Government to take it up officially, despite the fears of some ministers that it would prove futile except as a moral demonstration.[3] Thus in reality the Committee of the Stock Exchange, large majorities in both Houses of Parliament, and even the Government itself (though not unanimously) showed themselves more, and not less, anxious than their predecessors to prohibit the flow of British capital to the enemy. There was indeed a small and select minority of bankers and business men who urged the futility of interfering with the free play of economic forces,[4] but their views did not prevail. Nor do either the continued payments during the Crimean War in connexion with the Russo–Dutch loan or the quotation of pre-war Russian bonds in London furnish proof of any abandonment of financial weapons under the influence of

[1] e.g. *Herapath's Journal*, 22 December 1855.

[2] Clarendon to Cowley, 23 June 1854, Clarendon dep., c. 129, fo. 75, and e.g. Bloomfield to Clarendon, no. 360, 30 June 1854, F.O. 64/373. It is worth noticing that the French Government also took a strong line (Cowley to Clarendon, 22 June 1854, F.O. 519/213/109).

[3] 3 *Hansard* cxxxv, cols. 520–5, 767–84, 886–9, 1145–74, 1386–94, 1478–83 (21, 26 and 27 July; 2, 7 and 9 August 1854). The Act is 17 & 18 Vict. c. cxxii.

[4] Notably James Wilson (*The Economist*, 15 July 1854).

laissez-faire ideas. The former illustrates a principle not yet discarded — that a bilateral treaty which explicitly provides for what should happen in the event of war between the parties is not abrogated when war breaks out — and the latter merely perpetuated the ideas and practices of former wars.[1] British capital was pressed into service in this war more, not less, than it had ever been before.

Thus British financial policy in the Crimean War does indeed possess a certain unity, but it is not a unity provided by any remarkable adherence to the lessons of political economy or even of Pittite war finance. For in the atmosphere of deepening gloom and hysteria which developed after the failure to achieve a quick victory in the Crimea, when the war was transformed from an optimistic picnic into an exacting struggle to retrieve a ruined military reputation, British financial policies and financial thinking were largely transformed also. Military necessity seemed both to require and to justify heavy borrowing at home and considerable lending to foreign allies. Thus despite profound changes in the British economy since 1815 and a striking development and acceptance of economic theory, the British public's lust for victory enforced acceptance of increasingly traditional and pragmatic policies. More often than not, dogmas and attitudes which had been influential at the beginning of the war, were by its end substantially discarded in the effort to overcome disaster and achieve military success. In the last resort it is not economic theory nor smugness about the nation's wealth and resources which offer the best key to British financial policy in this war, but the country's determination not to be beaten in what seemed to that generation its darkest hour.

[1] This is argued by the present author in a comment on F. W. Fetter, 'The Russian Loan of 1855: A Postscript', in *Economica*, November 1961, pp. 525–6.

CHAPTER SEVEN

Monetary Policy

T HROUGHOUT the nineteenth century monetary questions loomed very large in British minds, for the chief source of economic fluctuations was found in price movements, and these were regarded as the result of monetary factors. The onset of the Crimean War made them loom still larger. So obvious was it that war would create an increased demand for bullion, particularly when it was fought in an area like the Black Sea which was largely outside the European network of credit facilities, that it was not only the theoretically minded who feared serious monetary consequences as soon as a military expedition was despatched to the East in February 1854 — although as it happened monetary thinkers in the 1850s were already particularly concerned with external specie flows. In any case another war was bound immediately to push the dramatic monetary history of the Revolutionary and Napoleonic Wars into the forefront of men's minds. It was after all the suspension of cash payments and the resort to a paper pound, followed by serious inflation and the controversy around the report of the Bullion Committee of 1810, which had set in train that acrimonious monetary debate in which the resumption of gold convertibility in 1819 and the passage of the Bank Charter Act in 1844 had been the most bitterly contested stages. Since this debate was still unfinished in the 1850s, it was inevitable that the participants should seize upon and often distort the monetary history of the war in an effort to find therein proof of their opponents' errors. Thus historical recollections and contemporary concerns combined to convince both economists and laymen that the monetary strains of the forthcoming war would throw a significant and probably decisive light upon each of the three monetary

questions around which argument centred at that time. First
and foremost, what were the consequences of the automatic
correlation of the Bank of England's note issue with the
reserves in its Issue Department prescribed by the Bank
Charter Act of 1844? Second, how and why should alterations
in the Bank's rate of discount be made and what were the
effects to be expected from such alterations? Third, and least
widely canvassed, could a case be made out for abandoning the
gold standard?

As has already been noticed,[1] many weeks before the war
began the opponents of the gold standard and of the automatic restriction of the currency were prophesying that it
would reveal the inadequacies of the existing system, and
even that system's stoutest defenders feared that it was about
to be confronted with a challenge which would prove hard to
meet. Partisan exaggeration as well as serious argument
about the country's monetary prospects thus appeared at
once. When Gladstone laid before Parliament his first proposals for the financing of the expedition to the East, several
members of the Banking School (the opponents of the system
established in 1844) at once asked him whether he was prepared to carry on the war with a restricted currency. They in
their turn were quickly and quite unjustifiably charged by
supporters of the opposite school of thought with wanting to
restore the 'Little Shilling' of 1797–1819 and with 'an in-
curable addiction to the nostrums of Inconvertible Paper'. A
fortnight later, on 21 March, the forebodings inspired by the
bullion drain of the previous war were made more explicit in
a second financial debate.[2] Thus even before war was declared, its probable effects upon the currency had furnished
welcome ammunition to the controversialists in Parliament,
as well as to the pamphleteers outside.[3]

[1] See above, p. 14.

[2] 3 *Hansard*, cxxxi, cols. 395–8, 439–40, 1094–113 (6 and 21 March
1854).

[3] See, for example, Hamer Stansfeld, *A Remedy suggested for our
Financial Difficulties* (1854), and Anon., *The Bank Charter Act in the*

Far more important, the monetary circumstances which developed at the very beginning of the war did indeed prove to be such as to provoke doubt and dismay, even among the uncommitted. It happened that the Exchequer balances were then very low because of the failure of Gladstone's conversion scheme of the year before, and Gladstone was obliged to make heavy demands upon the Bank for Deficiency Bills. This provoked a great deal of criticism and uneasiness. By the end of April 1854 an alarming drain of bullion from the Bank appeared to have set in. On 21 April Gladstone himself was sufficiently disturbed to write to James Pennington (a writer on currency and banking much consulted by Peel) about 'the state and prospects of the Bank's reserve', asking for his views on 'the probable draft of bullion which may be caused by our military expedition abroad and by other circumstances of the war'.[1] Gladstone also sought the advice of Peel's veteran Chancellor of the Exchequer, Henry Goulburn, upon an extension of the fiduciary issue. Under the Bank Charter Act two-thirds of the country bank notes unissued in 1854 could be added to the Bank's fiduciary issue, and this step had been mooted in the House of Commons when war was imminent by the banker G. C. Glyn, and a little later in the Press and by the Treasury as well.[2] But to such a wholehearted believer in the classical theory that a drain of gold could only be stopped by contracting the circulating medium in order to lower prices, any increase of the fiduciary issue was obviously dangerous, and Goulburn accordingly advised Gladstone against it.[3] Within the Treasury itself, however, opinion was divided. James Wilson, the Economic Secretary to the Treasury, was well known as an opponent of the Bank

---

crisis of 1847 (1854). Copies of both are in the Goldsmiths' Library, London.

[1] Gladstone to Pennington, 21 April 1854, Add. MS. 44529, fo. 86.

[2] 3 *Hansard*, cxxxi, col. 397 (6 March 1854); G. Arbuthnot to Gladstone, 24 and 29 March 1854, Add. MS. 44096, fos. 37 and 43.

[3] Goulburn to Gladstone, 5 May 1854, Add. MS. 44162, fo. 115.

Charter Act, and believed, as Peel's old private secretary George Arbuthnot warned Gladstone, that 'no commercial crises can be owing to over issues of notes'.[1] Arbuthnot himself, then Auditor of the Civil List, took a wider view than Goulburn. He pointed out to Gladstone his mistake in watching the bullion in the Issue Department instead of the Banking Reserve, and went on 'war is a great absorber of specie, and when there is added to this the unfavourable balance of trade which must have been occasioned by the large imports of corn, I think that without seeking to trace the course of exchange in particular countries, there is sufficient to account for our loss of bullion'.[2] By 6 May, when Gladstone next made a financial statement to the House, he was obliged to admit that the heavy demands which the failure of his earlier conversion operations obliged him to make upon the Bank, together with this drain of bullion provoked by the war and by heavy corn imports was subjecting the Bank to considerable inconvenience.[3] On 11 May Bank Rate was raised to 5%, and Consols fell to 87, and according to *The Economist* the money market was more stringent than at any time since the crisis of 1847. After a mere couple of months of war it looked as though the prophecies that war and the Bank Charter Act would prove incompatible were about to be fulfilled.

It was in this atmosphere of monetary strain that John Elliot Cairnes felt it apt to publish a paper he had delivered a year earlier on the principles of currency involved in the Bank Charter Act. 'At the present moment,' he explained early in June 1854, echoing the common predictions of the time, 'at the opening of a European war, we may expect drains of gold more extensive than we have for many years experienced.'

[1] Arbuthnot to Gladstone, 24 March 1854, Add. MS. 44096, fo. 37.

[2] Arbuthnot to Gladstone, 29 April 1854, Add MS. 44096, fos. 56–60. Privately Gladstone was prepared to contemplate amending the Act of 1844, which he admitted to be a cause of panic (Gladstone to Graham, 10 October 1854, Add. MS. 44163, fos. 159–60).

[3] Gladstone to J. G. Hubbard (Governor of the Bank), 6 May 1854, Add. MS. 44095, fo. 194; 3 *Hansard*, cxxxii, cols. 1429–39.

Cairnes assumed that convertibility was a settled question, but he strongly attacked the contraction of the circulation which under the provisions of the Bank Charter Act must result from the drain of gold which had developed in the last two months. Again and again he repeated that the war would most probably introduce 'disturbing forces' which that Act had already shown itself unfit to control. To Cairnes the violent contractions of the currency which the Act enjoined could only be harmful; a 'timely and gradual rise in the rate of interest' was far preferable. In the last resort the issue of notes inevitably must be discretionary.[1] Cairnes's paper, however, distinguished though it was, failed to inspire a new debate on the monetary aspect of the war at that stage, for, contrary to all expectation, by the time it was published in the middle of June 1854, the tide had already turned. From 3 August Bank Rate was steadily reduced, until it reached 3% on 14 June 1855. At this low point it remained until 6 September 1855. The financial stringency which had developed so quickly at the beginning of the war disappeared as quickly as it had come, and with it the incentive to a renewed theoretical debate.[2] It was widely agreed that the prospect of an unexpectedly good harvest was the chief explanation of this surprising turn of affairs. When a Day of General Thanksgiving was finally held for the harvest on 1 October 1854 more than one allusion was made to the divine solicitude shown therein for the country's balance of payments: the plentiful harvest had added £30 million to the resources of the

[1] J. E. Cairnes, *An Examination into the Principles of Currency involved in the Bank Charter Act of 1844* (Dublin, 1854), pp. 3, 5, 40, 76.

[2] The Goldsmiths' Library contains a lecture by Edmund Taunton 'On the permanent national measure of value' delivered at Birmingham on 5 July 1854, which declares it impossible to carry on the war with vigour 'with our right hand cut off, for our free *silver* power is greater than our gold power', and a pamphlet by the indefatigable Hamer Stansfeld dated January 1855, *A Few Reasons for the immediate reconsideration of the Bank Charter Act of 1844*; but in general there is a marked absence of discussion of the repercussions of the war on monetary problems between June 1854 and the autumn of 1855.

country, one popular preacher told his congregation.[1] Another factor from whose operation much had always been anticipated, and rightly, was the constant influx of gold as a result of the Australian and Californian discoveries. Ardent supporters of the gospel of war finance by taxation alone found a third explanation in Gladstone's declarations of his intention to rely upon taxation, which were held to have checked speculation and saved the money market from the strain of financing Government loans.[2] Altogether, this episode of monetary strain, and the calm which followed, contributed little to the monetary controversies of the day. Extraneous factors were obviously the country's saviours, and the compatibility of war with the existing monetary system remained an open question.

But in August 1855 the monetary situation dramatically changed once more, and the Cassandra-like warnings so common at the beginning of the war at last began to seem justified. Trade and banking were sound, there was no considerable capital shortage among exporters, imports were not excessive nor the exchanges unfavourable,[3] yet the Bank's reserves fell heavily and its discount rate went up steeply between 6 September and 18 October from 3% to a peak of 7%. At first the Chancellor of the Exchequer's attitude was casual. On 26 September 1855 Lewis confided to Sir James Graham that the alarm about the export of bullion was overdone, and that he could see no reason why it should continue.[4] His brother-in-law Clarendon (who took his cue in financial matters from Lewis) repeated this verdict to Lord Cowley, the British Ambassador in Paris, adding that it was French proceedings which gave the chief cause for alarm. 'The men of business here are frightened at the proceedings of the Crédit Mobilier,' he wrote, 'and fear some of these days that there will be an

[1] W. Cadman, 'National Thanksgiving', *Penny Pulpit*, November 1854.
[2] e.g. *The Economist*, 26 August 1854.
[3] Ibid., 13 October 1855.
[4] Lewis to Graham, 26 September 1855, Graham MSS., Microfilm 45.

almighty smash in that Establishment.'[1] A fortnight later although things looked graver Lewis was still absent in the country, to the disapproval of his friend Henry Reeve, that minor official and leading journalist. Reeve and his circle placed the blame entirely upon the Bank of France and the Crédit Mobilier. 'Every sovereign exported from this country now is bought at a loss [because of the steep rise in bank rate],' he wrote to Lewis, 'yet the export goes on: and I suppose the Bank of France and the Crédit Mobilier are running a race against the Bank of England. . . . It must end in a suspension of cash payments either on one side of the Channel or the other.'[2] The financial state of France was indeed precarious. By 16 October James Rothschild was in London on a mission from the Bank of France to ask for a loan of £2 million sterling from the Bank of England. By this time English ministers had ceased to belittle the alarm in the money market. But neither did they attach as much blame as the City to the activities of French tripoteurs. 'The financial crisis in France and the approaching one here are the source of great uneasiness,' Clarendon told Cowley on 20 October, 'as they are not common crises which contain within themselves some elements of cure . . . but originate in causes which are constant and increasing and which time will only make worse, viz. the exportation of gold for war purposes none of which returns either in manufactures or produce or in bullion.' The Cabinet refused the French request for a loan, on the ground that it would entail an immediate summoning of Parliament to sanction the suspension of the Bank Charter Act — a step which both Governments agreed would be highly imprudent.[3] However the Financial Secretary to the Treasury was despatched to Paris to investigate the situation and consult with Fould, the French Minister of Finance. 'No man in England understands banking affairs better than James Wilson,' wrote

[1] Clarendon to Cowley, 28 September 1855, F.O. 519/172.
[2] Reeve to Lewis, 12 October 1855, Harpton Court MSS. c. 2273.
[3] Clarendon to Cowley, 16, 17 and 20 October 1855, F.O. 519/172.

Clarendon to the British Ambassador enthusiastically. Nevertheless Wilson does not seem altogether to have shared his chief's analysis of the situation. Although both agreed that the unavoidably heavy remittances to the Commissariat in the East were a large factor,[1] in Wilson's opinion speculative French exports of silver to India and China were a more important reason for the drain of gold than the war-induced operations of the Bank of France. (France had a bimetallic system, and as there had been a relative rise in the value of silver, used silver to make payments to the East, replacing it by gold drawn from England.) He also believed that Lewis's 'system of loans' was to blame for 'the derangement of the [English] money market'.[2] However, by the beginning of December stringency was rapidly disappearing, although the Bank's bullion reserve was slightly smaller than it had been at the beginning of October. One brief relapse occurred because of indirect operations upon London through the Crédit Mobilier on the part of continental subscribers to the new Russian loan, which entailed a loss of reputedly £200,000 of gold from the Bank,[3] but by the end of the year the crisis was clearly over.

By the standards of the crises of 1825, 1836, 1847 and 1857 there never was in 1855 a situation which deserved that name. Among the commercial public there was much serious uneasiness, but no panic, and these events have long been overshadowed by the far graver ones of 1857. Nevertheless the debate which the crisis of 1855 provoked deserves more attention than the comparative mildness of that crisis might suggest. In 1856 the Bank's privileges became subject to re-

[1] After his visit to Paris Wilson described to Lewis the English Commissariat's system of drawing bills upon Marseilles instead of London, which increased the pressure upon the Bank of France (Wilson to Lewis, 28 October 1855, printed in E. I. Barrington, *The Servant of All* (1927), i. 285).

[2] *The Economist*, 6 and 13 October and 24 November 1855.

[3] Clarendon to Cowley, 20 December 1855, Clarendon dep. c. 134, fo. 507; *The Economist*, 22 December 1855.

demption, and this precipitated a fresh round of discussion in the course of which many of the letters to the Press of the previous year were republished in pamphlet form and much play made with the events of the war. Not only does this debate throw light upon the rather obscure history of nine-teenth-century thought upon the monetary consequences of a state of war, but it also has some significance for the de-velopment of monetary theory in general. In so far as the crisis of 1855 was very obviously entirely the result of exo-genous factors, and not of the state of trade or credit at home, it hastened recognition of the inadequacy of the classical analysis of drains, and forced even the least committed to consider whether, if drains were caused by other factors than unduly high domestic prices, the only proper remedy was indeed contraction of currency and credit along the lines practised by the Bank. In addition, the part played by French silver exports in precipitating this drain encouraged some re-newed debate upon the gold standard itself. Few contem-poraries indeed would have agreed with the modern authority who wrote that 'in the money market the war caused scarcely any disturbance'.[1]

What then were the lessons contemporaries drew from these vicissitudes? The plain man commonly remained to the end the victim of what *The Times* once called 'the vague terror that war and financial confusion are inseparably connected'.[2] To him it was the *lack* of any bullion drain between June 1854 and August 1855 which called for explanation, rather than its existence in the autumn of 1855. By then, the number of men in the Crimea had more than doubled[3] and the Commissariat's demands for bullion had increased correspondingly. Moreover,

---

[1] Clapham, op. cit. ii. 365.

[2] 1 January 1856.

[3] 'After beginning the campaign last year with 25,000 men and well nigh losing all — we now have 51,000, our Turkish legion is good for 20,000 and regiments of the Foreign Legion will by the spring amount to 10,000,' wrote Prince Albert to Stockmar on 19 November 1855 (T. Martin, *Life of the Prince Consort*, 5th edn. (1878), iii. 388).

by that time the attempt to finance the war by taxation alone and without foreign subsidies of any kind had been given up. *The Economist* on 8 September 1855 calculated that as much as £47 million would have to be contributed by the money market to various Government or Government-sponsored loans within the next six months. When to these war-induced strains was added the fact that a very moderate harvest in 1855 made some corn imports necessary, monetary difficulties seemed obviously unavoidable. It was only the particularly well-informed who realized that they would never have attained the serious proportions they did without the operations of both the Bank of France and the Crédit Mobilier, which together were making heavy demands upon the Bank's resources. To the ordinary thoughtful citizen it seemed mere common sense that a war, if long and serious, would involve a drain of gold so heavy that inconvertibility and inflation were only a matter of time. By the end of the war the opinion was very widespread that if the war had continued at the same rate of expenditure as in 1855, the Bank Charter Act would have had to be suspended, and probably convertibility as well. (The two were all too commonly confused.) The economist J. R. McCulloch, a fervent supporter of the Act, summed up the experience of the war thus to Cornewall Lewis in October 1856: 'It appears to me that the operation of the present system in the late war was, in all respects, eminently satisfactory. It stood in the way of no legitimate transaction, but was a powerful obstacle to the creation of artificial credit and was therefore,' he went on to admit, 'highly unpopular. Had the war gone on half a dozen years longer you would have been compelled to inconvertible paper. The ignorance and shortsightedness of the public on such subjects is quite lamentable. I doubt whether they have made any progress since the days of the Mississippi scheme.'[1]

There was indeed a great deal of impatience with the Bank Charter Act at the end of 1855, but McCulloch was over-hasty

[1] McCulloch to Lewis, 1 October 1856, Harpton Court MSS., c. 1997.

to dismiss it as the result of public ignorance and short-sightedness on monetary matters. It sprang at bottom from the widespread realization that the best chance of avoiding disastrous economic difficulties in the midst of war, despite the heavy demand for gold which war entailed, lay in maintaining trade at as high a level as possible. It was very easy to argue that the crisis of 1855 was an artificial one, created not by a shortage of capital but by a shortage of money induced by the war and greatly aggravated by the restrictive effect of the existing monetary system;[1] and thus that it could be ended by a policy of cheap money — which would stimulate trade. Because it seemed impossible to deny Britain's vast material strength — which after all had been a favourite commonplace among publicists for years — this argument that her difficulties were artificial ones, made acute only by faulty monetary institutions, seemed all the more plausible. Thus in the autumn of 1855 the various exponents of discretionary control of a convertible currency and even of inconvertibility found a very responsive audience. 'Those who have paid but little attention to the subject hitherto,' wrote one pamphleteer triumphantly, 'begin to see that war and the present system cannot co-exist for any great length of time,'[2] and the claim was fully justified. The incompatibility of the war with the Bank Charter Act became almost a catchphrase,[3] and one which was made widely familiar when *The Times* took to remarking that although British resources were large, they were 'not illimitable', and that if war expenditure rose beyond a certain point, suspension of cash payments might again be unavoidable. Thus the leading journal itself by its doubts about the wisdom of raising Bank Rate and so depressing trade, at one point could be claimed as an ally by the

[1] These views were put forward for example by R. H. Patterson in 'The Gold-screw and its consequences', *Blackwood's Magazine*, lxxix (1856), 1–20, and by Alexander Alison, *Bank Reform* (1855).

[2] John MacFarlan, *Our Monetary Affairs* (1856), p. 51.

[3] 'Whether the War or our Currency Laws must be abandoned', I. C. Wright, *The War and our Resources* (1855).

opponents of the existing system.[1] In November and early
December many political prophets were predicting a suspension of the Act, particularly after the announcement on 14
November that the Governors of the Bank had had an inter-
view with the Chancellor of the Exchequer. 'I think I see a
disposition to tamper with the currency evinced in the
Government papers,' wrote Sir James Graham to his fellow
disgruntled Peelite, Gladstone. 'I always knew that this war
would be the reversal of Peel's policy.'[2] A considerably less
distinguished politician, James Parkes, told 'Bear' Ellice on
1 December: 'The *Post* today hints the 1844 Act is to be
revised,'[3] and this impression must have been strengthened by
the leaders published in the next few weeks in that quasi-
ministerial journal, so closely associated with Palmerston,
urging that elasticity was essential and a fiduciary issue of
£14 million much too low for the needs of war.[4] There is no
evidence that Lewis himself favoured suspension, although he
certainly felt that some parts of the Act deserved revision,[5]
and that there must be a discretion in the management of the
currency.[6] However it was in response to his request that on
7 December an Order in Council authorized the Bank to issue
additional notes to the amount of £475,000[7] — this being two-
thirds of the notes which certain country bankers had ceased

[1] *The Times*, 5 October, 7 December 1855. By 1 January 1856 however
The Times had come to believe that the Bank must 'unflinchingly
keep its charges up to the general level of those upon the Continent'.

[2] 19 November 1855, Add. MS. 44163, fo. 206.

[3] 1 December 1855, National Library of Scotland, Ellice Papers.

[4] *Morning Post*, 1, 10, 11, 14 and 18 December 1855. On this question
the radical *Daily News* for once shared the *Post*'s views (cf. *Daily News*,
18 December 1855).

[5] 3 *Hansard*, cxl, col. 1530 (28 February 1856). In 1857 he believed
that the Act had tended to increase the crisis of that year (Lewis to
Overstone, 20 November 1857, Harpton Court MSS., c. 2921).

[6] Lewis to Wilson, 30 October 1856, Barrington, op. cit. i. 332.

[7] *London Gazette*, 11 December 1855; Lewis to Palmerston, 2 November 1855, Broadlands MSS. Lewis's impression was that the Governor
of the Bank wanted suspension, but the Deputy Governor did not
(Lewis to Palmerston, 17 October 1855, ibid.).

to issue since 1844 and therefore permissible under the Act. Thus the measure suggested by the Banking School on the eve of the war was finally adopted in the crisis which at last seemed about to prove their gloomy forebodings warranted.

Fortunately for the supporters of the Bank Charter Act, however, their opponents could easily be given an often quite undeserved aura of eccentricity and unreliability. 'The present system' could be taken to mean not only the automatic correlation of the currency or of Bank Rate with the Bank's bullion reserves, but also the quite distinct and much less controversial questions of the Bank's banking privileges and the gold standard. Those who opposed the first alone were almost invariably weakened and discredited by being associated, usually quite unjustifiably, with the opponents of the other two aspects of the system, aspects which had won widespread acceptance and respect. It was this confusion, for example, which lessened the impact of the petitions for the suspension of the Act of 1844 drawn up by the Chambers of Commerce of Edinburgh, Glasgow, Liverpool, Nottingham and Birmingham, despite the fact that they deliberately did not raise the question of gold convertibility.[1] (There was considerable commercial distress in these areas that autumn.) The letters sent to *The Times* by one of the most notorious inflationists, T. C. Salt, conveniently enabled that journal to denounce 'currency Philosophers' at length and without distinction throughout December.[2] A crowded meeting held in the London Tavern on 5 December in favour of paper money served the same purpose.

Nevertheless by the end of the year the Bank Charter Act was sufficiently endangered for its chief begetter and defender, S. J. Loyd, first Lord Overstone, to publish an important pseudonymous series of letters in its defence in *The Times*.

[1] In Birmingham considerable manœuvring was necessary to prevent this question being raised in the petition (cf. G. H. Wright, *Chronicles of the Birmingham Chamber of Commerce, 1813–1913* (1913), pp. 128–31).

[2] *The Times*, 13, 20 and 26 December 1855.

In Scotland, another series of letters in *The Scotsman*[1] by George Combe (the famous phrenologist and publicist) performed the same service — perhaps even more necessary there, where the Bank Charter Act had always been unpopular and was opposed by the rest of the Press. Both took it for granted that only the Act ensured convertibility. They also argued that the Act was not responsible for starting the drain — rather unnecessarily, since serious writers agreed that it had been caused by war expenditure, corn imports or continental silver operations, and probably a combination of these factors. The real point at issue was whether the currency laws and the Bank's interpretation of them had aggravated and prolonged the drain once it had begun. This too they of course denied: if the circulation is increased, interest will fall and gold will be carried away, wrote Overstone on 30 November.[2] Eighteen months later, Overstone still refused to accept what it had by then become platitudinous to say — that if the war had continued, the Act would have had to be suspended. He insisted too that war expenditure abroad need not necessarily lead to an overall drain of bullion. Giving evidence before a Select Committee on the operation of the Bank Acts in June 1857, both Overstone and J. G. Hubbard (who had been Governor of the Bank during the war) made it clear that in the event of war they relied upon rectifying the exchanges through affecting the rate of foreign lending as well as the international trade balance.[3] This view that the currency acts were irrelevant to the cause, and beneficial to the course, of the crisis was widespread in 1855 among supporters of the Currency School. It was preached for example in the newly founded *Saturday Review* by G. L. Rickards, the Oxford economist, who blamed the absorption of capital by

---

[1] Reprinted as *The Currency Question Considered* (1856), these ran through nine editions by 1858.

[2] Letters of Mercator to *The Times*, reprinted in S. J. Loyd, Lord Overstone, *Tracts and other publications on metallic and paper currency* (1858), p. 314.

[3] *P.P.*, 1857, sess. 2, x, pt. 1, questions 2388–99, 3658, 3708–12.

the war, and by the young Bagehot, who exclaimed upon the 'peculiar covetousness of coin' of the oriental area where the war was fought.[1] It was left to James Wilson to point out that the fact that the Bank Charter Act was not responsible for this particular crisis was no argument for retaining it. Wilson agreed that a high rate of discount was essential in the autumn of 1855 and therefore approved of the Bank's policy.[2] But he pointed out (as he had done for many years) that the Bank's control over the circulation was in reality an indirect one, exercised through its banking advances, and that the Act was therefore irrelevant and its effects upon the public mind misleading and mischievous.[3]

Wilson, however, was the most moderate of the Bank Charter Act's critics. The main body of criticism came from representatives of the commercial community, and they naturally concentrated not upon the responsiveness to money rates of international transfers of capital, nor upon the shortage of domestic capital induced by government borrowing — both of which might be argued to justify a high bank rate — but upon the trade depression which was suffered when Bank Rate rose. By far the ablest exponent of their views was R. S. Somers of Glasgow. His pamphlet, *The Errors of the Banking Acts of 1844–5, as exhibited in the late monetary crisis*, although not published until February 1857, discusses the events of 1855 and incorporates newspaper articles published at the time. Somers stressed that the crisis of 1855 was unique, in that trade was obviously sound, but he did not find the explanation in the war. The drain of gold which the war entailed was 'trivial' compared with the country's gold imports, and the net loss of capital obviously much less than the gross war expenditure. To him the chief explanation lay in the immense

[1] *Saturday Review*, 3 November 1855, 2 February 1856. (These attributions are given in the bound volume belonging to Sir James Fitzjames Stephen, now in the possession of the London Library.)

[2] *The Economist*, 8 and 15 September 1855.

[3] Ibid., 20 October and 22 and 29 December 1855, and Wilson to Lewis, 28 October 1855, Barrington, op. cit. i. 285.

European silver exports to the East, and consequent demand for gold to take their place. The remedy for the drain was to stimulate trade, and therefore the Government's policy should be one of cheap money. Nevertheless he thought the war a sufficiently important aggravating influence to repeat the common view that had it continued much longer, the existing monetary system would have been found 'wholly insupportable'. Whatever its causes, the drain of 1855 had demonstrated that not every drain was 'the sign of an over extended state of trade and a scarcity of capital', and thus, claimed Somers, had proved that the Act's assumptions were out of date and its policies harmfully inflexible.[1] These were the views of commercial circles, but some academic economists' minds were moving in the same direction. On 4 December 1856 the question John Stuart Mill proposed for discussion by the Political Economy Club was, 'Is it incumbent on the Bank of England to restrict its discounts, on the setting in of a drain of gold, without reference to the causes in which that drain originates?'[2] The necessity for flexibility and discretion, the fallacy of supposing that any device could be found which would automatically regulate currency and credit in all circumstances, or that £14 million was the only proper figure for the fiduciary issue, became much more familiar and respectable ideas as a result of the exceptional crisis of 1855, so plainly the result of external factors. Thus Thomas Tooke in his pamphlet, *On the Bank Charter Act of 1844*, which was published late in December 1855, found a much more favourable audience than he would otherwise have done for his attack upon the Bank's mechanical adjustment of its discount rate to its Banking Reserve throughout 1855, and his charge that it was the sharp fluctuations thus involved which turned

---

[1] *The Errors of the Banking Acts of 1844–5*, pp. 15–16.

[2] *Minutes of Proceedings*, vi. 73. In the edition of his *Principles of Political Economy* published in 1857, Mill inserted a reference to 'the late war with Russia' as furnishing an example of a drain not caused by the state of currency or credit (ii. 219).

what would otherwise have been merely a delicate situation into something far graver in the autumn of 1855.[1] However, although Tooke's argument has been given pride of place by later students (his pamphlet was reprinted as part of volume v of his *History of Prices*, published in 1857), at the time more ephemeral contributions in the newspaper press and the serious periodicals attracted quite as much attention. These make it very clear that it certainly should not be said that 'when the war ended without the anticipated disaster, people were forced to acknowledge that the Bank of England deserved well of the country'.[2] The anticipated disaster had seemed very imminent; and the wisdom of the Bank's policy (and the Act of 1844 by which it was inspired) was more in dispute than it had ever been. Some thought it had been right for the wrong reasons, others that it had in any case not been of decisive importance; but some held that it had been positively harmful, not only because they believed it had followed the swings of the market too blindly, but also because they challenged the fundamental position that contraction was the proper remedy under all circumstances for an outflow of bullion. The appearance of a drain of a kind which, prima facie at least, would not be stopped by 'the spirit of 1844', whose purpose was to stop all drains, spread the feeling that Peel's Act was useless, if not positively harmful. Tooke was indeed right to remark that at the end of 1855 there was 'considerable impatience in the public mind for the institution of a parliamentary inquiry into the operation of those novel restrictions imposed on the Bank by its last Charter'.[3] As the

[1] T. Tooke, *On the Bank Charter Act of 1844*, pp. 100–1.

[2] A. Andréadès, *History of the Bank of England*, 2nd edn. (1924), p. 344.

[3] Tooke and Newmarch, op. cit. v. 485. Soon after Parliament reassembled a motion was debated for such an enquiry, but refused by Lewis at that juncture on the grounds that it would inevitably and unfairly concentrate upon the exceptional, war-induced events of the previous autumn (3 *Hansard*, cxl, cols. 1481–542 (28 February 1856). A year later, however, he fulfilled his promise to initiate such an enquiry when peace had returned (ibid. cxliv, col. 320, 6 February 1857).

R

Morning Post more succinctly put it, there was 'general agreement that the Act needs amendment'.[1]

Thus in the end the experiences of the war had failed to settle the question whether a great war was compatible with a convertible currency and a Bank Rate regulated by commercial forces. Both had survived to the end of the war; but between September and December 1855 they had undeniably been under a very great strain. Those who opposed the system could plausibly claim that it had only been saved by the recent gold discoveries and consequent shiploads of bullion, and by a premature peace. It had also become more difficult to believe that 'the spirit of 1844' would unfailingly remedy all monetary crises, whatever their causes, whether in peace or war. Many moderate and open-minded men now believed that in certain kinds of crises the principles of the Act might well be harmful, even if they were normally of value; many more were convinced that it was the Bank's role as lender of capital that counted, not its role as issuer of currency, and that the Bank Charter Act was therefore irrelevant. It is thus easy to understand how the impression gained ground that the existing monetary system would not — perhaps ought not — have survived had the war continued.

One last consideration perhaps encouraged this impression: the particular importance attached by the Government in this war to trade. It was not merely that the commercial community felt that the events of 1855 proved that they were liable to be sacrificed to a narrow and arbitrary theory of the means of checking outflows of gold, however sound the state of trade might be, and however undeserving of being 'put to the pinch'. There was also the far more significant consideration that the maintenance of export trade had been deliberately made an essential element in the economic policy of the country during this war. It was thus very easy, if also over-hasty, for them to assume that a policy of dear money, often described as tantamount to a deliberate depression

[1] *Morning Post*, 21 December 1855.

of trade, would not have been allowed by the Government
for long. Commercial policy was, however, such a complicated and vitally important aspect of economic policy
during the Crimean War that it deserves separate consideration.

CHAPTER EIGHT

War Trade and Trade War

IT was in its commercial policy even more than in its
financial decisions that the British Government in the
Crimean War made an ambitious attempt to reconcile the
conflicting claims of military expediency, administrative
practicability, and the well-being of the national economy as
understood by the economic science of the day. Unfortunately
there was no consensus of opinion as to how this could best be
achieved. Trade policy was therefore always a highly controversial affair. How susceptible was Russian morale, currency and trade to economic pressure? How grave was the
risk of antagonizing neutral powers, above all the United
States, if British naval power was fully used to exert that
pressure? How practicable was it to check evasion and fraud
if official controls on trade were imposed? Did economic science
indeed prove that to attempt to control the course of trade was
to battle with impossibilities? Above all, how high a price
would Britain's own industrial and commercial economy have
to pay, if economic warfare were resorted to on a large scale?
To all these questions conflicting answers were given inside
and outside Government circles and at different stages of the
war. At the beginning, as has already been pointed out,[1] the
Cabinet reached a clear enough conception of its objectives:
not to allow Russian shipping out of Russian ports, to cut off
Russian imports totally but Russian exports only in so far as
this would not damage Britain's own economy, and to avoid
offending the all-important neutral powers. In practical terms,
these objectives implied a policy composed of three apparently
incongruous parts. First, control of the export from Britain
of war material; secondly, abstention from seizing enemy

[1] See above, p. 18.

248

property on neutral ships and from privateering, combined with the blockade of enemy ports and capture of contraband of war and enemy despatches; and thirdly, the legalizing of British trade with the enemy, apart from the actual entry of British ships into Russian ports.

The first began to be evolved six weeks before war was declared. In an urgent attempt to prevent certain contractors exporting large quantities of marine engines to Russia,[1] the export of arms, ammunition, military and naval stores and every component part of an engine or boiler was wholly prohibited on 18 February 1854. The onus of making this quite impracticable proclamation work was thrown upon the Customs Officers, who were at first instructed to use their discretion and allow such goods to be cleared if they were satisfied they were not going to Russia,[2] but after a few days were ordered to do so only if the trader gave a bond that they would be landed at a specified port. This was not to be cancelled until a certificate of landing had been received from the British Consul at the port in question.[3] The Foreign Office at once expressed its doubts about the adequacy of this safeguard and was not altogether satisfied by the Treasury's assurance that bonds would only be accepted for materials commonly used for peaceful purposes, or for warlike stores professing to be shipped 'to the regular and distant markets of the world'.[4] This however was the system which was relied on for the rest of the war, after being given legal force by an Order in Council on 11 April 1854. This prohibited the export of certain enumerated articles to those northern and eastern parts of Europe from which they could easily be re-exported to Russia, but allowed their export to other places against a bond that the goods

[1] Aberdeen to the Queen, 17 February 1854, Add. MS. 43048, fo. 251; 3 *Hansard*, cxxx, col. 914 (20 February 1854) and *The Economist*, 29 April 1854.

[2] Treasury Minute of 21 February 1854, Public Record Office, T[reasury] 29/554/401.

[3] Treasury Minute of 24 February 1854, ibid. 429.

[4] Treasury Minute of 24 March 1854, ibid. 642.

would be landed and entered at their declared destination. Export to northern and eastern Europe under bond was only allowed by special licence of the Privy Council, which considered each case on political grounds, and did not readily grant such permission.[1] Nevertheless there was undoubtedly much British profiteering in war material destined for the enemy,[2] fostered by the loopholes left at first in the Channel Islands and the Isle of Man and later in Canada and the West Indies,[3] and by the tardiness with which the list of enumerated articles and prohibited areas was adjusted in the light of experience. The most serious gap was in the control of exports of saltpetre, which by October 1855 had increased so alarmingly as to make it obvious that indirect British trade with Russia in this essential chemical must be very extensive. The Privy Council was accordingly obliged after Cabinet discussion to impose far stricter controls.[4] But in any case, as the Government's chief adviser on questions of international law, that pessimistic traditionalist, Sir John Harding, rightly urged from the beginning, 'if arms are allowed to be exported at all to places which trade with the enemy, they will reach him',[5] for re-export from such places was always very easy. Moreover America and Belgium were good alternative sources of supply of the marine machinery and chemicals[6] which the system

[1] This is the impression gained from Public Record Office P[rivy] C[ouncil] 6/7–8, *passim*. The diarist Charles Greville was the official chiefly responsible for the issue of these licences.

[2] Denounced, for example, in the *Illustrated London News*, 17 February 1855, *The Economist*, 1 September 1855, and *Punch*, 6 October 1855.

[3] Cf. the Orders in Council of 8 June 1854 and 27 December 1855.

[4] The Financial Secretary to the Treasury to the Clerk of the Council in waiting 27 October 1855, T. 9/10/267–9, C. Greville to Granville, 31 October 1855, P.R.O. 30/29/33, J. Buchanan to W. L. Marcy, 25 January 1856, *The Works of James Buchanan*, ed. J. B. Moore (Philadelphia, 1908–11), x. 17–18. The Admiralty, Ordnance and Foreign Office were always more alert and suspicious than either the Treasury or the Council Office.

[5] P.R.O., F.O. 83/2280, 22 March 1854.

[6] The Russian chemical industry was quite inadequate (cf. P. I. Lyashchenko, *History of the National Economy of Russia to the 1917*

was chiefly intended to withhold. Export control thus never
played more than a specialized and somewhat ineffectual part
in the attempt to undermine the enemy's belligerent capacity.
The main effort, it was always realized, must be a naval one.

Why then, it may be asked, was the right of capture at sea
drastically curtailed and privateering forsworn at the very
outset of the war? The notion that this decision was baffling,
secretive and irresponsible is entirely a legend created by later
controversialists on belligerent rights at sea.[1] In reality expediency was the Government's guide,[2] as was well enough
understood at the time — although some contemporaries also
welcomed what they believed to be advances in 'morality' and
civilization. 'Immediate interests and manifest dangers are
worth more than precedents,' was the Government's motto.[3]
These concessions were made to avoid quarrels with the
Scandinavian and German neutral powers and above all with
the United States, and to secure uniformity with the French
in the exercise of belligerent rights at sea. But less well-known
considerations were quite as important, above all with that
distinguished Peelite Sir James Graham, whose arguments as
First Lord of the Admiralty were probably decisive in the
Cabinet. He saw that the fundamental question was, 'whether
we try to intercept the whole maritime commerce of Russia,
or not', and believed a negative answer was dictated by the

Revolution, tr. L. H. Herman (New York, 1949), p. 331), and Russia's
position with regard to munitions was frequently critical.

[1] Above all by Sir Francis Piggott in the only detailed treatment of the
subject, *The Declaration of Paris, 1856* (1919) (vol. iv in his unfinished
'Law of the Sea' series). Piggott, a former Chief Justice of Hong
Kong, devoted himself to demonstrating in the tradition of David
Urquhart and T. G. Bowles that any relaxation of her maritime rights
endangered Britain's safety and greatness. Unfortunately his work is
chiefly valuable to the historian of maritime polemics in the early
twentieth century.

[2] Cf. Graham to Clarendon, Clarendon dep. c. 14, fo. 290, and Add.
MS. 43355, fo. 156.

[3] Clarendon to Graham, 16 February 1854. Graham MSS., Microfilm
44.

profound change in the basis of Britain's power since she was last at war. That power now rested on her position as 'the great Emporium of the Commerce of the World' and as a manufacturing nation, and on the policy of importing freely which she had accordingly adopted. The right of search for Russian goods in neutral ships should therefore be abandoned (since it would check the flow of imports) and privateers need not be used against Russian trade. The stimulus this might give to neutral shipping should no longer be feared, since our colonial and coasting trade were already deprived of protection against competition. On the other hand, he emphasized, these concessions were in no way to absolve neutrals from their duty of impartiality; they were not to be allowed to carry Russian goods from one Russian port to another, which would benefit Russia alone; and the continuance of the concessions envisaged was to be dependent on their 'willing acquiescence' in the vigorous use of Britain's remaining maritime rights of blockade and the seizure of contraband of war. Graham went on to add the familiar arguments about the importance of a common policy with France and the diplomatic advantages of conciliating the neutrals, and particularly the United States, which might possibly be used almost as a privateering base by Russia.[1] He wound up by pointing out the moral attractions of his plan.[2] Such widely assorted arguments convinced even

[1] Nevertheless, it was not fear of neutral-aided privateering which led Britain to abandon privateering herself, nor were her concessions to neutrals made to induce them to support this decision, as is suggested by H. W. Malkin, 'The Inner History of the Declaration of Paris', *British Yearbook of International Law*, 1927, pp. 1–4. The present author has discussed these points more fully in *Law Quarterly Review*, lxxvi (1960), 379–85.

[2] Graham's Memorandum as finally amended for use as a public document is in F.O. 96/24. It was prepared in February 1854 after consultations with Stephen Lushington (Judge of the Admiralty and Consistory Courts) and Clarendon (Clarendon dep. c. 14, fos. 172, 194, 270). Graham was also in communication with Cardwell (P.R.O., 30/48/8/47/10) and George Cornewall Lewis (Graham MSS., Microfilm 44).

Aberdeen's variegated Cabinet. Until the last moment they resisted French pressure to open the enemy's colonial and coasting trade to neutrals[1] and refrain from explicitly reserving the right to resume the search of neutral ships and the issue of letters of marque. Only when the United States attempted to exploit this difference, and the French gave 'a solemn engagement . . . to enforce blockades with the utmost strictness', did the Cabinet yield on these two points and thus make possible a common Allied Declaration to the Neutrals.[2] Substantially Graham's policy triumphed; that is to say, any drastic interruption of the flow of imports into Britain was to be averted by giving immunity to neutral shipping, while strict blockade and the seizure of contraband were to wipe out Russia's merchant marine, throttle her normal import and export trade, and deprive her of imports vital for her war effort.

Unfortunately the positive part of this policy never really tallied with the outlook of Napoleon III and his ministers, and this for more fundamental reasons than the much publicized differences between the Allies in matters of maritime law. The French Government lacked economic and political confidence. Few of its members shared the free trade doctrines of the Whig and above all the Peelite British ministers. They shared still less their confidence that hardships and economic dislocation were unlikely to arise from the interruption of direct trade with Russia. Least of all did they believe that if such hardships and dislocation did come, they would be

[1] Graham thus tried to maintain 'the Rule of 1756' lest England should be debarred from crippling the coastal and colonial trade of *France* in that future Anglo–French war which he believed the French Government even then contemplated (Clarendon dep. c. 14, fo. 252).

[2] Cowley to Clarendon, 20 April, enclosed in E. Hammond to the Secretary to the Admiralty, 22 April 1854, Ad. 1/5635. For Cowley's private reports to Clarendon, see Clarendon dep. c. 16. The account given in 1868 by the French Foreign Minister, Drouyn de Lhuys (printed in the Appendix to the Report of the Neutrality Laws Commissioners, H.C. (1867–8), xxxii. 56–9), is not altogether accurate.

patriotically and loyally accepted by French commercial and industrial interests. They knew the regime to be insecure and the war not popular. Above all the consequences in 1848 of famine in 1847 had taught them to dread a shortage of grain supplies. They were thus never prepared to weaken the enemy at the risk of economic damage to themselves.

This divergence between Britain and France became more obvious as the British Government worked out the implications of the Declaration to the Neutrals. Edward Cardwell, the impressively competent Peelite President of the Board of Trade, was the first to argue that its corollary should be the legalizing of trade with the enemy, for 'the moment that the trade of neutrals with the enemy is recognized, the justification for prohibiting it to our own subjects is gone.' As the law stood, he contended, Russian trade, for so long predominantly in British hands, would simply fall into those of neutrals; 'our own resources, and not those of Russia' would be impoverished. Cardwell's arguments convinced the three ministers most concerned — Clarendon and Gladstone, respectively Foreign Secretary and Chancellor of the Exchequer, and Granville, Lord President of the Council[1] — and were strongly supported by Lushington, the Admiralty Judge.[2] On 11 April a Committee of the Privy Council under Granville rejected the alternative and traditional system of only allowing trade with the enemy under licence as fostering fraud, privilege and monopoly (three fashionable economic bugbears), as futile in view of the immunity already granted to neutral trade, and above all as incompatible with strict blockade, 'the chief

---

[1] Cardwell to Aberdeen, 3 April 1854, Add. MS. 43197, fos. 280–6 and minutes thereon. Cf. *Edinburgh Review*, c. 216. This article was based upon materials given by Graham to his friend Cornewall Lewis, then editor of the *Edinburgh Review* (Graham to Lewis, 24 February 1854, Graham MSS. Microfilm 44).

[2] P.R.O. 30/29/23, 5 April 1854 and Add. MS. 43355, fos. 141–2. Lushington also pointed out that prohibiting trade with the enemy would no longer withhold intelligence from him, in the days of the telegraph and the Press.

weapon the allies have now reserved to themselves to be used against the commerce of the enemy.'[1] The subsequent Order in Council legalizing trade with the enemy except with blockaded ports astounded the trading public, which had been flooding the Council Office with applications for licences. It not only astounded but enraged the French, who had already proposed an extensive licensing system and a mixed English and French Licensing Commission, and were now confronted with the *fait accompli* and its corollary of 'strict blockade, and no licences'. Only when his undertaking of 28 March 'to enforce blockade with the utmost strictness' was invoked did the French Foreign Minister agree not to grant licences, and then he did so upon conditions.[2]

The Allies' economic strategy had now been defined, and evidently chiefly by Britain: they placed no merely legal obstacles in the way of trading with the enemy, but at the same time they intended vigorously to enforce *de facto* blockades and capture contraband of war and enemy shipping. This represented a deliberate attempt to reconcile military expediency with economic stability at home; to weaken the enemy, yet also to build up Allied strength. Its very ambivalence made it at first widely acceptable.[3] On the one hand it accorded well with the ideas and interests of which the influential middle classes were most aware. It respected the free play

---

[1] Ad. 1/5642, C. Greville to E. Hammond, 13 and 15 April 1854. Cf. 3 *Hansard*, cxxxii, cols. 1022, 1030 (28 April 1854). The Council Office had been against a licensing system from the beginning (cf. *Memoirs of the Life and Correspondence of Henry Reeve*, i, 320, and P.C. 7/8/216). These proposed licences to trade with the enemy were entirely distinct from the licences required to export enumerated articles to certain areas (discussed above, p. 250).

[2] Cowley to Clarendon, 20 April, enclosed in E. Hammond to the Secretary to the Admiralty, 22 April 1854, Ad. 1–5635. Walewski, the French Ambassador in London, had already found Clarendon adamant on 19 April (F.O. 27/1038).

[3] Neither the Declaration nor Orders in Council provoked discussion in Parliament, and *The Times* pointed out the lack of clamour on the subject (3 and 21 April 1854).

of economic forces in shipping and imports and wore some of the aspects of a moral crusade (the suppression of the slave trade and of privateering were often compared). It allayed their anxiety over supplies of raw materials, assuaged their Cobdenite dread of any interruption of international trade and even their more sophisticated fear lest foreign industrial competition should be stimulated by adverse changes in price levels. On the other hand the strict naval complement of the Government's loose import policy appealed to the nation's war fever and satisfied the British tradition of a vigorous effort at sea. Moreover it did not involve great economic risk, since (as *The Economist* assured the thoughtful) Russia's economic importance to Britain had been steadily dwindling in the last few years. Between 1848 and 1852 British exports to Russia had declined in value by 43% (there had been an increase only in hardware, cutlery and machinery). A high proportion of British imports of bristles, flax, hemp, hides, linseed, tallow and raw wood (in that order) still came from Russia, but alternative sources of supply could easily be developed, while the Government's import policy ensured that some supplies from Russia would continue to reach Britain indirectly, probably at no great additional cost.[1] Both the ruin of the enemy's economy and the preservation of her own were thus at first confidently anticipated.[2] But the convinced believers in either objective were inevitably offended, in their consciences and pockets alike. Thus the Russian merchants and shippers, while they urged that Russia's economic vulnerability was not being fully exploited, suffered

[1] *The Economist*, 18 February; cf. also ibid. 25 February, 1 April, 13 May, 17 June 1854. Russia supplied one-sixth of Britain's imported wheat and one-third of her imported oats, but these important supplies were largely removed from the scope of allied economic policy by the Tsar's prohibition of grain exports from the great southern exporting areas. There was, however, some re-routing of grain through Poland and the Baltic, whence exports were not prohibited until the end of 1855.

[2] Cf. *Edinburgh Review*, c. 193–224 and *The Times*, 21 and 25 April 1854.

from upstart rivals who cornered her re-routed trade;[1] many naval officers found their duties much complicated and their prize money decreased by the new deference to neutral rights; and most important of all, most international lawyers defended ancient belligerent practices[2] — and lost some fees through the decrease in prize business. The opposite school, if more strikingly vocal, was far less powerful. Nevertheless rigid free-trade theorists[3] deplored the exercise of any maritime rights at all, and ridiculed the whole idea of economic warfare — 'let us seek in political science instead of in the usage of former wars our views of national policy and international law,' urged T. E. Cliffe Leslie, then Professor of Jurisprudence and Political Economy at Belfast, arguing in favour of total abandonment of blockade.[4] The apostles of the peace party[5] were of course prepared in any event to find the country ruined by the war.

The framers of British policy were thus running the risk inherent in every attempt to make the best of both worlds — they might well seem to make the best of neither, and find themselves confronted by an unholy alliance between their diverse critics, temporarily at least supported by those very

---

[1] It was repeatedly argued that since Russia's foreign trade was chiefly carried on by British capitalists, they were the chief losers by its dislocation — a view developed later by J. Dumas, *Les Aspects Economiques du Droit de Prise avant la Guerre Mondiale* (Paris, 1926), i. 22.

[2] Cf. Buchanan, op. cit. ix. 308. Even the Queen's Advocate was hostile to the new policy and consequently a source of 'impediments and crotchets innumerable' (Clarendon dep. c. 14, fo. 372). On the other hand one of them, Arthur Waddilove, urged the complete sanctity of private property at sea (*Journal of the London Statistical Society,* xviii (1855), 21–32).

[3] J. L. Ricardo's *The War Policy of Commerce* (1855) furnishes the chief exposition of these views.

[4] *Journal of the Dublin Statistical Society,* i. 105.

[5] Cf. John Bright's *Letter to Absalom Watkin on the Russian War* (1854) and his speech in the Commons on 7 June 1855. Bright, himself a carpet manufacturer, suffered from the rise in the price of flax (*Diaries of John Bright* (1930), p. 169).

middle-of-the road men originally most appreciative of their plan. By the autumn of 1854 disappointment had already brought even many members of the Government to this point of uncertainty. In the Black Sea no blockade whatever had been established, and British merchants who had arranged their affairs in the expectation of blockade had suffered heavily while huge profits had been made by Levantine traders.[1] In the White Sea none was established until 1 August;[2] and the notifications of the Baltic blockades had been held irregular so that the validity of many prizes was doubtful.[3] Russian trade had been successfully re-routed through Austria and above all through Prussia to a quite unexpected extent, and contraband of war was reaching her freely through the same channels. Even the attempt to wipe Russian shipping off the seas had been partly frustrated by its large-scale transfer to accommodating neutral owners.[4]

[1] In particular producers and importers of Indian linseed for the British market lost heavily when the expected dearth of Russian linseed did not materialize. (The mouths of the Danube were however blockaded from 1 June 1854).

[2] This was to avoid the worse evil of granting licences for French-owned timber to pass out (Ad. 2/1698/29, Ad. 1/5367, 30 June 1854, Clarendon dep. c. 14, fo. 344). On the representations of the Swedish and Norwegian Governments the peasant barter trade in ryemeal and fish was exempted even after 1 August (Ad. 1/5634, 24 March, Ad. 1/5637, 30 June, Ad. 1/5638, 29 August 1854), a concession which proved mistaken (Ad. 1/1690/50).

[3] The publication of a *precise* geographical description of an *actual* blockade was required, but was often not given, conspicuously with regard to the blockade of the Gulf of Riga. In the famous test case of the *Franciska*, restoration was ordered on appeal (*Reports of Prize Cases*, ed. E. S. Roscoe, ii (1905), 346–70; cf. T. Pemberton Leigh to Granville, 25 August 1855, P.R.O. 30/29/23, discussing his reasons for this judgment).

[4] Danes and Tuscans were the worst offenders. French and British consular reports about doubtful sales were pooled, and naval officers then instructed to seize the ships and send them for trial. But such sales were recognized by the British courts if shown to have been completed according to the law of the buyer's country, although no *post bellum* transfers whatever were recognized by the French. Hence the desperate advice finally given by the Queen's Advocate on 19 December

It seemed all the more necessary to reconsider the original policy since these disappointments could not fairly be laid at the Government's door, however much the public persisted in doing so. Graham had steadily ordered naval commanders to enforce his policy[1] and, bolstering up Clarendon, had resisted all pressure for further relaxations, insisting that 'we have nothing left but Blockade and Contraband of War; and if these be pared away, our Claws will be harmless.'[2] The loose notifications in the Baltic, which seemed to smack so deplorably of the Berlin and Milan Decrees, were published in spite of repeated Admiralty attempts to instruct commanders in the requirements of the Queen's Advocate.[3] True, the Admiralty must bear some blame for Napier's shortage of the small gunboats which alone could prevent a flourishing coastal trade in the Baltic shoals,[4] but in the Black Sea it was the Crimean invasion alone which made the fleet inadequate for blockade duties.[5] In any case French lack of sympathy with the whole British concept of blockade was far more hampering. Granville was not greatly exaggerating when he confided on

---

1855 that such ships if ordered to be restored by the British Courts should be reported to the French for them to deal with. F.O. 83/2271, 8 July, 8 August and 19 December 1855, F.O. 83/2288, 19 October 1855, Ad. 2/1698/142, Ad. 1/5637, 16 June 1854, and *The History of the Baltic Campaign*, ed. G. B. Earp (1857), pp. 170–4.

[1] Cf. *The Russian War, 1854, Baltic and Black Sea Official Correspondence*, ed. D. Bonner-Smith and A. C. Dewar (Navy Records Society, 1943), *passim*, but especially p. 348.

[2] Clarendon dep. c. 14, fo. 344; cf. also ibid., fo. 295. Their attitude is made clear in Ad. 1/5636, 1 and 26 May, Ad. 1/5638, 4 July 1854, and Ad. 2/1698/23, 51, 104, 134, 169, 229.

[3] Cf. *The Russian War, 1854*, pp. 51, 60, Ad. 1/5636, 27 May 1854, and Ad. 1/5639, 30 August 1854.

[4] A point made much of by W. Treue, *Der Krimkrieg und die Entstehung der Modernen Flotten* (Göttingen, 1954), p. 115. Cf. Earp, op. cit. pp. 149–51, P. H. Colomb, *Memoirs of Sir Astley Cooper Key* (1898), p. 248 and *The Russian War, 1855, The Baltic*, ed. D. Bonner-Smith (Navy Records Society, 1944), e.g. p. 85. Clarendon remarked that Memel 'for all practical purposes is now the port of Courland and Livonia.'

[5] *The Russian War, 1854*, pp. 326, 348.

24 February 1855 that 'the deficiencies in blockading Russian ports have arisen in almost every case from the French. In the north they objected to blockades whenever any Frenchman asserted that he had property in the Russian ports which he wished to bring away. In the Black Sea, Hamelin [the French Admiral] had not the will or the means to establish effective Blockades, and was extremely jealous, probably in compliance with orders from home, of giving any sanction to what they deem to be the loose theories of Blockade adopted by us.'[1]

But all these obstacles might be overcome. The strongest reason for doubting the wisdom of the original policy lay in the revelation of its vulnerability to forces almost entirely beyond the Allies' control. It has long been recognized that the Crimean War was as much a diplomatic struggle as a military one. In the matter of war trade as in all else the neutrals ultimately called the tune. Geography and technology alike played into their hands. Russia's long land frontiers conveniently bordered those of the two vital Central Powers, and improvements in transport (above all certain railway building) together with the growing internationalization of trade made it easy and cheap to re-route Russian trade with impunity.[2] Thus the vital twentieth-century issues of 'ultimate destination' and neutral 'leaks', and the dethronement of sea power alone as an instrument of economic war, were both foreshadowed in the Crimean War. But although Aberdeen's Government had discarded much of the practice of the Napoleonic Wars, it could hardly anticipate the methods used in the two World Wars. War-trade agreements, control at source

---

[1] P.R.O. 30/29/23; cf. *The Russian War, 1854*, pp. 257, 271, 371. 'Loose theories' chiefly because the British held that a ship breaking blockade need not be warned beforehand to be liable to capture. For other differences see P. Fauchille, *Du Blocus Maritime* (Paris, 1882), pp. 110, 146.

[2] Especially since there was normally a certain transit trade through Prussia (M. L. Tegoborski, *Commentaries on the Productive Forces of Russia* (1855–6), ii. 426).

and similar devices were unthinkable to mid-nineteenth-century governments; the most they could expect from neutrals was prohibition of trade with a belligerent in contraband of war. If this were not enforced, the diplomatic objectives of the Crimean 'war for the neutrals' overrode all economic considerations, above all where Prussia — by far the most serious leak — was concerned, at least for the British Government. (The wider public was far less conscious of diplomatic difficulties, and often impatient to teach the neutrals a lesson.)[1] Over other trade — and it must be remembered that the definition of contraband of war, though widened by Britain to include coal and machinery,[2] was still very narrow by twentieth-century standards — no neutral control could really be expected, and certainly none was exercised, however inflated its volume.

It was Clarendon who in September 1854 touched off that thorough reappraisal which already seemed necessary. He had never been a very enthusiastic supporter of the policy. Only diplomatic considerations had won him over in the first place, and he was now under pressure from the Russia merchants. Was it true that the Allies' policy had failed to impair Russia's economy? If so, should the import of Russian produce into Britain be prohibited through the Customs, and the principles of free trade be waived in order to hasten the peace which would allow their full restoration? The Board of Trade's report may have surprised Clarendon, for they produced tables suggesting that in spite of re-routing, only about two-fifths of the tallow and hemp normally imported from Russia was entering Britain, and about two-thirds of the flax. They

---

[1] Sober expression was given to this impatience, for example, by the barrister J. T. Danson as early as 19 June 1854 (*Journal of the London Statistical Society*, xvii. 193–218).

[2] Graham insisted on this (e.g. Ad. 2/1698/51), urging that 'the whole Baltic supply of Coal is drawn from England: and while England possesses her Coal Field and the command of the Sea, Russia for all steam purposes of War is crippled, if we withhold her supply and treat Coal as a Contraband of War' (Clarendon dep. c. 14, fo. 158).

S

surmised that there had also been a decline in Russian imports, especially of raw cotton, which 'must have inflicted serious loss, on the Capitalist, the Operative, and the Public Revenue', while 'commercial interests must have been seriously injured by the unemployment of Russian shipping'.[1] But Clarendon's doubts had greatly impressed James Wilson at the Treasury, always a most persuasive and lucid reasoner on economic affairs. On 30 September he wrote in *The Economist* a striking leader entitled 'Our War Commercial Policy. Can it be continued?', which Clarendon boasted to Graham was 'all my thunder'.[2] The British blockade, Wilson showed, was preventing Russia from importing tropical and colonial produce, hence heavy British imports from Russia could no longer be paid for indirectly thereby, and there was imminent danger that the exchange might actually be turned in favour of St. Petersburg. Moreover, he argued, the circumstances which had justified the original policy had completely altered. With the fall of Sebastopol (believed to be imminent) Russia would be open only to economic attack, while the neutrals' profits from the re-routing of Russian trade were now deterring them from joining the Allies, and at home alternative sources of supply and a bumper harvest were assured. In an official memorandum written a month later Wilson sketched his idea of the war commercial policy now appropriate — one of directly checking British imports of Russian produce in the traditional style. The diplomatic position forbade all but domestic measures. He therefore urged that trade with the enemy should be made illegal once more, and the entry of articles normally imported from Russia allowed only on pro-

---

[1] P.R.O. B.T. 3/47/412–25. The Russian official trade figures support the conclusions of the Board of Trade (see p. 270 below). Clarendon also sought information about the state of Russia's finances from British consuls in the Baltic.

[2] Clarendon to Graham, 2 October 1854 (Graham MSS., Microfilm 44). It is typical of Gladstone's remoteness that he sent Clarendon a cutting of this article, 'as it may otherwise fail to come beneath your eye' (Clarendon dep. c. 14, fo. 641).

duction of certificates from British consuls that the goods were not of Russian origin.[1]

Lord John Russell, Granville, and Clarendon's Under-Secretary at the Foreign Office, Wodehouse, never shared Clarendon's enthusiasm for this proposal. They foresaw fraud and evasion, and feared a permanent diversion of trade and stimulus to foreign industries.[2] But they admitted that 'there will be an appearance of rigour in the measure' and were prepared 'to knock under if Cardwell sees no objection'.[3] The debate on whether Britain should return to 'obsolete restrictions on commerce during war' thus turned into a duel between Wilson and Cardwell. Cardwell asserted (with his department) that the blockade had already justified itself, and that Wilson's policy was out of date and impracticable and if it did work, would be disastrous. The argument turned on the incidence and effects of the increased cost of Russian produce in the British market if its import were prohibited — neither side, it should be observed, hoped to interrupt British imports of Russian produce completely. Cardwell held that Wilson's quantitative comparisons — showing for example that England provided 50% of Russia's export markets, but Russia only 1% of Britain's — were quite misjudged, since the effect of a dislocation of trade on a country producing raw materials and on an industrial economy were entirely different. For Russia the question might indeed be a simple one of profit and loss, but for Britain what was at stake was

[1] Memorandum on the Commercial Policy pursued with respect to Russian produce since the commencement of the war, 23 October 1854, Add. MS. 43355, fos. 144–9. Wilson consulted the Customs on the details of this plan (P.R.O. 30/29/23, 23 and 24 October 1854) and Clarendon the Board of Trade (B.T. 3/47/426–9). Prohibitive duties were also mooted.

[2] Add. MS. 43355, fos. 156–9. Lord John had never believed that economic pressure would have any effect on Russia (P.R.O. 30/22/11, 22 May). For Clarendon, cf. Barrington, op. cit. i. 253.

[3] P.R.O. 30/29/23, Lord John Russell to Granville, 29 and 30 October 1854 and P.R.O. 30/22/11, Granville to Lord John Russell, 29 October 1854.

the advantage which might be given to her industrial rivals if the cost of Russian produce was raised to her alone — in short, her competitive position in world markets. Cardwell's arguments were impressively thorough and had a good deal of elegance and refinement. If they ran counter to the views of important commercial interests,[1] they kept intact the new tariff orthodoxy and also a war policy on which the Government had already staked much political capital. They expressed that sense of the precariousness of raw material supplies which was to prove increasingly acute in the 1850s. It was a hard-fought struggle, but Cardwell, and Cardwell alone, carried the Cabinet completely,[2] and within the Government the original policy was never challenged again.

Outside the Government, however, things were far otherwise. In February 1855 indignation against the Coalition found one of its chief outlets in a parliamentary attack on this policy, powerfully supported by the shipping and trading interests whose resentment about neutral gains underlay much of the patriotic enthusiasm which demanded the total interruption of Russian trade. This debate in the Commons[3] was inevitably

[1] Anxious, Cardwell astutely suggested, to keep up prices by inducing a shortage of Russian produce (Add. MS. 43355, fos. 160–2).

[2] Cardwell's Memorandum of 29 October 1854 (Add. MS. 43355, fos. 160–2) was brought by Granville to the Committee of Council held on 30 October, at which his views triumphed (*The Greville Memoirs*, vii. 195). The question then went before the Cabinet, which considered a further memorandum from Wilson (Add. MS. 43355, fos. 168–78) and one from Cardwell (ibid., fos. 152–5). Lord John Russell had predicted from the beginning the Cabinet's acquiescence in whatever Cardwell's views might be (P.R.O. 30/29/23). Many more points were argued than have been indicated here, especially with regard to the exchange. Clarendon may have yielded partly because the French would not contemplate imposing a similar prohibition on imports of Russian goods. They preferred the plan of blockading Prussian ports (Cowley to Clarendon, 19 October 1854, F.O. 519/214/137).

[3] 3 *Hansard*, cxxxvi, cols. 1659–706 (20/21 February 1855). T. A. Mitchell, of a firm of Riga merchants, one of the committee of management of Lloyd's shipping register and an Assistant of the Eastland Company, took a leading part, assisted by the Members for the two great centres of Russian trade, Hull and Newcastle. J. L. Ricardo's

less thorough and realistic than that inside the Government four months earlier, but politically it made its mark. The next day (22 February) the Peelites resigned. In war trade as in so much else, however, the change in government turned out to mean surprisingly little change in policy. If Russia ever feared that Palmerston would indeed attempt 'total' economic warfare, as one peer suggested,[1] her fears must soon have been allayed. There was, it is true, a steadily growing public feeling that the economic attack against Russia must be pressed home[2] and a persistent demand that Prussian ports should be blockaded or Prussian ships coming from Prussian ports searched, or at least heavy differential duties imposed on specified imports from Prussia. The more learned urged the application of the Rule of 1756 and a summons to Prussia to end the breach of neutrality which her abnormal trade with Russia represented. But none of these courses was diplomatically practicable.

The new Government therefore concentrated on fully enforcing the original policy exactly as their predecessors had been doing.[3] The machinery for notifying blockades was im-

---

call for the total removal of restrictions on Russian trade won no support. The excitement provoked by this commercial debate contrasts sharply with the apathy felt about the legal aspects of the policy (cf. 3 *Hansard*, cxxxiv, col. 1091, 4 July 1854). Even in this crisis *The Times* continued to support Cardwell's policy.

[1] 3 *Hansard*, cxxxviii, col. 591 (15 May 1855).

[2] Expressed for example by Clarendon (*Greville Memoirs*, vii. 262) and Napoleon III (J. H. Harris, third Earl of Malmesbury, *Memoirs of an Ex-Minister* (1884), ii. 17) after the failure of the Vienna Conference. For a naval expression of the same view see *Life and Letters of Admiral Sir Bartholomew James Sulivan*, ed. H. N. Sulivan (1896) pp. 297, 319. Cf. *Hansard*, cxxxvii, col. 1850, cxxxviii, col. 591 (27 April and 13 May 1855); *The Times*, 17 May 1855.

[3] Admittedly the blockade of the mouths of the Danube had been raised in January 1855, but this was to avoid the worse evil of complying with the French desire to allow grain to come out under licences. At the end of 1855 renewed French anxiety to get grain induced the Admiralty to allow certain ships to pass through the blockading squadron in the Sea of Azov. But these were the only concessions made,

proved,[1] the Aaland Islands' immunity was ended,[2] and tremendous efforts were made to keep ships at their stations till the last possible moment, in order to check the very considerable traffic which began as soon as they withdrew, and included a good deal of armament running, often over the ice.[3] Above all, they endeavoured to check neutral trade with Russia in contraband of war. This was not easy. There was no ground in international law for a belligerent to prevent munitions of war going from one neutral port to another unless they were found concealed or were very clearly intended for enemy use,[4] and even then officers who sent in a ship for adjudication acted at considerable legal risk.[5] Consuls were therefore urged to send prompt, full and reliable information about suspected cargoes for the assistance of naval officers, but nevertheless the only ships which could be searched without much hesitation were those of the small Hanseatic towns,[6]

---

apart from a *de facto* concurrence in the permission given by France to previously laden neutral ships to leave newly blockaded ports.

[1] Consuls were given 'a new and serious duty' in this respect (F.O. 83/2280; cf. Ad. 1/5661, 5 February, and Ad. 1/5662, 17 April 1855).

[2] Ad. 1/5663, 28 June 1855, Add. MS. 49563, fos. 42, 65. The Islands had become 'un véritable lieu d'entrepôt pour le commerce russe'.

[3] Cf. *The Russian War, 1855, The Baltic*, pp. 354, 362, Add. MS. 49565, fo. 112, and cf. F.O. 64/399, no. 203. Sir Charles Wood, Graham's successor at the Admiralty, tried to get Napoleon III to send more gunboats to the Baltic to check this, but found 'the North interests him very little' (Add. MS. 49555, fo. 210). Cf. *The Russian War, 1855, The Baltic*, pp. 264, 297, 383, and Add. MS. 49564, fo. 124.

[4] This was the constantly repeated opinion of the Queen's Advocate, in which Clarendon found Palmerston concurred (F.O. 96/24, 23, 24, 25 April 1855, F.O. 83/2288, 10 December 1855, Ad. 1/5665, 18 September 1855).

[5] Especially after the decision of the Privy Council in the case of the *Ost See* that officers who made a capture which was held improper might be required to pay an indemnity to the owners.

[6] All vessels entering and leaving the Elbe in the spring of 1854 were searched for contraband (Ad. 2/1698/173; cf. G. B. Henderson, 'Problems of Neutrality, 1854: Documents from the Hamburg Staatsarchiv', *Journal of Modern History*, x (1938), 239, who suggests that this was intended as a menace to Prussia).

and of course British ships. The problem was not a naval but a diplomatic one, and its best solution was the prohibition of the trade by neutral governments themselves. Here the Foreign Office had little success. Denmark, Hanover, Hamburg and Lübeck, for example, and finally, on 8 March 1855, Prussia herself, issued such prohibitions, but they were often little more than formal. The Prussian ordinance exempted 'articles of Zollverein manufacture' and so allowed widespread evasion, connived at, the Foreign Office believed, by the Prussian Government. Yet Clarendon hesitated to demand an outright prohibition of trade with all belligerents in all contraband of war, for this would simply mean that 'the Russians would get what they want just the same and the new regulation would be rigorously applied to ourselves.'[1] Only at the very end of December 1855 did Britain's much stronger military and diplomatic position warrant a firmer tone. Clarendon's underlying object, however, was to alarm Prussia into supporting the Austrian peace ultimatum to Russia. His defensive treaty with Sweden of 17 December gave him his opportunity. Bloomfield, the British Minister at Berlin, was ordered to point out that neutrality in the Baltic would probably become impossible if the war continued, since the north was to be the theatre of the next season's campaign, and that Sweden certainly, and perhaps Denmark, would be on the Allied side.[2] But Prussia's attitude remained unchanged. On 29 December Bloomfield dismissed impatiently Stratford Canning's ill-informed suggestion that Prussia and Austria might prohibit trade with Russia: 'How can we expect any such general measures to be established, when the German Governments will not even put an effectual stop to the trade

---

[1] F.O. 64/399, no. 186, Clarendon's Minute of 12 November 1855. The French Minister at Berlin seems to have been prepared to make this sacrifice (E. de Guichen, *La Guerre de Crimée, 1854–56, et l'Attitude des Puissances Européennes* (Paris, 1936), p. 300). The British Embassy had confined itself to collecting evidence of the flouting of the ordinance with a view to securing its enforcement.

[2] F.O. 64/400, no. 357. Cf. ibid., no. 362.

in contraband?'[1] On 5 January, however, he at last clearly threatened naval coercion of Prussian trade[2] — a threat which has been considered decisive in ending the war, since it induced Frederick William IV to warn the Tsar that even his neutrality could no longer be relied on.[3] But British bitterness against Prussia long remained acute — and with reason. For if Denmark and Tuscany had been the chief protectors of Russian shipping, and America and the Low Countries a great source of armaments, it was the overland and coasting routes through Prussia which to the very end shielded Russia from the Allies' commercial attack.

Diplomatic practicability thus seriously distorted British trade policy during the Crimean War. Distorted though it was, however, did it nevertheless succeed in injuring Russia while keeping the British economy unimpaired? Its effects on Russia are difficult to ascertain. 'It is very annoying', complained Sir Charles Wood justifiably in October 1855, 'that we know so little of what goes on in Russia. How I wish we could make them a present of half a dozen of "our own Correspondents".'[4] As has already been shown, Russia was never effectively prevented from importing much-needed war material, except perhaps machinery.[5] The blockade certainly

[1] F.O. 64/400, no. 365. (Stratford Canning's suggestion is in F.O. 78/1091, no. 927.) In F.O. 64/411, no. 5, Bloomfield reported and explained an increase in the contraband trade at this time. For an example of some similar trade through Austria, see F.O. 64/399, Clarendon's minute on no. 188.

[2] F.O. 64/411, no. 7. His instructions had been sent on 26 December.

[3] Cf. G. Rothan, *La Prusse et son Roi pendant la Guerre de Crimée* (Paris, 1888), pp. 229, 238, F. Charles-Roux, *Alexandre II, Gortchakoff et Napoléon III* (Paris, 1913), p. 73 and K. Borries, *Preussen im Krimkrieg* (Stuttgart, 1930), p. 385 (a document which shows that other motives also weighed with Frederick William, if not with Manteuffel).

[4] Add. MS. 49564, fo. 71.

[5] The figures of total Russian imports given in A. F. Yakovlev, *Ekonomicheskie Krizisy v Rossii* (Moscow, 1955), p. 63, show that machinery imports dropped from 4·8 of the total in 1853 to 0·49 and 0·46 in 1854 and 1855 respectively. (I owe these references to Yakovlev's work to the kindness of my husband.)

caused much distress among the islanders and peasants of the
Baltic provinces, especially the Finns; but even the strongest
believers in economic pressure realized that their sufferings
would not produce any impression on the Russian Government.[1] It was the town dwellers and industrialists, and above
all the landowning classes, who counted. It seems fairly clear
that there was no catastrophic drop in the volume of goods
imported for their consumption (coffee, sugar, tea and so on)
and no sharp rise in their prices, since transport costs, however
inflated, represented only a small fraction of their final value.[2]
Many industries enjoyed a war boom,[3] although the stoppage
in imports from Britain of coal (which was not re-routed
through Prussia) and of raw cotton and cotton yarn seriously
affected the Baltic area and Russia's young cotton industry.[4]
But it was Russia's export trade in raw materials which the
Allies always considered to be her Achilles' heel. Certainly her
foreign trade had become increasingly important,[5] with

[1] Add. MS. 49563, fo. 100 (cf. ibid., fo. 116 and Add. MS. 49564,
fo. 47), *The Russian War, 1855, The Baltic*, pp. 165, 342 and Sulivan,
op. cit., pp. 301, 346, 358, 364. The return of naval prizes dated 11
August 1855 (in Ad. 1/5668) shows that most of the Russian ships captured were small boats carrying salt for curing the fish which these
people lived on in winter.

[2] Imports fell much less heavily than exports (Yakovlev, op. cit.,
p. 63; cf. Sulivan, op. cit., p. 311).

[3] Yakovlev quotes an economist of the 1860s, V. P. Bezobrazov,
as saying that many industrialists regarded the Crimean War as a golden
age. His figures show a boom in the metal working, leather, linen and
woollen industries (op. cit., pp. 64–5). Cf. Sulivan, op. cit., p. 362, for
the stimulus given, for example, to working salt mines and making
roads.

[4] Tegoborski, op. cit. ii. 245, 269; Yakovlev, op. cit., pp. 62–64;
The Economist, 11 August 1855; F.O. 96/24, Clarendon's note of 30
October 1854.

[5] According to W. McK. Pintner, 'Inflation in Russia during the
Crimean War Period' (*American Slavic and East European Review*,
xviii (1959), 84), in the early 1850s it exceeded the total turnover at all
the major internal market fairs combined by 38%. Tegoborski on the
other hand, writing controversially ('Les Finances de la Guerre. Res-
sources Financières de la Russie', *Revue des Deux Mondes*, seconde
série de la nouvelle période, viii (1854), 795), puts it at only one-sixth

Britain as her chief customer, and did shrink very markedly,[1] far more than was generally realized in Britain, in spite of the statements of the Board of Trade and the arguments of *The Economist*. Moreover some at least of the extra costs imposed by the Prussian route fell on Russian producers.[2] On the other hand many landowners benefited from the stimulus given by military demand to prices for hides, flax, raw wool and, in the south, grain. Economic pressure never created a peace party among the nobility. The chief sufferer in fact from the Allies' measures was the state itself, since it lost a substantial proportion of its customs revenue, which in turn was responsible for a large share of the total government revenue.[3] Even if this loss was not absolutely very large (perhaps 5% or so of total revenue), it aggravated a rapidly mounting deficit and stimulated that issue of paper money which carried Russia through the war, but at the cost of galloping inflation afterwards.[4] Russia's vulnerability was fiscal, not commercial. Yet as it turned out, naval attacks on economic objectives, especially on government stockpiles in the Sea of Azov, were probably as decisive as all the Allies' efforts at economic

---

of her internal trade. The annual Russian departmental statistics which are constantly used have apparently never been critically analysed, although C. Skalkowsky's remarks about 'les chiffres fantastiques de la statistique officielle' (*Les Ministres des Finances de la Russie, 1802–1890* (Paris, 1891), p. 103) were surely justified.

[1] Yakovlev's table of total exports excluding grains (whose export was prohibited by the Tsar and not by the blockade) shows a fall in value from 91 million roubles in 1853 to 48 million in 1854 and 34 million in 1855, op. cit., p. 63. These figures however exclude not only Finland but also Poland, the most important route for evading the blockade. Pintner's inclusive table shows a drop of much the same order (loc. cit., p. 87).

[2] Cf. *The Economist*, 20 January 1855.

[3] Perhaps just under a quarter in 1838 (cf. L. Dussieux, *La Force et la Faiblesse de la Russie* (Paris, 1854), p. 40), and it had certainly risen since then. Even Tegoborski in 1854 expected a drop in Customs' yield of about a fifth (*Revue des Deux Mondes*, loc. cit., p. 801).

[4] Cf. the discussion in the *Revue des Deux Mondes*, loc. cit., between Léon Faucher and Tegoborski, and Pintner, loc. cit., p. 87.

warfare — and Russia's vast internal problems and her final
diplomatic isolation were certainly far more important than
either.

On the other hand, did the policy of preserving British imports from dislocation keep the British economy unimpaired,
as Cardwell and his supporters intended? Its effects are difficult to isolate. The great Russian merchants and shippers
inevitably suffered heavily, and the re-routing of Russian
trade through Prussia was never of course complete. There was
thus some permanent and much temporary alteration in the
sources of British imports. For example, since the cost of trans-
porting Russian timber through Prussia was prohibitive, it
was replaced by Swedish — permanently, as it proved.[1]
Similarly, Russian raw wool was replaced by colonial and
home supplies.[2] Italy became temporarily the Navy's largest
supplier of hemp,[3] and India Britain's chief source of oil seed.
But this amounted only to a rapid acceleration of that ousting
of Russia from British markets which had begun some years
earlier, and involved little shortage of 'Russian produce'. Nor
did the prices of articles normally imported from Russia show
a constant steep rise, although they were subject to heavy
speculative fluctuations — especially tallow, oil seeds and
flax.[4] The story spread by critics of the Government's policy,
of virtually uninterrupted supplies from Russia itself selling

[1] *The Economist*, 12 January 1856; T. Milner, *The Baltic* (1854),
p. 139; J. Potter, 'The British Timber Duties, 1815–1860', *Economica*,
N.S., xxii (1955), 128.

[2] *The Economist*, 2 February 1856.

[3] Add. MS. 49558, fos. 48–9.

[4] Cf. *The Economist*, 2 September 1854, 25 February 1855, 5 January
1856. Flax prices rose partly because of increased demand, tallow prices
because Australian and American supplies were inadequate (even the
Navy ordered Russian tallow, Add. MS. 49558, fols. 48–9). Tooke and
Newmarch point out that prices of Russian produce fell in 1855 as
compared with 1854 (op. cit. v. 323). *The Economist* is a most valuable
guide to this question, although it consistently understressed the
economic effects of the war in general, which were probably less negli-
gible than is usually assumed.

at extremely high prices,[1] is largely legendary. But it is very doubtful how far all this can be attributed to the Government's war import policy, although of course this claim was frequently made by its supporters. Certainly Britain's competitive position as a world exporter was less fragile than Cardwell and his school of thought feared. The verdict clearly should not be one of much ado about nothing, but equally it is clear that trade war and war trade proved much less decisive than most contemporaries expected.

It is, however, surely significant that at the end of the war the Cabinet had no doubts about the wisdom of their policy. This is clear from the fact that at the peace conference Britain took a leading part in securing the Declaration of Paris, which embodied as a permanent part of international law the temporary concessions made over maritime rights in March 1854. True, the association of the abolition of privateering with these proposals transformed them into an irresistible chance for Britain to score off her most troublesome thorn in the flesh at that time, the United States. (The Americans were anxious to retain privateering, but had been trying to isolate Britain by rallying the smaller maritime powers around 'free ships, free goods'.) But in any case after two years' experience the Cabinet remained convinced that Britain had nothing to lose by these concessions, once a clause had been inserted which safeguarded her in case of America's employment of privateers in the event of a future war. They still believed not only that the value of privateering was diminishing, but also that a power which enjoyed naval preponderance could gain quite as much from seizure of contraband of war and *de facto* blockade as from the seizure of enemy property in neutral ships,[2]

[1] Cf., for example, the remarks of W. S. Lindsay (the Cobdenite shipowner and opponent of maritime rights), *History of Merchant Shipping* (1875), ii. 312, n. 1, and Tooke and Newmarch, whose conclusion (op. cit., p. 666) is quite inconsistent with their earlier discussion (ibid., p. 346).

[2] A packet of documents in Ellenborough's papers reveals the vigorous interpretation Clarendon placed upon the Declaration of Paris. He was

and moreover without the risk of diplomatic imbroglios. 'No one would contend that the power of blockade was not infinitely more effective than stopping the trade carried on by neutrals,' claimed the Government spokesman, the Duke of Argyll, in the debate in the Lords on the Declaration of Paris, and he predicted: 'Exactly in proportion as a country possessed a predominance of naval power would recourse be had to the more effective stoppage of commerce by blockade.'[1] Whatever the views of the public — and there were always some who thought the Government was parting with 'the birthrights and bulwarks etc. etc. of Britain' and others who, again in Clarendon's phrase, liked to see the thing '*grandement* and pay homage to the civilization of the age' — the attitude of Ministers had never been anything but practical. They saw themselves as balancing advantages and disadvantages. 'It was a balance of prudential considerations, which determined our policy,' insisted one of them.[2] Confidence in British naval power, sensitivity to neutral reactions and anxiety to safeguard Britain's commercial and industrial economy originally brought the balance down in favour of the complex policy which has been discussed. At the end of the war the same considerations continued to seem conclusive.

In trade as in finance the Crimean War generation realized that economic policy was a vital part of military success. Most of them came to appreciate that no simple guide, inspired by economic liberalism or any other dogma, could be found as to what the content should be of that policy. It was only clear what should be its purpose: to inflict maximum damage on the enemy while safeguarding British economic strength as far as

prepared to define contraband very widely indeed, to consider that blockades would not cease to be continuous if interrupted by stress of bad weather, and that the renunciation of privateering did not debar the Crown from arming private vessels for the defence of British coasts (P.R.O. 30/12/23/7).

[1] 3 *Hansard*, cxlii, col. 517 (22 May 1856).

[2] Sir James Graham on 10 April 1854 (Clarendon dep. c. 14, fo. 290)

possible. This was the inspiration behind the debate over war loans or war taxes, over cheap or dear money, over neutral immunity or maritime rights. Britain's economic strength must be preserved and exploited for victory. Whether this could best be done by new methods or old was a matter for dispute. As the war went on men's minds became more sympathetic to the experiences of the past, and Government policies began to move closer to those of their predecessors in time of war. The sudden end of hostilities just as the war effort was becoming fully developed, prevented these tendencies from becoming fully apparent. But they had gone far enough for it to be clear that if the financial and commercial policies of the Crimean War were exceptional, they were not so in the way that has usually been supposed. For if this war begins a new era in war-time economic policies, it does so not because it rejected the policies of the past in favour of economic liberalism, but because whether it accepted or rejected them (and in some measure it did both), it did so in the light of a relatively sophisticated and informed conception of the complicated issues at stake for the whole economy, and therefore for the nation's military position in the most fundamental sense. This was no 'war for arms and a peace for commerce'; 'business as usual' was not its motto, nor was it remarkable for any attempt to keep war and economic life separate. Rather it was distinguished by an unaccustomed grasp of the interconnexion of military and economic strength, and a deliberate determination to preserve the latter to the utmost possible extent in order to increase the former. In short, the Crimean War saw in England the beginning of a coherent appreciation of *Wehrwirtschaft*, cut short though that beginning was by a sudden peace.

CONCLUSION

The Verdict

WHAT the public and even the experts expect on the eve of any war rarely comes to pass, and the Crimean War was no exception to this rule. For although it was not the utterly futile episode depicted by neo-Cobdenites in later demonstrations of the pointlessness of war, neither was it the Armageddon which contemporaries expected it to be. Moreover, however substantial its repercussions upon international power-relationships proved in the long run, its immediate effects were remarkably unspectacular. Certainly in 1856 the British public believed that a premature and disappointing peace had been made, and the great expectations of a vast and decisive conflict entertained at the beginning of the war made this anti-climax all the more difficult to accept. But British discontent and impatience at the end of the war sprang still more from the feeling that Britain had been deprived of a full opportunity to prove her strength as a belligerent, and that the world was being left with a humiliating impression of military and political weakness which even one more campaign would have wiped out.

As it was, to the foreign observer the brief two years of fighting seemed to have fully justified his suspicions that a constitutional state of traders and manufacturers could never be a first-rate military power. Those very aspects of British public life which distinguished her from the rest of the world appeared to have been her undoing in war. Constitutional government had proved a broken reed. 'In the most critical time for this country four Governments, perfect and imperfect, have existed in four weeks, and we have now to see how a fifth can be constructed.'[1] This despairing cry from a senior

---

[1] Sir Charles Wood to Grey, 21 February 1855, Grey MSS.

275

SWINDLING THE CLARENDON.
(By a Distinguished Russian.)

Mr. Bull (*Landlord of the British Lion*). "WHAT! QUITE THE GENTLEMAN! WHY, HE HAS LEFT NOTHING BUT A PORTMANTEL FULL OF BRICKS AND STONES, AND GONE OFF WITHOUT PAYING THE BILL!"

(*Punch*, **April 12, 1856**)

British minister in February 1855 was a bald statement of fact which could not be gainsaid. More serious still, freedom of public discussion, for so long the core of the British conception of liberty, seemed merely to mean the irresponsible despotism of one anonymous clique of journalists who proclaimed the total breakdown of English military administration in one breath and supplied the enemy with abundant military information in the next. Nor had the wealth and economic resources for which Britain was renowned enabled the country to furnish a clear demonstration of a new system of war finance or war trade. In the end loans and indirect taxation had met the cost of this war almost as much as in less scientific periods of war finance; convertibility and a strictly limited fiduciary note issue had survived only by a narrow margin; and although neutral shipping had been allowed to carry enemy cargo unmolested, extensive blockade and a wide definition of contraband had made it clear that this did not imply any general exemption of trade from the rigours of war. Least of all had the world been shown that under constitutional government a nation could still be relied upon to rise to patriotic heights of self-sacrifice and united effort in time of need. On the contrary, class bitterness, at least between the middle classes and the aristocracy, had rarely been so intense or so outspoken in England as in the crisis of this war. Virtually the whole gamut of existing social and political institutions had been called in question. Altogether it is not surprising that on the Continent at least the spell of 1815, 1830 and 1848 had been decisively broken. The Crimean campaigns had revealed as a mirage the vision of Britain as a country uniquely happy in combining naval and military prowess with constitutional freedom, the pursuit of wealth with political and social stability. British prestige abroad had sunk very low indeed, and in the process the political and economic relationships which she exemplified — constitutional liberalism and *laissez-faire* economic policy — had been discredited also.

Yet it is important to realize that all these things looked

T

very different to native eyes. Not for the first or last time, the British placed a far more rosy interpretation than foreign observers upon their war-time experiences. They did not emerge with their faith shattered in their country's capacities as a belligerent, nor with fundamental doubts about the compatibility of military success with constitutional government and a 'scientific' fiscal, monetary and commercial policy. For a few months early in 1855 there had indeed been a national loss of nerve and an almost hysterical revulsion against the country's social and political institutions and sophisticated policies of trade war and war finance. But too many scapegoats were found for this loss of nerve to provoke fundamental questioning of English politics, society or economic policy for long. In the spring of 1855 'the System' was a vast, amorphous national bogy; but by the autumn of that year indignation had been transferred to specific individuals, institutions and practices — to Lord John Russell and the Peelites among the politicians, to defects in the composition of Parliament and in the selection of the executive, to administrative centralization and the dwindling away of direct contact between freeholders, Parliament and government; to the Bank Charter Act of 1844 and Prussia's unscrupulous assistance in the re-routing of Russian trade; above all, to *The Times*, for its exploitation and exaggeration of a national emergency. With such an impressive assortment of whipping-boys to hand, most Englishmen found it quite possible to convince themselves in the second winter of the war that the events of the previous year had condemned not the essence of British institutions or policies, but perversions which had arisen as a result of personal ambition or error, unhistoric innovation, or the sheer play of external circumstances. With very little encouragement — in the shape of successes first in the Sea of Azov and then on the Tchernaya — confidence returned at home. It was this renewed optimism and self-satisfaction which was responsible for English disgust when peace was signed and Englishmen found they were not to be allowed to demonstrate that the conclusions the world had drawn from the events of 1854–5 were the wrong ones.

While then the Crimean War was a serious blow to Britain and all she stood for abroad, at home its effects were not so simple. The humiliation and discontent it brought were intense but also brief, for most people were not in the end prepared to find such feelings warranted by the state of the nation and its institutions as a whole. The real mainsprings of the country's political and economic life, they persuaded themselves, were sound and strong. Yet the shocks of 1854–5 had been traumatic. It could no longer be taken for granted that aristocratic dash and heroism would win a war, that the times would call forth the man, or even that in the hour of need the Queen's Government would be carried on. The financial and commercial expedients of previous struggles could clearly not after all be disregarded, nor the complacent Fourth Estate entrusted with the role of national leadership in default of leadership from the politicians. Tradition and habit had proved disastrous, but innovation and the reasoned application of means to ends had brought mishaps also. Thus these brief but deeply felt experiences brought neither a sweeping break with those many traditions and habits which seemed to have been found wanting, nor a chastened renunciation of novelty and experiment. Like many other vaster struggles, the Crimean War simply strengthened and accelerated certain political and social developments which were in reality already present although not yet obvious: it represented (as, despite appearances to the contrary, wars have often done), not a turning point but a landmark.

In the event the emergence of certain aspects of the nation's political life in the later 1850s was powerfully assisted by the country's Crimean experiences, but that life was not thereby transformed. Impatience with the narrow cliquishness exhibited in Government-making and with the remoteness of the House of Commons from much of public opinion had been heightened; fear of one great daily newspaper, contempt for bureaucracy and resentment of central direction had increased; and the myth of the independent freeholder in his local assembly as well as the newer romanticization of trade and technology been given new life. A great impetus was thereby given to the spread of dissatisfaction with existing parliamentary institutions, but even more to the related cult of local self-government and of the practical man of affairs — the cult of provincialism and the philistine amateur. The cry to bring in new men had had to be heeded a little, despite the difficulties such outsiders made for the practising politicians. At the same time the middle classes' impatience with aristocratic cliquishness had been stimulated enough to encourage them to return to political co-operation with the respectable working classes in a way rare since the 1830s, but soon to become vitally important. Developments like these would no doubt have come even if the long post-Napoleonic peace had never been broken. But war brought them sooner and made men more conscious of their significance, and it was after all their advent which promoted that frequent first-hand experience of local politics and administration and that remarkably widely diffused culture of respectability, self-improvement and hard work, which together smoothed the transition to mass democracy in Britain in the later nineteenth century.

In economic policies and attitudes the Crimean War was a landmark in much the same limited sense. The denunciation of Mammon-worship had a short life; few people believed for long that opulence conflicted very seriously with defence. A decisive check was indeed administered to Peelite fiscal policy, with its surplus revenues and temporary income tax imposed solely to achieve planned reductions in other forms of taxation. With the war this era of public finance disappeared, as the young Stafford Northcote was soon to demonstrate,[1] though Gladstone always refused to admit it. Yet in any event the whole course of international affairs after 1856 would have

[1] In his book *Twenty Years of Financial Policy* (1860).

made an increasing volume of defence expenditure inevitable; the days of Peelite finance were numbered. Similarly the Bank Charter Act was more suspect than ever; but the monetary debate was not given a new twist by the war, merely a new lease of life. The most decisive precedent was set in the field of foreign trade. Here the modern era of economic warfare had perceptibly arrived, with its emphasis upon seizure of contraband and vulnerability to neutral pressures — and above all with its careful calculation not merely of shipping losses but of comparative effects, indirect as well as direct, to the economy as a whole on both sides.

Had the war ended in the spring of 1855 with some overwhelming disaster, England might indeed have undergone a political and social revolution of the kind which then, as on so many other occasions, seemed very near. On the other hand, had Napoleon III been willing to go on fighting in 1856, British forces would probably have won successes and French arms met with difficulties which might have entirely changed later judgments of their respective military calibres. At the same time another campaign or two might well have made clearer the political moral to be drawn at home from the war, by allowing events to set an indisputable seal of success upon either 'the wisdom of ancestors' or 'the spirit of the age'. But as it was, an abrupt, artificial peace — forced upon the country by the attitude of her ally, and not the result of British policies or wishes — prevented the war from playing any such decisive role. If the traditionalists were not prepared to concede total defeat, neither could the new men claim total victory. 'Had the war continued, it would have shown that ——' became for a time the controversialists' favourite opening gambit, but it was a sterile one, since it could be concluded entirely according to taste. In 1856 that experienced radical journalist, John Wade, then in sober middle age, could end his discussion of the war by assuring his readers that 'manifestly the civilisation of science, of wealth and of freedom are the true sources of power in war and peace'.[1] Only a year earlier such an assertion would not have seemed in the least manifest. But a premature peace had combined with rationalizations and red herrings to make Wade's claim widely acceptable. Buckle and Herbert Spencer could still believe consent arising from benefits to be as firm a basis for political solidarity as military discipline and coercion; John Stuart Mill could still explain that free men could display a second, higher set of martial qualities, made up of moral and not pugnacious attributes.[2] Lesser men more gropingly followed these lights. The compatibility of military success with the pursuit of wealth and free institutions remained a common English article of faith, despite the acute disbelief which was almost universal in 1855 and never lost in some circles, and despite increased continental cynicism.

The Crimean War thus takes its place with those many other unresolved contests which distinguish the history of Britain in the mid-nineteenth century. It is their existence which gives the years between 1846 and 1867 their particularly ambiguous character, a character well described by that now classic phrase, 'the age of equipoise'. But the country's experiences during the Crimean War serve as a reminder that this phrase, however apt, may be misleading without a gloss. For this was not an age of balance achieved through the resolution of conflict, or even through agreement to differ; it was not an age of political quiescence or social peace. Its balance sprang from the holding in suspense of conflicting forces unable to give a knock-out blow, and it was thus only in the sense of tension and fundamental uncertainty that this was an age of equipoise. During the Crimean War parliamentary government and the creed of political economy had both been on trial, and neither had made a very creditable showing; yet neither had been proved intrinsically defective, and each continued to command respect. Their trial by combat had resulted only in yet another open verdict to vex and perplex

---

[1] John Wade, *England's Greatness* (1856), p. 781.
[2] Mill to Wentworth Holworthy, 11 July 1855, *Letters*, i. 185.

mid-Victorian society. The abandonment of the constitutional assumptions of 1832 and the spread of disillusionment with the doctrines of free trade were both experiences which befell the next generation, and not the men of the Crimean War, despite their bitter foretaste of them in the spring of 1855. But that this was so provides no evidence that this was an age of political complacency or crude confidence in Cobdenite economic ideas. It proves rather that these were years distinguished by a multitude of undecided battles and inconclusive contests.

Bibliography

This is a list of all the sources cited in the footnotes to the text. Unless otherwise stated, the place of publication of printed sources is London.

A. MANUSCRIPT SOURCES

1. BRITISH MUSEUM (ADDITIONAL MANUSCRIPTS)

Aberdeen Papers

Bright Papers

Broughton Papers

Cobden Papers

Congreve Papers

Gladstone Papers

Halifax Papers

Iddesleigh Papers

Layard Papers

Palmerston Letterbooks

Ripon Papers

Sturge Papers

2. PUBLIC RECORD OFFICE

Cardwell Papers

Cowley Papers

Ellenborough Papers

Granville Papers

Russell Papers

Stratford Canning Papers

Certain classes of the records of the Admiralty, Board of Trade, Foreign Office, High Court of Admiralty, Privy Council, Treasury and War Office.

3. OTHER ARCHIVES

The Royal Archives, Windsor Castle.

Chadwick Papers, University College, London.

Clarendon Deposit, Bodleian Library, Oxford.

Disraeli Papers, Hughenden Manor, Buckinghamshire.

Ellice Deposit, The National Library of Scotland, Edinburgh.

Graham Papers, microfilm of, deposited Cambridge University Library.

Grey of Howick Papers, Prior's Kitchen, University of Durham.

Harrison Papers, London School of Economics and Political Science

Holyoake Collection, Bishopsgate Institute.

Lewis Papers, Harpton Court Collection, the National Library of Wales, Aberystwyth.

Newcastle Papers, Clumber MSS., University of Nottingham.

Palmerston Papers, Broadlands Archives.

Panmure Papers, Dalhousie Muniments, Scottish Record Office, H.M. General Register House, Edinburgh.

Urquhart Papers, Balliol College, Oxford.

B. PARLIAMENTARY PUBLICATIONS

Hansard's *Parliamentary Debates*, third series.

House of Commons Papers:

1854–55, ix, part 1, Reports on the Army before Sebastopol.

1857 (sess. 2), x, part 1, Report on the operation of the Bank Act of 1844.

1860, vii, part 1, Report on the effects of the alterations as to the War Office and Board of Ordnance, 1855.

1867–8, xxxii, Report of the Neutrality Laws Commissioners.

1868–69, xxxv (366), part ii, Return of Public Income and Expenditure.

C. PERIODICALS, PAMPHLETS AND POEMS

1. NEWSPAPERS

Daily News	*Morning Post*
The Economist	*Newcastle Courant*
Examiner	*News of the World*
Free Press	*Nonconformist*
Globe	*People's Paper*
Guardian	*Press*
Herapath's Journal	*Punch*
Illustrated London News	*Reasoner*
Journal des Débats politiques et littéraires (Paris)	*Record*
	Reynolds News
Leader	*Saturday Review*
London Gazette	*Sheffield Free Press*
Manchester Guardian	*Spectator*
Morning Advertiser	*The Times*
Morning Chronicle	*Watchman*
Morning Herald	

2. OTHER PERIODICALS

Blackwood's Magazine

Eclectic Review

Edinburgh Review

Journal of the Dublin Statistical Society

Journal of the London Statistical Society

North British Review

Penny Pulpit

Quarterly Review

Revue des Deux Mondes (Paris)

Westminster Review

3. PAMPHLETS AND POEMS

ANON. The Bank Charter Act in the Crisis of 1847 (1854).

The Bank Screw . . . A letter to W. E. Gladstone by Malagrowther the Less (1854).

Administrative Reform Association, Official Papers.

ALISON, A. Bank Reform (1855).

Anti-Centralization Union, Government and its Measures in 1857 (1857).

BALLANTYNE, T. Prophecy for 1855 (1855).

BARNES, R. W. Public Opinion, considered in Letters between one of his Friends and R. W. Barnes, M.A. Vicar of Probus (1855).

BRIGHT, J. Letter to Absalom Watkin on the Russian War (1854).

CAIRNES, J. E. An Examination into the Principles of Currency involved in the Bank Charter Act of 1844 (Dublin, 1854).

COMBE, G. The Currency Question Considered (1856).

CONGREVE, R. The Roman Empire of the West (1855).

DOUGLAS, J. Passing Thoughts (1856).

ELLIOTT, E. B. The Downfall of Despotism (1853).

ELTON, A. H. Tracts for the Present Crisis (1855–6).

An inquiry into the alleged necessity and justice of the war with Russia (1855).

Where are we drifting? (1855).

GASSIOT, J. P. Four Letters to J. A. Roebuck, Esquire (1856–7).

HOWITT, W. ('John Hampden, Junior') The Aristocracy of England (1846).

JONES, E. *The Emperor's Vigil and The Waves and the War* (1856).

KENNAWAY, C. E. *The War and the Newspapers* (1856).

MACCALL, W. *National Missions* (1855).

MACFARLAN, J. *Our Monetary Affairs* (1856).

MASSEY, G. *War Waits* (1855).

MAURICE, F. D. *Administrative Reform and its connexion with Working Men's Colleges* (1855).

'M. B.' *The Public Debt, its influence and management considered in a different point of view from Sir H. Parnell's* (1831).

MAXWELL, P. B. *Whom shall we Hang? The Sebastopol Inquiry* (1855).

NORMAN, G. W. *The Pressure of Taxation in this and other Countries* (1850).
Papers on various subjects (n.d.).

OVERSTONE, S. J. LOYD, LORD. *Tracts and other Publications on Metallic and Paper Currency* (1858).

PALGRAVE, Sir F. *Conciliatory Reform* (1831).
Observations on the Principles to be adopted in the establishment of new Municipal Corporations (1832).

RICARDO, J. *The War Policy of Commerce* (1855).

RICKARDS, G. K. *The Financial Policy of War* (1855).

SMITH, J. TOULMIN. *The Home Policy which the present War-Time needs* (1855).
Local Self-Government Un-mystified (1857).

SOMERS, R. S. *The Errors of the Banking Acts of 1844–45* (1857).

STANSFELD, H. *A few reasons for the immediate reconsideration of the Bank Charter Act of 1844* (1855).
A remedy suggested for our financial difficulties (1854).

TOOKE, T. *On the Bank Charter Act of 1844* (1855).

URQUHART, D. *Answer to Mr. Cobden on the Assimilation of War and Peace* (1862).
Naval Power suppressed by the Maritime States (1873).
The Queen and the Premier (2nd ed., 1857).

URQUHART, H. H. *The Story of the War* (1857).

WRIGHT, I. C. *The War and our Resources* (1855).

D. OTHER PRINTED WORKS

1. ARTICLES IN LEARNED REVIEWS, ETC.

ANDERSON, O. 'Further light on the inner history of the Declaration of Paris', *Law Quarterly Review*, lxxvi (1960).

'The Russian Loan of 1855: An example of economic liberalism?', *Economica* (November 1960).

'Economic warfare in the Crimean War', *Economic History Review*, xiv (1961).

'The Russian Loan of 1855: A Comment', *Economica* (Nov. 1961).

'Wage-earners and income tax: a mid-nineteenth century discussion', *Public Administration*, xli (1963).

'Loans versus Taxes: British financial policy in the Crimean War', *Economic History Review*, xvi (1963).

'Great Britain and the beginnings of the Ottoman Public Debt', *Historical Journal*, VII. i (1964).

'Cabinet government and the Crimean War', *English Historical Review*, lxxix (1964).

'The Janus Face of mid-nineteenth-century English Radicalism: the Administrative Reform Association of 1855', *Victorian Studies*, viii (1965).

'The reactions of Church and Dissent towards the Crimean War', *Journal of Ecclesiastical History*, xvi (1965).

ARMYTAGE, W. H. G. 'Sheffield and the Crimean War; Politics and Industry, 1852–57', *History Today*, v (1955).

BRIGGS, A. 'The Crimean Centenary', *Virginia Quarterly Review*, xxx (1954).

'David Urquhart and the West Riding Foreign Affairs Committees', *Bradford Antiquary*, N.S., xxxix (1958).

BURN, W. L. 'The Age of Equipoise', *Nineteenth Century and After*, cxlvi (1949).

FETTER, F. W. 'The Russian Loan of 1855: A Postscript', *Economica* (November 1961).

GUTCHEN, R. M. 'Local improvements and centralization in nineteenth-century England', *Historical Journal*, iv (1961).

HARRISON, J. F. C. 'The Victorian gospel of success', *Victorian Studies*, i (1957).

HART, J. 'Sir Charles Trevelyan at the Treasury', *English Historical Review*, lxxv (1960).

HENDERSON, G. B. 'Problems of Neutrality, 1854: Documents from the Hamburg Staatsarchiv', *Journal of Modern History*, x (1938).

HILL, C. 'The Norman Yoke', in *Democracy and the Labour Movement*, ed. J. Saville (1954).

'FR. DE J.' 'Ernest Jones and Chartism circa 1856', *Bulletin of the Institute of Social History*, v (1950).

KNAPLUND, P. 'Finmark in British Diplomacy, 1836–55', *American Historical Review*, xxx (1925).

LAMBERT, R. 'Central and local relations in mid-Victorian England: The Local Government Act Office, 1858–71', *Victorian Studies*, vi. 2 (1962).

MACCOBY, S. 'Newspaper politics: A footnote to nineteenth-century history', *Politica*, i (1934).

McGREGOR, O. R. 'Social research and social policy in the nineteenth century', *British Journal of Sociology*, viii (1957).

MALKIN, H. W. 'The inner history of the Declaration of Paris', *British Yearbook of International Law* (1927).

PINTNER, W. McK. 'Inflation in Russia during the Crimean War Period', *American Slavic and East European Review*, xviii (1959).

POTTER, J. 'The British Timber Duties, 1815–1860', *Economica*, N.S., xii, (1955).

RAMM, A. 'The Crimean War', in *The New Cambridge Modern History*, x (1960).

ROBBINS, M. 'The Balaklava Railway', *Journal of Transport History*, i (1953).

RUBEL, M. 'Les Cahiers d'Étude de Karl Marx, II, 1853–56', *International Review of Social History*, v (1960).

SHANNON, H. A. 'The coming of general limited liability', *Economic History*, ii (1931).

SUTHERLAND, L. S. 'The City of London and the Devonshire–Pitt Administration, 1756–7', *Proceedings of the British Academy*, xlvi (1960).

ZELDIN, T. 'English ideals in French politics during the nineteenth century', *Historical Journal*, ii (1959).

2. SEPARATE WORKS

ANDRÉADÈS, A. *History of the Bank of England* (2nd edn., 1924).

ANSCHUTZ, R. P. *The Philosophy of John Stuart Mill* (Oxford, 1953).

ANSON, SIR W. *The Law and Custom of the Constitution* (5th edn., 1922).

ANSTEY, T. C. *A Guide to the History of the Laws and Constitution of England* (1845).

ARGYLL, GEORGE DOUGLAS CAMPBELL, 8TH DUKE OF. *Autobiography and Memoirs* (1906).

ASPINALL, A. *Politics and the Press, 1780–1850* (1949).

ATKINS, J. B. *Life of W. H. Russell* (1911).

ATLAY, J. B. *The Victorian Chancellors* (1908).

BAGEHOT, W. *Biographical Studies*, ed. R. H. Hutton (1881).

BARRINGTON, E. I. *The Servant of All* (1927).

BASTABLE, C. F. *Public Finance* (1892).

BENSON, A. C., and VISCOUNT ESHER (eds.). *The Letters of Queen Victoria, 1837–1861* (1907).

BINKLEY, R. C. *Realism and Nationalism, 1852–71* (New York, 1935).

BISHOP, M. C. *A Memoir of Mrs. Urquhart* (1897).

BLAISDELL, D. C. *European Financial Control in the Ottoman Empire* (New York, 1929).

BONNER-SMITH, D., and DEWAR, A. C. (eds.). *The Russian War, 1854, Baltic and Black Sea Official Correspondence* (Navy Records Society, 1943).

BONNER-SMITH, D. *The Russian War, 1855, Baltic Sea Official Correspondence* (Navy Records Society, 1944).

BORRIES, K. *Preussen im Krimkrieg* (Stuttgart, 1930).

BOURNE, H. R. FOX. *English Newspapers* (1887).

BOWLEY, M. *Nassau Senior and Classical Economics* (1937).

BRIGGS, A. *Victorian Cities* (1963).
   The Age of Improvement (1959).

BRIGHT, J. *Diaries* (1930).

BRODRICK, G. *Memories and Impressions* (1900).
   Political Studies (1879).

BURN, W. L. *The Age of Equipoise* (1964).

BUXTON, S. *Mr. Gladstone as Chancellor of the Exchequer* (1901).

CARLYLE, T. *Latter-Day Pamphlets* (1850).

CAVOUR, Camillo Count di. *Cavour e l'Inghilterra*, Carteggio con V. E. D'Azeglio a cura della commissione reale editrice (Bologna, 1933).

CHARLES-ROUX, F. *Alexandre II, Gortchakoff et Napoléon III* (Paris, 1913).

CLAPHAM, SIR J. *An Economic History of Modern Britain*, ii (1932). — PARTS

CLEVELAND-STEVENS, E. *English Railways: Their development and their relation to the state* (1915).

CLOKIE, H., and ROBINSON, J. *Royal Commissions of Inquiry* (1937).

COLLETT, C. D. *The History of the Taxes on Knowledge* (1899).

COLOMB, P. H. *Memoirs of Sir Astley Cooper Key* (1898).

COMTE, A. *Lettres à Richard Congreve* (Paris, 1889).

CONNELL, B. *Regina v. Palmerston* (1962).

CORRY, B. A. *Money, Saving and Investment in English Economics 1800–1850* (1962).

DEWAR, A. C. *The Russian War, 1855, Black Sea Official Correspondence* (Navy Records Society, 1945).

DRESCHER, S. *Tocqueville and England* (Cambridge, Mass., 1964).

DUMAS, J. *Les aspects économiques du droit de prise avant la guerre mondiale* (Paris, 1926).

DUSSIEUX, L. *La Force et la Faiblesse de la Russie* (Paris, 1854).

EARP, G. B. (ed.). *The History of the Baltic Campaign* (1857).

ENFIELD, VISCOUNTESS (ed.). *Leaves from the Diary of Henry Greville*, second series (1884).

FAUCHER, L. *Études sur l'Angleterre* (Paris, 1845).

FAUCHILLE, P. *Du Blocus Maritime* (Paris, 1882).

FIELDING, K. J. (ed.). *The Speeches of Charles Dickens* (Oxford, 1960).

FINER, S. E. *The Life and Times of Sir Edwin Chadwick* (1952).

FITZMAURICE, LORD E. *The Life of Granville George Leveson Gower, second Earl Granville* (1905).

FONTANE, T. *Journeys to England in Victoria's early days* (1939).

FORTESCUE, SIR J. *History of the British Army*, xiii (1929).

GLEASON, J. H. *The Genesis of Russophobia in Great Britain* (Cambridge, Mass., 1950).

GOOCH, G. P. *The Later Correspondence of Lord John Russell* (1925).

GORDON, H. *The War Office* (1935).

GOSDEN, P. H. J. H. *The Friendly Societies in England* (Manchester, 1961).

GUICHEN, E. DE. *La Guerre de Crimée, 1854–56, et l'Attitude des Puissances Européennes* (Paris, 1936).

HARDCASTLE, M. S. (ed.). *The Life of John, Lord Campbell* (1881).

HAWTHORNE, N. *The English Notebooks*, ed. Randall Stewart (New York, 1941).

HAYEK, F. A. *John Stuart Mill and Harriet Taylor* (1951).

HAYWARD, A. *The Correspondence of*, ed. H. E. Carlisle (1886).

HELPS, SIR A. *The Life and Labours of Mr. Brassey* (1872).

HERR, R. *Tocqueville and the Old Regime* (Princeton, 1962).

HEWETT, O. W. '... *and Mr. Fortescue*' (The Diaries of Chichester Fortescue, Baron Carlingford) (1958).

HIRST, F. W. *The Political Economy of War* (1915).

HODDER, E. *The Life and Work of the seventh Earl of Shaftesbury* (1887).

HOGARTH, G., and DICKENS, M. *The Letters of Charles Dickens* (1882).

HOLDSWORTH, SIR W. *History of English Law*, xiv, ed. A. L. Goodhart and H. G. Hanbury (1964).

HOLYOAKE, G. J. *Sixty Years of an Agitator's Life* (1906).

HUGHES, J. R. T. *Fluctuations in Trade, Industry and Finance* (Oxford, 1960).

JENKS, L. H. *The Migration of British Capital to 1875* (New York, 1927).

JENNINGS, L. J. (ed.). *The Croker Papers* (1885).

JEPHSON, H. *The Platform* (1892).
The Sanitary Evolution of London (1907).

JOHNSON, A. H. (ed.). *The Letters of Charles Greville and Henry Reeve, 1836–65* (1924).

KEETON, G. W. *Trial by Tribunal* (1960).

KEITH, A. B. *The Constitution of England from Queen Victoria to George VI* (1940).

KINGLAKE, A. W. *The Invasion of the Crimea* (1863).

LAMBERT, R. *Sir John Simon, 1816–1904* (1963).

LANGFORD, J. A. *Modern Birmingham and its Institutions* (1877).

LAUGHTON, J. K. *Memoirs of the Life and Correspondence of Henry Reeve* (1898).

LECANUET, R. P. *Montalembert* (Paris, 1895–1902).

LEDRU-ROLLIN, A. A. *De la Décadence de l'Angleterre* (Paris, 1850).

LEWIS, SIR G. F. (ed.). *Letters of the Right Honourable Sir George Cornewall Lewis to Various Friends* (1870).

LINDSAY, W. S. *History of Merchant Shipping* (1875).

LONGFORD, E. *Victoria R.I.* (1964).

LYASCHENKO, P. I. *History of the National Economy of Russia to the 1917 Revolution*, trans. L. H. Herman (New York, 1949).

MACCOBY, S. *English Radicalism, 1853–86* (1938).

McCULLOCH, J. R. *Taxation and the Funding System* (Edinburgh, 1845).

Dictionary of Commerce and Commercial Navigation (1832–9).

MACDONAGH, O. *A Pattern of Government Growth, 1800–1860* (1961).

McGILCHRIST, J. *Life of Henry, Lord Brougham* (1868).

MACKINTOSH, J. P. *The British Cabinet* (1962).

MALMESBURY, J. H. Harris, third Earl of. *Memoirs of an ex-Minister* (1884).

MARKHAM, V. *Paxton and the Bachelor Duke* (1935).

MARTIN, B. K. *The Triumph of Lord Palmerston* (first edn. 1924).

MARTIN, T. *Life of the Prince Consort* (fifth edn., 1878).

MARTINEAU, J. *Life of Henry Pelham, fifth Duke of Newcastle* (1908).

U

MARX, K. *The Eastern Question*, ed. A. M. and E. Aveling (1897).

MARX, K., and ENGELS, F. *Correspondence, 1846–95* (Calcutta, 1945).

MAURICE, F. (ed.). *The Life of F. D. Maurice* (1884).

MAXWELL, SIR H. *The Life and Letters of George, fourth Earl of Clarendon* (1913).

MILL, J. S. *Autobiography* (World's Classics edn., Oxford, 1924).
   Principles of Political Economy, ed. W. J. Ashley (1909).
   Letter of, ed. H. S. R. Elliot (1910).

MILNER, T. *The Baltic* (1854).

MONTALEMBERT, C., COMTE DE. *De l'Avenir politique de l'Angleterre* (Paris, 1856).

MOORE, J. B. (ed.). *The Works of James Buchanan* (Philadelphia, 1908–11).

MORLEY, J. *Life of Gladstone* (1903).

MORRIS, H. *Portrait of a Chef* (1938).

NASH, T. A. *Life of Richard, Lord Westbury* (1888).

NORTHCOTE, S. *Twenty Years of Financial Policy* (1860).

Panmure Papers, ed. Sir G. Douglas and Sir G. D. Ramsay (1908).

PARKER, C. S. *The Life and Letters of Sir James Graham* (1907).

PEARDON, T. P. *The Transition in English Historical Writing 1760–1830* (New York, 1933).

PEMBERTON, W. S. CHILDE-. *Life of Lord Norton* (1909).

PIGGOTT, SIR F. *The Declaration of Paris, 1856* (1919).

PIGOU, A. C. *The Political Economy of War* (1921).

POCOCK, J. G. A. *The Ancient Constitution and the Feudal Law* (Cambridge, 1957).

POLITICAL ECONOMY CLUB. THE *Minutes of Proceedings*, vi (1921).

PROUTY, R. *The Transformation of the Board of Trade* (1957).

REDFORD, A. *A History of Local Government in Manchester* (1940).

REDLICH, J. *The Procedure of the House of Commons* (1908).

REEVE, H. (ed.). *The Greville Memoirs* (1903 edn.).

REID, T. W. *The Life, Letters and Friendships of Richard Monckton Milnes, First Lord Houghton* (1890).

ROBBINS, L. *The Theory of Economic Policy* (1952).

ROBINSON, G. *David Urquhart* (Oxford, 1920).

ROSCOE, E. S. (ed.). *Reports of Prize Cases*, vol. ii (1905).

ROTHAN, G. *La Prusse et son Roi pendant la Guerre de Crimée* (Paris, 1888).

SEYMOUR, C. *Electoral Reform in England and Wales* (New Haven, 1915).

SIMPSON, F. A. *Louis Napoleon and the Recovery of France, 1848–56* (1923).

SIMPSON, M. C. M. (ed.). *Correspondence and Conversations of Alexis de Tocqueville with Nassau Senior, 1834–59* (1872). *Many Memories of Many People* (1898).

SKALKOWSKY, C. *Les Ministres des Finances de la Russie, 1802–1890* (Paris, 1891).

SMILES, A. *Samuel Smiles and his Surroundings* (1956).

SMITH, J. TOULMIN. *The Parish* (2nd edn., 1857). *Local Self-Government and Centralization* (1851).

SOYER, A. *A Culinary Campaign* (1857).

SPENCER, H. *Autobiography* (1904).

STEEVES, H. R. *Learned Societies and English Literary Scholarship in Great Britain and the United States* (1913).

SULIVAN, H. N. (ed.). *The Life and Letters of Admiral Sir Bartholomew James Sulivan* (1896).

TEGOBORSKI, M. L. *Commentaries on the Productive Forces of Russia* (1855–6).

THACKERAY, W. M. *The Four Georges* (1856).

THOMAS, J. A. *The House of Commons, 1832–1901* (Cardiff, 1939).

Times, The History of The, vol. ii (1939).

TOCQUEVILLE, A., COMTE DE. *Memoir, Letters and Remains* (1861). *Œuvres complètes*, ed. J.-P. Mayer (Paris, 1954).

TOCQUEVILLE, MADAME DE. *Œuvres complètes d'Alexis de Tocqueville* (Paris, 1866).

TODD, A. *On Parliamentary Government in England* (1867).

TOOKE, T., and NEWMARCH, W. *A History of Prices, 1792–1856* (1857).

TREUE, W. *Der Krimkrieg und die Entstehung der Modernen Flotten* (Göttingen, 1954).

TUCKER, G. S. L. *Progress and Profits in British Economic Thought* (Cambridge, 1960).

URQUHART, D. *Turkey and its Resources* (1833).
The Pillars of Hercules (1850).
Constitutional Remedies, showing how the law is designed to control the acts of the Government (1855).

VALSECCHI, F. *Il Risorgimento e l'Europa. L'Alleanza di Crimea* (Milan, 1948).

VELAY, A. DU. *Essai sur l'histoire financière de la Turquie* (Paris, 1903).

VITZTHUM VON ECKSTAEDT, COUNT C. F. *St. Petersburg and London* (1887).

WADE, J. *England's Greatness* (1856).

WILSON, D. A. *Carlyle to Threescore and Ten (1853–1865)* (1929).

WOODWARD, E. L. *War and Peace in Europe, 1815–1870* (1931).
The Age of Reform, 1815–1870 (Oxford, 1938).

WRIGHT, G. H. *Chronicles of the Birmingham Chamber of Commerce, 1813–1913* (1913).

YAKOVLEV, A. F. *Ekonomicheskie Krizisy v Rossii* (Moscow, 1955).

Index

Aaland Islands, 266

Aberdeen, fourth Earl of, 75, 165; weakness as war leader, 34, 111; attitude to reform of military administration, 55–56, to public opinion, 89, to subsidies, 217, 223

Acts of Parliament, Bills of Exchange, 177; Bribery at Elections, 169; Common Law Procedure, 169; Constitution of New South Wales and Victoria, 175; Deputy Speaker, 177; Ecclesiastical Courts Procedure, 171; Education of Pauper Children, 177; Feudal Tenures, 152; Friendly Societies, 175; Liberty of Religious Worship, 176; Limited Liability, 175; Local Government, 138; Merchant Shipping, 170; Metropolitan Local Management, 174; Nuisances Removal, 137, 174; Oxford University, 169; Public Libraries, 175; Railway and Canal Traffic, 170; Registration of Incumbrances, 177; Revenue Collection, 170; Sale of Beer, 178; Summary Jurisdiction, 177; Usury Laws, 170; Youthful Offenders, 170

Adderley, Charles, later first Lord Norton, 170

Administrative Reform Association, 83–86, 104–8, 114–15, 160; attacked, 120–2; failure, 122; and working-class leaders, 125; and Anti-Centralization Union, 137; and Urquhart, 145, 148; and ideal of political independence, 155–7

Admiralty, Board of, 68, 259

Albert, Prince, 36, 63 n. 3, 68, 91, 154, 237 n. 3

Anglo-Saxons, study of, 130–1; cult of, 132, 139, 140

Anstey, T.C., 140

Anti-Centralization Union, 134–8

Arbuthnot, George, 14, 232

Argyll, George Douglas Campbell, eighth Duke of, 39, 273

Aristocracy, expected war-time role of, 101, 103; prestige of, 102, 103, 158–60; discredit of, 104, 106–11, 115, 124; defended, 120; charged with perverting constitution, 152, 154

Army, lack of distinguished generals in, 36; and aristocracy, 102, 111, 115; education of officers, 115; medical service, 115; administration of, dissatisfaction with, 10–12, 51–53; proposals for reform, 54, 57, 62; changes not satis-

Piedmont, 219–22

Pigou, A. C., 212

Pitt, William, the Younger, financial errors of condemned, 15, 192, 193, 195; defended, 200 n. 2, 215

Political Economy Club, 244

Press, freedom of, much valued, 31, 70–71, 87; censorship, 72–74; conduct criticized, 75, 77; repercussion of conduct during war abroad, 78–81, and at home, 81–82, 88–89. *See also* Newspaper Stamp Duties

Press, The, 120

Primogeniture, 154

Privateering, abstention from, 16, 251–3; abolition of, 272–3

Prussia, and Russian trade, 258, 260 n. 2, 261, 270; British attitude to, 265, 267–8

Public meetings, much valued, 70, 72, 83; use of during Crimean War, 83–84

Public opinion, 142; free expression of, much valued, 31, 32, 70; doubts upon, 74, 81, 89; final complacence about, 92; influence of, on House of Commons, 85–86

Punch, 7, 106, 115, 226

Puseyism, 168

Radicals, 3, 22, 85, 91; diverse responses to war, 98–100; various ideals of, 129–63; gains from war, 171–82.

Raglan, Lord, 36, 60, 72, 75

Reasoner, The, 179, 181

Record, 76

Reeve, Henry, 75, 103, 235

Representative Government,

compatibility of, with war, 7, 31; criticisms of, 31, 89–93; final complacence about, 91–92

Revolutionary and Napoleonic Wars, recollections of drawn upon, 1–2, 8, 13–16, 22, 188–9, 190, 195, 229

Ricardo, J. L., 117, 257 n. 3

Rickards, G. K., 210, 212, 214, 242

Roebuck, J. A., 43, 49, 50, 146

Rule of 1756, 265

Russell, Lord John, 34, 39, 62; and Parliamentary Reform Bill, 8, 10; and military administration, 11, 12, 40, 54–62 *passim*; and Vienna Conference, 44; and the Press, 75, 78, 89; and the House of Commons, 167, 168; and war finance, 203, 217; and maritime rights, 263

Russell, W. H., 71, 73, n. 1, 76

Russia, shipping, 16, 258; chemical supplies, 250 and n. 6; foreign trade, 249–50, 256, 260–3; effects of British maritime policy on, 268–71

Sabbatarian legislation, 178, 181

St. Leonards, Lord, 166

Salt, T. C., 241

Saturday Review, 78, 122–3, 242

Scotland, and the Bank Charter Act, 242

Scott, Sir Walter, 130

Sebastopol Committee, 40, 43, 47; ineffectiveness of, 49–50, 86; attempt of Palmerston government to avert, 63–64

Printed in Great Britain by Richard Clay (The Chaucer Press), Ltd., Bungay, Suffolk